THE HAPPINESS THEN

R.H. Ellis

MINERVA PRESS

LONDON

MONTREUX   LOS ANGELES   SYDNEY

THE HAPPINESS THEN
Copyright © R.H. Ellis 1997

ISBN 1 86106 591 4

First Published 1997 by
MINERVA PRESS
195 Knightsbridge
London SW7 1RE

Printed and bound in Great Britain by
Antony Rowe Ltd, Chippenham, Wiltshire.

THE HAPPINESS THEN

To Bill, Cathy and Emma, who loved and lost her too.

Acknowledgements

My thanks are due to Jeanette, my Cruise Bereavement Care counsellor, for her endless patience in listening to me, and to her and to Carol Jack for their original suggestion that I should write something.

I am deeply grateful to my daughters Emma and Cathy, my son Bill, my daughter-in-law Sue, and my son-in-law Simon, for their love, help and encouragement to finish this book and to try to want to live.

I wish to thank those kind friends who have shown interest and willingness to hear about my writing and my feelings.

I would also like to thank my two typists, Val Burgess, who started the book, and Ros Boase, who finished it, for their hard work and tolerance of my changes of mind, Dee Austin for her help with photocopying and Robina Jeffreys for tidying up the odds and ends, a safe pair of hands at long stop.

Cover photo: South Pacific sunset on Bora Bora.

About the Author

Dr Ellis was born and bred on the edge of the Fens in Cambridgeshire. A fourth generation doctor, he was educated at Marlborough College and followed his father to St Catharine's College, Cambridge, where he won a Hockey Blue. He followed both his father and grandfather to St Bartholomew's Hospital, London, where his grandfather had been a fellow student and shared rooms with W.G. Grace.

At Barts he met and married the love of his life, a nurse, and they had three children, a son who is a gastroenterologist and twin daughters, one a student counsellor, the other a psychologist, who provided them with five grandchildren.

After thirty-three years as a consultant physician on the staff of Gloucestershire Royal Hospital specialising in Lung Disease, he retired and developed his interest in Life Assurance Medicine. He continues as Consultant Medical Officer to Allied Dunbar, and Medical Director of Lincoln Assurance.

Dr Ellis maintains a keen interest in travel as a director of D.J. Executive Travel in Cirencester, and both he and his wife shared a love of travel, tennis, cricket, bridge, opera, history, and current affairs.

This is his first book.

The pain now is part of the happiness then, that is the deal.

Shadowlands, C.S. Lewis

Without Her

I miss her in her month of May
I miss her in high summer's flame
I miss her in the fragrant rain
of June time
I miss her in the morning mists
The bright clear days and evening cools
of autumn
I miss her all the hours of all the days
of all the years that never end
Without her

Contents

Prelude

This book is about travel, about love and about grief. It is a description of happenings that happened and of feelings felt.

Esmé was a free spirit: she never needed the security of sameness, any more than she required the reassurance of repetition; her refreshment was by new faces lit by faraway suns in foreign lands, and she loved them for their very difference and for the new perspectives they provided for her. She was a traveller rather than a tourist, her mind was ever open, she accepted strange people and strange places for what they were and not for what she would have preferred them to be. She was ever ready to jettison preconceived ideas; she expected every new experience to change her a little. Her curiosity was boundless and insatiable, and thus was my own life so enriched; we both knew that over every blue horizon there were ever wider yonders beckoning us. The lure of the unknown never left her and her heart never failed to quicken at the prospect of things new. She had that precious alchemy which enabled her to see the ordinary and lustreless as potential gold; for her the elixir of life could be found anywhere if you really wished to look for it. If an optimist is somebody with a disposition to take a bright hopeful view of things, then that was my wife. When she agreed to marry me, I knew that she had placed a fortune in the palm of my hand, she was the composer of my every cherished melody and she orchestrated the whole concert that was my life.

After many years of happy family holidays, mostly on the Gower Peninsula where Esmé was born and bred, and then across Europe with tent and motor caravan, the children grew up and away. Esmé and I found Kassiopi at the northern end of Corfu, went there for five or six years, and felt that we would never want to go anywhere else. In 1978, however, we started to get itchy feet, and felt that we really ought to go further afield and see as much of the world as we could;

we were in our late fifties and fit, and had a burning desire to see other countries and other people in far flung places. Esmé had read much more about the world than I had; she was familiar with the travels of Somerset Maugham, Graham Greene and Robert Louis Stevenson, and had read some of Joseph Conrad. By 1978 we felt that we could afford to travel widely, and we made this our top priority for the next fifteen years, cutting back if necessary on other things.

Esmé had the gift of very rarely being bored, and every experience for her seemed to have intrinsic value; her enthusiasm and happiness over little things and little experiences, and her joys over big ones, fed me during the whole of our married life. It was impossible not to share them with her, and when difficulties arose during travel as they often do, she was the ideal companion; she never took anything for granted, and we told each other a thousand times how lucky we were to be seeing the world together; she often asked what had we done to deserve it.

Starting in the Caribbean, our journeys took us far and wide. We saw the oceans of the world, except the Arctic and Antarctic; most of the major seas, and many of the great rivers and mountain ranges. As we loved the sun, most of our trips were to the tropics, often to the southern hemisphere, and especially to the east. The daily diet of sights sounds and smells in different countries became an addiction, and before each journey we saw to it that we had already made plans for the next.

The excitement would grow in the weeks before departure, while we read in the travel guides what we should see. Esmé was a great planner, and loved planning her wardrobe, and in detail what she would wear each day and night while she was away. She compiled The List, two sides of foolscap with small writing, covering every conceivable thing that we might need while we were away, and it enlarged as the years went by. Her Yellow Bag for the cabin was much beloved; it had a rigid lower compartment for bottles and toiletries, and a roomy soft upper compartment with a rigid base, the two joined by a circumferential zip; it covered the world with us and we never saw another like it. Her excitement was utterly infectious, and she often told me that I was a true catholic convert, and that seeing the world had become more essential to me than to herself.

The journey and the enjoyment of it would begin as we walked out of the door. The drive to the airport, arriving at the terminal, checking in, the bookshop, pre-flight drinks and snacks, the departure lounge, all of this became very much part of our metabolism. Esmé said that just walking through the doors of Terminals 3 or 4 at Heathrow gave her an orgasm. When she told this to one of my less than kind colleagues who fancied himself as a humorist, he observed that she should carry on doing this, because being married to me it was the only way she was ever likely to have one.

The ritual in the terminal never changed, except that in later years we found that we could afford to fly business class and enjoy the cloistered half-luxury of the business class lounge. We would buy half a dozen paperbacks, go to duty-free for booze and perfume, and I would check my cabin bag endlessly to make sure that I had got everything, with prompts from Esmé. When friends complained about airports and long flights we really could not understand them.

Abroad I was the photographer and Esmé would keep up day by day with the travel guidebooks. Some years after we began travelling long distance, she said that we should write a daily journal; we should have done this from the start, and it was when we were in a bus in Bogota in Colombia that she suggested I should get out and buy an exercise book, and from then on wherever we were, we would write up the day's experience in the evenings, usually in the bar; one of us would write the narrative on the right side of the book, the other comments on the left.

Now that she has gone, these books and the photographs are very precious, and when I read what she wrote I can hear her beloved voice and the music of her laughter; when she laughed she made the flowers smile under lowering skies, and she could summon the sun and the moon from their nebulous hiding places to come share her happiness. She was my angel of light on the wing of day and night in all the seasons of the year.

Chapter One

The Caribbean

We both had a dream about the Caribbean since we were very young. Esmé's vision was of islands in the sun, mine was of the cricket played there, and when I was a boy I wondered if I would ever be able to watch a test match in Barbados or Trinidad or Jamaica. In 1978 we felt that we could afford to go to Barbados and Tobago; neither of us had been outside Europe, except for one short visit to America when our daughter Cathy was in Washington. On Barbados we heard that the Coconut Creek Hotel, run by an ex-RAF officer and his wife, was both cheap and adequate.

We landed at night after an eight hour flight, and there was a forty minute drive by taxi to the hotel where we had a small wooden bungalow near the beach, and we woke to a warm tropical morning sun. We went to breakfast, which was on a patio with low whitewashed walls; within a few feet there were clumps of bougainvillaea, hibiscus and oleander and we had never seen colour quite like it. In the bushes there were birds waiting to share breakfast with us, and the pretty little banana quits, small, bright yellow and black, fascinated us. Here we were at last, almost past middle age, sitting in the tropics, loving it all, and loving each other. If we were going to be able to do this sort of thing twice a year for the rest of our lives, we would die happy.

The beach was fine white sand, the sea was azure, there were palm trees and the casuarinas hung over the beach like huge ferns. We had our first experience of a Bajan buffet, with an extraordinary array of food. There was swordfish, snapper and dolphin with pepper and pickled small green bananas, breadfruit, plantain, sweet potatoes, yams and christophene, and the meal seeming to go on for hour upon hour. We were invited to a manager's party, with free drinks for all, and everybody dressed up in their tropical best. Esmé looked super, as she always did, but I did not have the right dress at all; I lacked the necessary white trousers, white socks and shoes, although I did have a gaudy Caribbean shirt. I decided that I would kit myself out properly for next time.

In the late evenings we could stand on the verandah of our bungalow within a few feet of the Caribbean, and the whispering wind of the night seemed to catch the palms unawares, as it hurried like an inquisitive tenebrio to share our secrets of love and contentment. On our last evening we stood for a long time just watching the sea, and the sky was lovely that night. As we turned to go into the cottage and to bed Esmé said that they had given us a wonderful welcome to the tropics, they had even polished the stars.

Barbados is a flattish island, covered with sugar cane, and its attraction lies in its beaches, particularly on the Caribbean side; on the other side on Crane Beach, there are huge Atlantic rollers and the surfing is good.

We flew to Trinidad and caught a smaller plane to Tobago, where the airport consisted of two or three sheds. On the drive to Turtle Beach Hotel, we went through dense plantations of coconut palms, and the interior of this island was very different from Barbados. There were monkeys shinning up and down the palm trees, and they had their share of coconuts, in spite of metal sleeves around the tree-trunks. Turtle Beach is a long beach of virgin sand, and the hotel is at one end; at the other we saw in the distance Pigeon Point, an attractive tree-covered promontory sticking out into the sea with a long jetty, and decided that one early morning we would find the energy to walk along there, hoping to see turtles laying eggs in the sand on the way.

We had a room on the ground floor and the sea was within thirty yards, through a tropical garden with brilliant flowers. When we arrived, I was battling with the suitcases and Esmé went missing. She came back half an hour later, and announced that she had been in deep conversation with a woman two rooms down, who had told her all about the troubles of her marriage and the abject failure of this holiday on Tobago to put them right; everybody always told Esmé their most intimate details and presumably this was why she was such a valued social worker. I told her that I had a few troubles of my own to discuss with her, not least that I could not open her suitcase.

Turtle Beach is a middle grade hotel and we were made to feel at home. In the evenings there was entertainment by steel bands and also by a group of men beating jungle drums, and we saw fire-eating and limbo dancing. Our first tropical sunset there was unforgettable; there was little cloud and we watched spellbound as the sun seemed to plummet like a livid cannonball, and the sea changed from blue to red-gold in minutes; the birds were suddenly quiet, a tremendous hush descended on everything, all was serene after the day-long roar of the sun's furnace and every living thing was thankful for the longed-for nocturne.

On Turtle Beach at sunset they pulled in the fishing nets; forty men positioned round a huge net, chanting the while, gradually pulled in hundreds of leaping fish. There were dozens of pelicans trying to help themselves to the fish, and every now and then one of them would become careless, and get caught in the net, when it was killed and taken away for consumption along with the fish. This scene, the sunset, the men chanting and pulling in the fish, and the pelicans, was our lasting memory of Tobago.

One afternoon we walked from Turtle Beach along the coast to Arnos Vale. As we sat on a balcony drinking some tea, the birds arrived at 4 p.m. sharp, as they did every day for their tea. There were banana quits, Tobago blue tanagers, ruby topaz humming-birds, and the king of the woods and boss of them all, the motmot; they all seemed to wait until the motmot had its fill, and then came down for the crumbs. On the way back there was a steel band practising for the morrow, a band festival of some sort in Scarborough, and they played 'Yellow Bird' and 'Island in the Sun' for us with gusto; Esmé asked why we had to go home.

Before we left Turtle Beach we met George. He was a local who made a bob or two selling small pieces of black coral and he joined us when we were sitting outside our room and passed the time of day with us. He was very dark with dancing eyes and a cavernous mouth, and when he laughed, which was most of the time, we could see right down his throat; we saw his red uvular stalactite behind turrets of pure white teeth unsheathed by lips like lorry tyres. He sold us two pieces of coral which he said came from a reef off Trinidad sixty metres down, and was difficult to get; he did not seem to mind whether he sold us any or not, his life was simple and he was happy with it. We liked George, and his coral formed the beginning of Esmé's tropical necklace.

We spent hours sitting and watching the seabirds and our favourites were the little sandpipers; we loved the way they ran up and down the beach with the pulse of the tide, their legs moving like the spokes of tiny wheels.

At the end of our holiday there was a strike in Trinidad, and the air crew would not take off for London until they got the pay rise they wanted. We were closeted for four hours, sitting on the floor of the airport while there was much arguing and shouting going on just outside; I remember thinking that if anything was guaranteed to give the pilot a heart attack when we finally got airborne, it was a violent row about money just before take-off.

On this our first visit to the Caribbean we had seen two islands; we had seen something of the culture and the beauty and we could not wait to return. Our only disappointment was the paucity of reef fish; when we went to the Buccoo Reef off Tobago, there was coral, but fewer fish than we hoped for, and in later years in the Seychelles and on The Great Barrier Reef, there was no comparison; a year or two later we met a young Englishman on Petit St Vincent who was running a boat and he told us that the Caribbean had been an undersea desert for many years.

In the spring of the following year we went back to Barbados. We had planned to go to Grenada for the first week, and to St Vincent for the second, but when we arrived in Barbados expecting to get the plane to Grenada we were told that a war had started, and that the Americans had invaded the island at the invitation of the government. We were also told that a volcano had erupted on St Vincent, and there was dust settling everywhere on Barbados from it. We sat in the airport wondering what would happen, and eventually a pleasant middle-aged woman took us into her charge, and we were taken to the Coral Reef Club on St James' Beach and installed in a three-bedroomed apartment. This was very palatial to us, and when they asked us if we would accept it as an alternative to what we had booked on the other two islands we readily agreed; we were some way from the beach, but this did not matter because the tropical garden was lovely.

We had heard about the Coral Reef Club, and we knew that it was run by a couple named O'Hara, who had gone out to Barbados from the Lygon Arms Hotel in Broadway, where Budge O'Hara had been assistant manager. It was reckoned to be up-market and I remembered that I had had a patient in Cheltenham with a heart problem, and he had asked me whether he was fit enough to spend some money and go to the Coral Reef Club; I told him that he would be perfectly all right, advised him to go ahead, and he dropped dead on the beach on the second morning. When I later discussed this with Budge he was very nice about it, and merely asked that in future I should send only my fitter patients to the Coral Reef, because people tended to die on holiday on Barbados, and fridge space was limited in the planes back to London! We got to know Budge and Cynthia very well during the next two or three years, they became good friends, and we met them whenever they came to England.

The Coral Reef was run as an upstage club, many of the people coming back year after year; you were expected to dress up a little in the evening and the planter's punch before dinner was an occasion for everybody to meet and get to know each other. There was always music and dancing later for those who wished to live it up.

When now I sit at my table for one and watch couples dining wordlessly, I wonder at their profligacy with time, for sooner or later they will lose each other. I want to shout at them that what they are wasting is more precious than all the gold, the jewels, all the riches in the world, and when it has gone they will never get it back. Perhaps that may not much matter to them, in which case they deserve not my criticism, but my sympathy.

Swimming in the sea at Coral Reef Club was difficult, because of rocks and coral close inshore. We walked along to Colony Club next door, where there was a large area of sea roped off for swimmers, and water scooters were kept out. We set ourselves the task of swimming round this rope each day in order to try and keep fit, and counter all the eating and drinking.

We returned to the Coral Reef in 1980, and decided to spend a week there, and a second week cruising in the Grenadines. The O'Haras knew us well by now and they kindly took us on their catamaran for swimming and lunch on Sundays; this made us feel that we were special guests, what Cynthia called "old Coral Reefers". The age factor applied, because when we were on the boat, getting into the sea was easy enough but getting out via a very short ladder was difficult, especially for Esmé, who had to be hauled aboard by the other men on the boat, while I pushed under her bottom. We got to know the coast of Barbados, sailing along the Caribbean side of the island where there seemed to be hotels every half mile or so. It was a major playground for the Americans who came in November/December and departed at the end of February, and it was because of them, most of them wealthy, that prices on the island were high; but hotel rates fell in mid-April.

After a week at the Coral Reef in 1980, we took a plane to Union Island with a view to picking up an old sailing boat which was to take us around the islands of the Grenadines. The plane in which we flew to Union was a small six-seater, and the descent to the island was hair-raising; the plane came round a mountain and there below was a small airstrip; banking around the mountain was tight and we were descending at the same time. I told Esmé not to look out of the window, but she did and was terrified; she said that if I really loved her I would not expose her to this sort of thing, and she hoped it was a seaplane because she was quite sure we were going to end up in the sea. The pilot made the runway, and we went to a tin shed, which was the terminal building, where two very lethargic officials waved us through without getting up from their chairs or putting down their cans of Carib beer.

We were met by a young Scotsman who owned the Scaramouche, an old inter island schooner which had lain as a wreck for years on Union. He was the son of a consultant neurologist in Glasgow, had quarrelled with his father and had gone out to the West Indies. He found the Scaramouche and set about repairing her and making her seaworthy, with a view to taking people round the islands. There was room on her for about twenty people sleeping in bunks, and there was one cabin aft which he offered to us, thinking that he had two elderly people who needed special comforts. He ran this boat with the help of his blonde girlfriend Kirsty, and we spent a lovely week weaving our way between these beautiful islands; we especially liked Palm Island, Tobago Cays and Petit St Vincent.

Food was tasty and plentiful, we enjoyed the conch soup which appeared regularly and the cold beer that went with it all. Accommodation was pretty basic and we slept on the floor of our cabin, enjoying the sound and the feel of the sea. The captain and Kirsty were next door, the other side of a thin partition, and it was obvious at night that they too were thoroughly enjoying the cruise and not wasting a moment. There was only one loo and the captain suggested that if it got crowded we should use the side of the boat. Esmé was a little dubious about this and he offered her a bucket with a length of rope attached to the handle to use in emergencies, he said it would be more dignified than sitting on the side rail and she agreed.

When we arrived off Petit St Vincent we thought that it was the most beautiful island we had ever seen; Esmé could not believe it when she saw that the white seabirds had brilliant blue breasts, due to reflection from the sea. We went over to the island to have a look round and decided that if we came again we would probably make it our base, at any rate for a week, and then move on to another island, perhaps Bequia which we could see across the water.

We spent two more holidays on Barbados at the Coral Reef in 1981 and 1982 and both times we stayed there for the full fortnight. In 1982, we flew out with Valerie and Peter McKeigue, Esmé's sister and brother-in-law; Valerie had been seriously ill with kidney and heart disease and this was a big trip for them because they had never been to the tropics. There were going to be problems with Valerie's very rigid renal diet, but they decided to take courage in both hands and come.

We stayed at the Coral Reef and Valerie and Peter at Treasure Beach a mile or so away, where they had a self-catering apartment so that they could monitor Valerie's diet. It was a highly successful holiday for them; they came over to the Coral Reef to have dinner with us several times and Valerie, although far from well and always uncomplaining, was able to enjoy the beach and swimming in the sea. Soon after this she went into renal failure and had to start dialysis, and this was to lead to a transplant. She died suddenly from a stroke months later while having lunch, and I will forever remember Peter saying that she died so prettily.

Esmé had by now discovered Cynthia's boutique at the Coral Reef and had bought several very nice things there; she bought shirts, one of which became a favourite, a white cotton shirt with small motifs over it, a palm tree on a little beach, a glass containing a tropical drink, the setting sun and suchlike. She bought swimsuits which did her proud for years; they are still in the drawer because I cannot bear to part with them.

In 1983 we went to Petit St Vincent. We flew to Barbados by British Airways and instead of being whisked away by taxi to a hotel, we were asked to wait at one side and told that our private plane would soon be available to take us on to Union Island, and we would then go by motor launch to Petit St Vincent. We felt that we were now part of the jet set, for not in our wildest dreams had we imagined that we would ever be in a position to charter a plane, but here we were being given special attention at the airport on Barbados. Esmé said that she could really get used to this sort of living and asked me why I had made her wait until she had one foot in the grave before she sampled it. I let that pass because I could not think of a suitable reply.

We experienced the same hairy descent to Union Island airstrip where we were greeted by a cheerful man wearing a yachting cap, who was the captain of the motor launch. The launch took thirty minutes to get from Union to Petit St Vincent, and on the beach there we were met by Haze Richardson and his wife who managed Petit St Vincent for American owners, and then driven across this very small island in a jeep to the far side, where we were to occupy two large bungalows which were side by side looking westward; the jeep driver was Liverpool and we wondered whether he had a brother called Manchester. When Esmé saw that we had two bungalows she said that it would be a great relief to have me doing my ablutions and eliminations on my own, but she was prepared for me to share her bungalow at all other times. I said that I thought that was very good of her and that there were times in a marriage when such generosity was very much appreciated. I could of course have said that if she really loved me she would want to share my mind and my body twenty-four hours a day, but as in the airport I let it pass; I could do this so easily because I knew that she would and she had. We knew the whole of each other and were happy with that knowledge. Esmé often told people that we did not have rows, though it was from time to time necessary for us to have long and earnest discussions about my shortcomings!

Petit St Vincent is delightfully relaxed and quiet, and it is so small that you can walk round it in fifty minutes. There are some eighteen chalets and bungalows at various points on the circumference of the island; there are no telephones, so if you want anything you write it down on a piece of paper and put it into a bamboo pole outside the bungalow, and every half hour or so Liverpool comes round in the jeep and collects the orders. Meals are taken in a central concourse where there is a bar and a restaurant, and over the top of the whole thing an enormous flame tree.

When we first arrived and stepped from the launch we were greeted by five yellow Labradors, who seemed very pleased to see us and licked us all over. Two of them accompanied us to our bungalow and stayed the night sleeping on the floor, obviously wanting to make sure that we would settle in properly. Haze Richardson told us that when Grenada was invaded by the American troops, Petit St Vincent was used as a helicopter take-off point, and one of the Labradors jumped into a helicopter with the soldiers and had to be forcibly ejected; the dog wanted to go to war to see what it was like.

We met some pleasant people here, mostly Americans, and became friendly with John, the Englishman who ran the sailing boat; he took us off on trips to other islands, uninhabited and dotted all around. I remember sitting one morning in the bar under the flame tree, and watching Esmé walk across from the bungalows to join me for a pre-lunch drink; she looked so pretty and happy wearing one of her tropical shirts and a huge floppy towelling sun hat, she was very brown, very fit and never lovelier and I wanted all this to go on and on for ever and ever. There was so much more of the world to see, we had only just begun, and I simply wanted to continue to share the joys of discovery with this gorgeous woman who filled my heart with such very special things, and with whom I had been in love for longer than I could remember. There were golden moments such as this when I looked at her from a distance and my deep love for her and my overwhelming sexual want of her would surge through my body like an electric current, would so excite me and distend my mind that I was sure my brain would burst, such was the tumescence of my feeling. To live without the total experience of her day by day and night by night was quite unthinkable.

After a week on Petit St Vincent we dragged ourselves across to the island of Bequia, much frequented by the yachting fraternity, and we went to a small hotel in the middle of a palm grove which was rather run down and badly managed. The manager was absent most of the time having a raging affair on the main island of St Vincent, which appeared to take his whole mental and physical energy, and he returned to the hotel only to catch up on sleep. We spent a week here, and the best thing about the island was the music: the steel bands were tremendous.

We were in a wooden chalet with a little verandah, surrounded by conch shells for a garden; there were mosquito nets over the beds and Esmé sprayed and anointed herself with anti-mosquito substances quite frantically; at the end of a week we boarded a motor launch to take us back to the main island of St Vincent and were quite ready to do so.

We were deposited on a jetty and immediately were jostled and pushed around by three menacing louts demanding money. This was frightening, and they threatened to break our spectacles and throw our bags into the sea; we had about an hour to wait before going to the airport, and it was difficult to know quite what to do. There was a small bar in a hut on the jetty and we sought refuge there. The louts waited outside for us, while Esmé fortified herself with rum punches I spent most of the time looking out of the window hoping desperately that our persecutors would go away, which eventually they did, and we made it to the airport unharmed. While we were in that little bar the barman said that it was pointless alerting the police, because mugging and robbing was quite out of hand on St Vincent, the police had become resigned to it all and were probably on the take anyway.

We returned to Petit St Vincent in the spring of 1984 aiming to combine a week there with a week on Young Island. We occupied a bungalow which was raised up a little on a promontory overlooking the tiny harbour and had a good view of the whole island, and the small boats coming and going. There were some fishing boats, and one afternoon we saw frigate birds swooping down and taking the fish from the nets, and the fisherman was unable to do anything about it. Frigates fascinated us, large birds with forked tails which normally circle very high in the sky, and appear not to be moving their wings at all; they swoop down on other birds and make them drop their fish, which they then take before the fish hit the water; they rarely catch fish for themselves. We were to see frigates in large numbers in the Seychelles, especially on Bird Island.

The second part of this holiday was on Young Island, a small island two hundred yards off St Vincent, and we were taken from the airport to a jetty and then across in a motor boat. The accommodation was in chalets built on the sides of a mini mountain and we were near the top with marvellous views. The showers were outside the chalet and there was a fence around them at shoulder height. It was an experience for us to be washing in the open air, while passing the time of day with the neighbours, something we had not done since camping days. The food was delicious and the speciality was lobster tails, a gustatory experience not be missed.

On the second morning we were swimming in the sea and saw a young Chinese couple in some trouble, the girl suffered a dislocation of her right shoulder, and the boy explained that he was an international cellist; I tried to reduce the dislocation but it was too painful and she had to be taken to hospital on St Vincent to have it reduced under anaesthesia. Later they gave us details of his next concert in London, and we promised to try to be there.

As always we found a man with a boat, this one a cheerful soul who offered to take us on a cruise to the island of Mustique. We noticed that he had a whale tooth on a thong round his neck and we asked where he got it; he told us that Bequia was an official whaling station and he offered to get us two whale teeth, one to add to Esmé's tropical necklace and one for me. The sail to Mustique took us through rough waters: there was a lot of wind, the boat lurched and rolled and I lost a hat and my sunglasses; Esmé clung to the rail as if her life depended on it, which it well might have done.

Mustique is not the prettiest of islands, but it is very quiet with few people. We beached and walked along a little lane to Basil's Bar, where we ordered a lobster lunch and felt that we could be rubbing shoulders with royalty. We were told that Princess Margaret had sat at the same table with her escort only a month earlier and we hoped she enjoyed the lunch. Our lobster was covered with thousand island dressing, presumably to suit the American palate; Esmé observed that the Americans had no palate so why should anyone try to suit it.

Vidal the manager on Young Island, and his wife, invited us one evening to their bungalow for drinks, they were a delightful couple and we talked of many things including cricket and music, they played some records, and he gave us an LP to take home. I asked him about tennis, having seen a court there, and he asked if we would like to play with them. I was dubious about this because I thought he might be fairly good, and the next day when I saw him playing with three friends, the standard was almost professional and I was glad we had opted out. Esmé and I were more comfortable hitting a ball at each other in private.

This combination of Petit St Vincent and Young Island in 1984 was our last visit to the Caribbean for many years. We did return ten years later in April 1994 but Esmé had suffered two strokes in June

1993 which destroyed half her vision and also her perception, a grievous deficit. We went back in order to see cricket, and we stayed at the sister hotel of the Coral Reef, The Sandpiper Inn, having been there many years before for dinner and liked the look of it. It was very difficult for Esmé to understand everything but she was so brave and uncomplaining, and the tropical heat seemed to give her a new lease of life. We spent ten days on Barbados, taking in the test match, and then went to Antigua for more cricket, staying at Galley Bay Hotel; Antigua is an unattractive island except for its beaches. We were taken each day to the cricket by a taxi driver named Charles, who immediately understood Esmé's problems, and he was there ready to pick us up outside the ground when we wanted to come home. He told us all about the politics of Antigua where Viv Richards was regarded as king, soon to be deified.

We had a bungalow on the beach at Galley Bay, and lying on a sunbed under a casuarina tree Esmé found that she could read again. She had lost her ability to read in June 1993, but here, at Galley Bay, she read five hundred pages of *Wild Swans* by Jung Chang, this was the last book she ever read, because three months later she suffered the onset of complex epilepsy. She enjoyed this final trip to the Caribbean, although it was difficult for her to get in and out of the sea at The Sandpiper where there was a very shelving beach. While we were there Kathy Croker, our very good Cheltenham friend, and her daughter Alison and family, who were staying in a nearby hotel, joined us from time to time; they came to lunch on water scooters and we dined out with Kathy one evening before we left. Kathy's Ted had been secretary of the Football Association, and she had lost him at Christmas 1992 after a long illness bravely fought and borne, and I think she had found that visits to Barbados had helped her to exist: after the loss of a love there is no living, only existence with hope but without conviction.

Soon after we were first married Esmé said that perhaps one day we would be able to afford a holiday in the West Indies, and little did we know that when we first went to Barbados in 1978, during the next sixteen years we would be privileged to see a great deal of the rest of the world. Little did we know that at the end of the sixteen years Esmé's final experience of the tropics would be on the same island of Barbados, and that just a year or so after that, not only would there be no more travel, there would be no more looking at each other, talking to each other, touching each other and no more loving each other. There is only the memory, and I am terrified that even that will dim. Thoughts of happiness gone are elusive as the swallows wheeling in the sky above me, immune to capture, whereas those of my loss and sorrow surround me like sitting ducks.

Chapter Two
Thailand

In the autumn of the same year that we first went to Barbados we decided that we would go to the far east; I had read in a medical journal about the possibility of holidays in Bangkok, and Esmé was always game to visit new places as far away as possible.

We flew from Heathrow in a temperature of minus 10°F and arrived early the next morning in Bangkok where the thermometer showed 75°F. To get from the international airport to the centre of Bangkok is a long and arduous drive; even in the early morning the traffic is dense and as you get toward the centre of Bangkok rules of the road are non-existent. Traffic chaos was one of the first things we noticed about Bangkok and we were told that measures to relieve it, such as flyovers and underpasses, were not possible because Bangkok is built on a swamp, and the water table is only just below the surface. Thailand, except for the mountains in the north, is really one gigantic swamp, one huge fen country, with criss-crossing dykes known as klongs everywhere, all draining into the enormous and utterly fascinating Chaeo Phraya river.

In 1978 the only possible hotel on the river was The Oriental, a very famous hotel at which many writers have stayed and have written about, and comparable to the Peninsula in Hong Kong, Raffles in Singapore, and The Peace in Shanghai. The original wing was preserved as a museum and the main hotel had been rebuilt beside it, a huge modern block, the interior marbled, and with great ambience and elegance.

We had a room on the eighth floor, and there below us was one of the great rivers of the east, very wide and absolutely packed with boats of every conceivable size and shape; most striking were the trains of heavily-laden barges, low in the water and with domed roofs like the wagons of the wild west. They were pulled by powerful tugs which clattered and strained and at most achieved no more than three knots, even going southwards downstream away from us, toward the warehouses near the mouth of the river where it empties into the Gulf of Siam; from a distance and above they looked like giant sluggish caterpillars. Apart from the tugs and barge trains there were the typical Thai long-tailed boats and busy water taxis carrying up to thirty people; the motorboats had a long tail sticking out at the stern on the end of which was the rudder and the propeller, and at the proximal end a powerful V8 engine; so designed in order to navigate the klongs which are very shallow. We found that by far the best way to traverse Bangkok was by water taxi and we used them extensively.

The Thai girls were quite beautiful; small and doll-like, they walked with such grace, and The Oriental must have had the pick of them; they looked marvellous in their panungs, a garment wrapped tightly around the hips and falling in a soft drape to the feet and with their waist-long gleaming black hair and tiny feet, we felt that they were the perfect picture of femininity. Esmé felt so angry that the Thais were prepared to sacrifice their women, arguably the most physically attractive in the world, to satisfy the revolting sexual needs of European and Australian tourists.

Boys in national dress circulated in The Oriental when there were messages for guests, carrying a board on a pole with bells hanging and tinkling, and on the board would be written the names of those guests for whom there was a communication. The Thai people were giving up their traditional style of dress for western clothes in the city, and we were told that they were abandoning a form of costume that could turn a festival or public holiday gathering into a 'painter's shimmering palette of vividly coloured sarongs and silk trousers'.

Looking at all the activity here, the horrendous traffic jams, and the people, it was difficult for us to believe that barely two hundred years before this was the site of a fishing village and a Chinese trading post on a swampy shore of this wide brown river. The river then would merely have been the way to and from the splendid capital of Ayutthaya, forty miles up and the centre of a vast kingdom covering much of what we now know as Burma, Laos, Cambodia and Malaysia, as well as Thailand.

We visited the old wing of The Oriental and Esmé was fascinated to find on display there letters and registers of hotel guests bearing the names of Joseph Conrad, Somerset Maugham, Graham Greene and

Noël Coward and she tried to imagine what it was like when these people were staying there; ever enthralled by history, she tried to live every minute of it.

We had only a week in Bangkok before moving on to Malaysia and the island of Penang. We visited the colourful royal palaces, their rooftops with curling snakes on each corner sticking up into the sky, but we knew that we would need more time to see the palaces properly, and there was much else, and we felt that we must come back to Bangkok before long. We saw the chapel of the Emerald Buddha, one of the world's most venerated Buddha images, less than three feet high and carved out of translucent emerald stone on a high altar with murals around it depicting the earthly life of the Lord Buddha, and in front of it row upon row of candles lit by the faithful; photography was allowed in the royal palace grounds but forbidden inside the Chapel of the Emerald Buddha. We saw the Reclining Buddha, mildly disappointing, a huge metallic figure lying on its side in a small building, and you could not stand back and view the whole. We entered the Temple of the Golden Buddha, in a pavilion with an open front in which there sat a huge solid gold Buddha, supposed to be made of five tons of pure gold; originally cased in plaster, the gold was only discovered when it was being moved by a crane and was accidentally dropped.

We made a day trip to the ancient capital of Ayutthaya, going up by coach and back by motor launch in the evening. On the way up we had a guide who was voluble and knowledgeable, and Esmé could hardly contain herself when she realised that in this country and indeed all over the east the letter 'l' was pronounced as an 'r' and vice versa; we were therefore told to expect to see in Ayutthaya "lerics" which were unique. Esmé said that she hoped that when we got there we would have time for a 'dlink' or 'thlee' and she needed to use the 'roo' soon. We toured the ruins of Ayutthaya which stands high on a wide fertile plain that is Thailand's rice bowl.

We travelled back to The Oriental on a large motor launch with the sunset to our right; the evening was balmy and we felt utterly content.

We went up the river another day on a rice barge and in a long-tailed boat to the Floating Market at Damnoen Saduak, a half-day excursion out of the city, and there were hundreds of stalls selling so many things, vegetables, orchid plants, mynah birds, puppies, antiques and jewellery, everything imaginable. These stalls were on a huge barge, the river in front of which was jam-packed with boats, each paddled by a Thai woman wearing a conical coolie type hat; but in 1978 it was considered that the Floating Market was no longer the fascinating experience of earlier years, due to the flood of tourists. Esmé bought a small ivory Buddha and felt guilty but was reassured by the fact that the elephant population in Thailand was increasing rapidly. She might perhaps think differently now, but when I look at this little Buddha in our corner cabinet I have a vivid recollection of her pleasure when she bought it.

We spent as much time as we could, when not sightseeing, in The Oriental itself because it was so comfortable and the atmosphere so pleasant. There is a heavy Conrad influence: besides a Joseph Conrad bar, the top restaurant was called Lord Jim, and each afternoon in the marbled foyer a string quartet played chamber music from four until six o'clock.

For this holiday Esmé had bought white and yellow knee-length dresses, one with a strap round the neck and the other with shoulder straps, and she looked lovely; she wore with the dresses white and yellow sandals with laces tied in front of the ankle which did justice to her lovely legs. After the buffet we watched Thai dancing, the hyperextension of the fingers and wrists demanded for the dancing was bizarre, and we wondered how much pain was caused to the children in their early training for this.

Just before we left Bangkok for Penang we visited a Thai village where we saw an exhibition of Thai boxing and a fight between a cobra and mongoose, which the mongoose won easily; we felt sorry for the snake. We had not appreciated before we went to Thailand that people may have ramshackle houses of one sort or another but in the east they seem to live entirely on the street: they cook and eat on the street, they sleep on the street, they do business on the street, and for all we knew they made love and had babies on the street. We had done so much in the time available in Bangkok but we felt that we needed to return, and we did this three years later in 1991.

In 1989 on our way home from the South Pacific we had planned to spend time in Australia but when we landed in Sydney there was a strike of Ansett airline pilots and all internal flights were cancelled; we did not fancy all those miles by coach to Queensland and we opted instead to go back to Bangkok and then over to the island of Phuket, hoping that we might be able to get into the Royal Yacht Club, which friends had praised so much, but it was nearly Christmas and the Royal Yacht Club was full. We ended up in the Meridian Hotel, a very large cosmopolitan hotel, and standing on the beach and looking back at it Esmé described it as looking like a giant wedding cake.

We had not been to Phuket before but knew that it was very beautiful. The Meridian was on the west side of the island with a fine beach in front of it extending right round to the headland miles away to the north; we made ourselves at home here and spent most of the time lying under a straw umbrella and reading our books, with the Andaman Sea only a few feet from us. The hotel catered for all ages; there was much and varied night entertainment, several restaurants and two large swimming pools. There were four hundred and fifty rooms and Germans outnumbered all other nationalities, Lufthansa flying in every other day, and the early morning placing of bags and towels on the sun-loungers reminded us of those camping holidays so very long ago in the South of France and Italy. Esmé quite liked the Meridian, where there were plenty of shops, and she was pleased when the Bangkok Post was delivered to our room in a long narrow plastic bag; she felt that these would be very useful for packing shoes on future trips, and she suggested that I should go and buy some from the staff quarters, which I did.

After two or three days lazing on the beach we got up the energy to go on a day trip to Phi Phi Island. We embarked on a large motorboat; there were hundreds of people on the jetty scrambling to get in and it was all a little reminiscent of Dunkirk. Esmé got on board before me and as was her wont got us two seats in the cabin. She was always very good at getting chairs and tables wherever we were, pubs in England, restaurants abroad, boats – she never failed. Phuket offshore is very beautiful, there are lots of tall vertical rocky pillars sticking out of the sea and covered with vegetation; further north than we went, Phanga Nga is supposed to be the most beautiful part of Phuket and a James Bond film was made there. Our cruiser moored in a bay off Phi Phi Island and we were taken ashore in narrow boats. We had a good lunch under some trees and explored quite a large shopping area; it was obvious that Phi Phi Island, which was small and unknown until a few years previously, was rapidly becoming a resort in itself, and hotels were going up behind the beach. Esmé recorded in the journal that the sea and cliffs of Phi Phi Island were breathtakingly beautiful, she also remarked that the crowding on the boat and the difficulty of getting on and off made her feel like a Vietnamese boat person, and she reckoned that if the Vietnamese boat people endured anything like this they deserved to be allowed to stay in Hong Kong. We were the oldest people on this trip by many years, and when we had to get off the bigger boat and into smaller boats to be beached on the island, I had so much equipment on my back, bag, snorkels, cameras, binoculars that I felt like an American marine storming Okinawa; but the Japanese here, though plentiful, were not armed with guns and flame-throwers; the way Esmé bumped and bored them out of the way to get us lunch filled me with admiration, as I watched her from the other end of the hut while trying to grab some cold beer, and I felt she could be an asset to the Welsh pack in the line-out at Cardiff Arms Park.

The flight between Phuket and Bangkok takes just short of an hour and poses no great problem. The domestic airport is twenty minutes' walk from the international airport and although there are courtesy buses they tend to be rather infrequent, and as there is usually a scrum to get onto them we felt that we would rather walk and push our trolley ahead of us. We spent a final night at The Oriental before boarding the plane for London and we met Tim and Valerie Ashby there quite by chance; we had originally met them on a tour of South India and had become good friends. We had dinner with them down the river at the Sheraton Hotel which had not been built when we first came to Bangkok, and had a very enjoyable evening watching some good dancing. The river traffic had changed, there were very few rice barges or barge trains now, and as much as possible was being shifted down to the river mouth by road; this seemed a pity, and change in boat traffic was also evident when we returned to Hong Kong after many years and discovered that there was an almost total absence of junks and many fewer sampans, which diminished the character of the place.

Three years later we returned to Phuket and made our first acquaintance with the Royal Yacht Club. We were met at the airport on Phuket by two of the hotel staff with a large air-conditioned Mercedes; they were dressed immaculately in white suits and Esmé was convinced that there had been some mistake and that they were expecting the King and Queen. We were driven in this grand style to the hotel fifty minutes away on Nai Harn Bay, and as soon as we arrived we knew that it was our type of place, there is no checking in on arrival, you are taken straight to your room where a cold tropical cocktail awaits and all your details are taken later. The Yacht Club is so named because the Royal Regatta is held there each December, and the King brings his party. The rooms are enormous with a long wide patio, part covered and part open, and the view is breathtaking across Nai Harn Bay. We quickly got to know the assistant manager and became good friends with Nid who was responsible for the arrangements on the beach. We had lunch each day in a small bar, a wooden shack where there was simple Thai food, excellent and so much cheaper than in the hotel, and there was plenty of Singha Thai lager beer.

We decided to take a day trip to Coral Island, and a minibus took us to the southern end of Phuket where there was a long and extremely rickety wooden jetty with many planks missing. We had to walk along this and get into a large motor vessel parked off the end of it, and Esmé walked it like a nervous cat. The cruise to Coral Island takes an hour and we were transferred to the beach in long-tail boats; snorkelling was profitless because there were few fish but there were two good beach restaurants, and we had some delicious Thai soup and seafood. We did not know it at the time, but this was to be the last holiday with Esmé in good health. Writing this now, and looking back and looking also at the photographs taken on that beach on Coral Island, she looked so fit, well and happy that I really cannot believe what was to happen to her, and end life as we knew it six months later.

Transferring from the larger boat into the small long-tailed boats to get to the beach and vice versa, Esmé required the help of three or four willing coolies, and when she got onto the big boat to go back to Phuket she announced that she was not quite as good as she used to be at getting the leg over, I felt that if ever there was a time for chivalry, assuredly this was it, and I hastened to reassure her that she was every bit as good as she ever was, in more ways than one.

Reading the journal of this holiday which had taken us across the world, she wrote on the last page on the last day that we had had a fabulous holiday, and because we had been to so many varied places there was so much to remember. In the situation that I am now my fear is that I will lose these memories even with the help of the photographs and journals. I still fear that many of them will melt away into the mists of time and they are all that I have left of her.

After her two strokes in June 1993, by September we took our courage in both hands, and somewhat against the advice of our doctors we went back to the Royal Yacht Club for a two-week holiday. With her vision impairment and loss of perception Esmé could not recognise objects, but in spite of this she tried hard and was very game and determined to enjoy the tropics again; she was equally determined that she should not spoil my holiday.

Backache had become a problem and she spent most of the time swimming in the pool which helped her greatly, and everybody at the Yacht Club who understood our situation was very kind and helpful. Esmé saw Nai Harn beach again, was made welcome in the beach bar, she saw Coral Island and even swam in the sea there and had lunch again, Thai fish soup, in the same beach restaurant. On the last evening, standing on the balcony of our room, she saw again the tropical sunset, she saw a glorious gold and crimson carpet rolled out as if specially for her across the Andaman Sea, with a Singapore Sling in her hand. We felt that provided there were no more serious setbacks we might be able to live some sort of life, and perhaps even continue some sort of travel.

We did return within three months to the Yacht Club: our son Bill and family had decided to visit Australia to see our eldest grandson, Barney, who was teaching in Melbourne. They arranged to go to Australia via the Yacht Club and they joined us there. Esmé was now very limited in what she could do but she made great efforts; she was able to lie on the beach, there are photographs showing her happy that everybody was enjoying themselves, and she even tried to write the daily journal; but because of her impaired vision writing had become a great labour. When the time came for us to leave she made a point of saying goodbye to Nid, to the people in the beach bar and to all our friends on the staff of the hotel, and I had a sickening feeling that she knew that she would not return, and this broke my heart. I know that wherever else I go, I can never go back there without her.

Chapter Three

Penang

In 1978 the second half of our holiday was spent on Penang. We had heard about Penang from our friends Steuart and Margaret BonBernard; Steuart had been a government officer there for some years after the war before returning to England to train and work as a solicitor in Cheltenham.

The island is beautiful and exotic and has an extraordinary mix of peoples. There is a colourful blend of Malay, Chinese, Thai and Indian cultures, and when we were there in 1978 there was little or no evidence of ruination of the island by the building of concrete jungles. In Georgetown trishaws, a combination of rickshaw and bicycle, were the commonest means of transport, easily outnumbering the motor cars. When we were considering going to Penang I had sought the advice of Odin Khoo, my house physician at Standish Hospital, Gloucester, who was Malaysian. His uncle was in the hotel business and he strongly advised us to stay at the Rasa Sayang Hotel on Batu Ferringhi Beach. This had a four storey wing and we had a room on the third level overlooking the beach; Odin Khoo had advised us what to eat on Penang, and we could not wait to sample what he described as "steamboat", a special type of local fish soup.

Always when we arrived at expensive hotels across the world, I would go outside to look for a cheaper source of beer; it was my experience that there was almost always a Chinaman or an Indian able and willing to peddle cost price drink nearby. Outside the Rasa Sayang I was not disappointed, there was an Indian in a tent by the side of the road with many boxes and cartons of beer behind him. I used my grey shoulder bag as a beer sack, and tried to walk back into the hotel looking as if I was not carrying a heavy load.

The beach was pleasant, there were trees for us to lie under and read our books, and the staff were very friendly. Esmé could not wait to go on a tour of the island because she had heard that there were many spice shrubs and bushes. On our second night we went to the restaurant for a Malaysian buffet. Esmé had gone over to the food to see what was available, and as I was about to join her two people sat down, who I assumed were Japanese, and asked if we would allow them to share the table. When I got to the buffet I said to Esmé that we were going to have to spend dinner with two middle-aged Japs, and when she had got her food she went back to the table and said politely to them that she was afraid that she did not speak Japanese, they said with smiles that neither did they, because they had been Chinese all their lives. From this point there started an extraordinary chain of events which led to us making friends with at least three extended Chinese families. The two people at the table were Doctor and Mrs Lau, Fook and Nonya. Fook had trained in medicine at Guy's Hospital in London, was a member of the Royal College of Physicians and was senior physician at the local hospital in Georgetown. They asked us to go the next evening for pre-dinner drinks at their house and on another day he took me round his hospital.

We received telephone calls in our room with invitations, and eventually we agreed to go to lunch the following Sunday at the Hotel Casuarina a few miles down the road, where three Chinese families awaited us; Raymond and Bernice Ng, Godfrey and Mai Ling Geh, Eng Toon and Theresa Goh, and also Fook and Nonya. Raymond was a merchant banker along with Eng Toon, his brother; Godfrey was a cousin and an English-trained plastic surgeon. We had a delightful lunch with these extremely pleasant people and they made available the next day a chauffeur-driven car so that we could tour the island, and asked us to join them for supper the next night at a restaurant up on the hill. It transpired that the Ngs and the Gohs had children at school in England at Cheltenham Ladies' College and Cheltenham College, and they saw the opportunity of having us, living in Cheltenham, in loco parentis. The dinner was a Chinese meal which went on for hours, and the conversation was stimulating. They were very interested in everything English and we discussed the previous Saturday's football results as well as English and Malaysian politics. On the tour of the island in their chauffeur-driven car Esmé was able to see all the shrubs and bushes that she wanted to, and she was tickled to death when she saw a cinnamon bush.

After we returned to England, and for the next few years, we saw most of them from time to time. Raymond and Bernice had a son, Winston, at Cheltenham College and he came to lunch on Sundays quite regularly. We also saw a lot of Linda and Lily Goh who were at Cheltenham Ladies College and when their parents came over to see them they always took us out for lunch. When Winston finally left Cheltenham College, Raymond and Bernice gave us a special bottle of champagne which they had had labelled 'Dr and Mrs Bob Ellis'; the bottle remains on the kitchen shelf with a candle stuck in it.

Our friendship with these Chinese people started at that table in the Rasa Sayang all those years ago when Esmé said that she was sorry that she did not speak Japanese!

The sea around Penang is not suitable for swimming, as there are biting insects in the plankton and there are rocks and reefs close in and shallow, but the hotel had a large pool and we were able to take our exercise there.

Before we left Penang we went to see Georgetown, and we saw Fort Cornwallis, where the island was first claimed for the British; a very complex temple called Kek Lok Sic and, most interesting of all, we saw the Snake Temple which was built in 1973 and is occupied by many deadly vipers, which were allegedly made sleepy by the heady fumes of the constant incense burning; sleepy they may have been, but we were disinclined to put a foot near them to test them out.

By the time we left Penang we had already seen enough to know that ahead, provided we could stay fit, lay years of exquisitely related experiences, and so many times did Esmé tell me that we must know and savour every moment, and not rely on an index of memories when we were too old to travel. We all have empty spaces in our minds which we tend to fill with the events and passions of others, through music, literature and art, but it did seem to us back in 1978 that we would have wonderful opportunities to fill most of our spaces with experiences of our own. Standing on Batu Ferringhi beach just before we left to go home, Esmé gazed at the sea, deep in thought for a long time before turning to me and saying that we had exchanged the sapphire of the Caribbean for the emerald of the Andaman; I waited, and then she said that one day we would lose each other and she could not begin to imagine how she could ever say goodbye to me. It is one of my very few comforts now, but a very important one, that she never had to.

Chapter Four

Hong Kong

When we were sitting beside the pool in The Oriental Hotel in Bangkok, we got into conversation with another English couple who had just come from ten days in Hong Kong, and they waxed lyrical about what they had seen there. We had it on our list of places to see without giving it much priority, but after this conversation we decided that we would go the following year in 1979, and combine Hong Kong with Bali. Esmé and I had both wanted to go to China since we were young, and we thought that if we could get across to Macau from Hong Kong we could go into Red China, because we had heard that the frontier was open from time to time for tourists to do a very limited trip inside the Chinese mainland.

We had acted in loco parentis for Richard Hardy in Cheltenham, whose parents Sue and Geoff had lived for two or three years in Hong Kong when Geoff was in the Foreign Office. They told us that we should stay in Kowloon rather than on the island of Hong Kong, and recommended the Hong Kong Hotel, close to the Kowloon terminal of the Star Ferry. When we told our Chinese friends in Penang that we were going to Hong Kong, they immediately gave us the name and telephone number of a relative who was a businessman in Hong Kong, and whose wife was the official flower arranger in the Hong Kong Hotel.

It thrilled us to think that we were going to a place which was face to face with Red China, a country whose borders had been closed for years, but in the event we were unable to get across into China, and we spent all our time exploring Hong Kong. We went across on the Star Ferry many times accompanied by thousands of Chinese; there were more than five million people in Hong Kong, ninety-eight per cent of whom were Chinese. The population exploded after the war and went from six hundred thousand in 1945 to four million in 1971.

Many of the immigrants to Hong Kong came over the Chinese border illegally, and the population had been swelled by the arrival of the boat people from Vietnam. Arrival at Hong Kong is quite an experience. As we flew into Kai Tak airport, there were blocks of flats on either side of the runway and it seemed that they were only feet from the wing tips. I had a pilot as a patient who was working for Cathay Pacific Airways, and he told me that he felt that when he flew into Kai Tak from the harbour side, if he sneezed he might kill three hundred people. He said that you had a choice, either you flew in from the landward side between mountain peaks, or you did a roof top skim over the skyscrapers in Kowloon, or you came in from the harbour with the problem of the wing-tip skyscrapers. In spite of these hazards Kai Tak Airport has one of the best safety records in the world.

Esmé, as usual, had done her homework: she knew what we ought to do during our week or so in Hong Kong and first priority was the harbour cruise. Hong Kong has an enormous harbour, probably the biggest in the world, which narrows to the channel between Hong Kong Island and Kowloon. This channel is getting narrower and narrower as years go by because more and more land is reclaimed, both on the island and the mainland side, for more building of more skyscrapers. We went on the harbour cruise in an adapted junk, and wended our way among all the shipping in the outer harbour, where there must have been a hundred ships waiting for unloading space on the jetties of Kowloon. We went to a far corner of the harbour where the liner Queen Elizabeth ended her days, destroyed by fire while arrangements were being made to convert her into an offshoot of Hong Kong University; locals, with a knowing look, said that the whole thing was an insurance scam. I hoped to see something of the wreck, but there was literally nothing remaining, and I was told that within six months of the liner being declared a wreck, salvage firms had taken away all the removable metal and sold it for scrap in China. When you think that the liner weighed 85,000 tons, they must have worked hard and fast, but that is what all Chinese do.

We were taken into the Typhoon Shelter, where there were hundreds and hundreds of junks and sampans moored side by side and end to end, and swarming all over them were millions of people; they all live on the boats and they seem to lead an absolutely communal life. These boats are powered by engines rather than sails, and the noise and the smell was incredible.

When we went back to Hong Kong for the third time many years later, we were sad to find that the Typhoon Shelter was no more, there were hardly any junks to be seen anywhere, and so much more building and land reclamation had gone on that Hong Kong did not seem quite the exciting place that we found when we first saw it in 1979.

On this first trip, after the harbour cruise, we went up to the Peak where the views are magnificent, and then crossed the island to Repulse Bay, named after a British man-of-war, and dined in a huge floating restaurant at Aberdeen. Next evening, we dined in a revolving restaurant, which towered high above Kowloon, and the view of the night skyline was so exciting that we took hours to get through the meal. On another evening we went across on the Star Ferry, and took a tram ride along the waterfront of Hong Kong Island, there the streets were packed with people, the noise was deafening, there were festoons of bright Chinese signs over the streets; the night streets of Hong Kong have to be seen, heard, smelled and even felt, and you cannot believe it all.

With only two days left we had to make difficult choices, and we decided that we must see the New Territories, where most of the people lived who had come across illegally from China. We took a train through the territories, and saw the hundreds upon hundreds of blocks of flats, each flat seeming to have people hanging out of the windows, and there must have been two or three families per flat. We knew that Hong Kong had been bursting at the seams for some time, but judging by the mass of population in the New Territories, which was increasing all the time from China, there was never going to be any more room for anybody.

Before we went home we felt we must see some of the outlying islands, and we went to Lamma. In much earlier times this was the haunt of pirates, but in 1979 it was a home base for a large boat population. There was a long jetty with sampans nudging and pushing, trying to find somewhere to tie up so that they could unload their produce and sell it in the market just along from the jetty. The noise was incredible, men shouting, young pigs tied up in oblong baskets squealing, Chinamen running this way and that carrying vegetables, meat, sacks of corn, wooden logs and heaven knows what besides. We walked along the waterfront where there were restaurants with tanks of fish swimming around, and if you decided to eat, you selected your fish which was cooked in front of you. Esmé was a little concerned about the general prospect of the pigs in the baskets and the fish in the tanks; she said that there was only one way for them to go and she did not much like it. She suggested that when we went back to the jetty to get into the boat, I should let loose some of the pigs as a parting gesture; I told her that if I did this, she would go on to Bali alone, because I would be in the sea with my throat cut!

Before we left Hong Kong we took afternoon tea in the Peninsula Hotel, walking past the ten gleaming Rolls Royces parked radially in the forecourt, like the spokes of huge wheel, the hub a large fountain. When we were sipping our tea Esmé told me to imagine that it was 1931 and Noël Coward was sitting at the next table, and that he was about to go on to Shanghai to the Peace Hotel, where he would write *Private Lives*; my love always had a vivid imagination.

On our last evening in Hong Kong we went out to dinner with the good lady who was the flower arranger in the Hong Kong Hotel and her husband. They took us to a Chinese restaurant where we were treated to a demonstration of noodle making, and it was amazing to see how they wound the long ropes of noodle around sticks, tossed them up in the air to the ceiling and caught them again; Esmé suggested that when we next had a dinner party at 8 Greenhills Road, I should be in the background making noodles like this; she thought it would impress our friends.

In all our travels Esmé was ever avid for new experiences, everything she saw or heard was taken in and assimilated, nothing was wasted, she said that it all added up to the reason for our being here, which was to live; that has reverberated through my mind during these last two years as her life was gradually and cruelly taken away from her.

We had the opportunity to renew our acquaintance with Hong Kong two years later in 1981. I discovered that the biennial Asia-Pacific Conference on Lung Disease was to be held in the Regent Hotel in Hong Kong in November 1981, and it seemed reasonable to go back there and complete our experience of the place, especially because Red China had become more liberal in allowing tourists to do limited tours of the country via Macau. We again stayed in the Hong Kong Hotel, and as much of the conference was low grade, I decided that my time would be more profitably spent on further sightseeing with Esmé.

My so loyal colleague at Standish Hospital, Gloucester, Anna Makamaska, also attended the conference and when we went to China, she accompanied us with an old friend whom she had met travelling in previous years. We took the hydrofoil across Hong Kong harbour to Macau which showed much evidence of Portuguese colonisation, with impressive mansions lining wide boulevards.

At the border we were marshalled about by Chinese customs officials and soldiers, who were courteous and polite, but obviously unused to dealing with tourists. We eventually got through, and on to a coach which took us along roads over flat farming country. There were many water buffaloes, the whole picture similar to Indonesia and Thailand. We were taken to a farm and shown through the house, the kitchen, the hovels and the stables and it seemed much like any farm anywhere else in the far east. We went to the house of Dr Sun Yat Sen, the father of the Chinese Republic which he created in 1911, and saw his bed, his wash basin, his study, his desk with pen and inkwell, and this seemed such a small house for a man who had created such an enormous republic. Many years later on a wide tour of China, we would see Dr Sun Yat Sen's memorial in Nanking, a huge mausoleum reached after climbing hundreds of steps, so different from this unremarkable house just across the border from Macau.

We stopped at a small town, and the lasting impression of this short trip to China was of rain, thousands and thousands of bicycles, and thousands and thousands of people all wearing, men and women alike, blue cotton suits and blue peaked caps.

We felt that the excitement and the thrill of Hong Kong was maximal on our first visit and we have an ever present reminder of that visit in our living-room, a large table lamp decorated with painted Chinese figures.

Like her father before her, Esmé was always fascinated by news and current affairs, and I remember her excitement on the first morning of our first visit to Bangkok when a copy of the Bangkok Post was pushed under the door of our room; she was similarly excited when the same thing happened with the Straits Times in Penang and the South China Morning Post in Hong Kong. She loved reading about far away people in their faraway places, and the last thing she ever wanted was to be insulated from the outside world; getting away from it all was never for her.

Chapter Five

Indonesia

After we had seen Hong Kong in 1979 we flew with Garuda
Indonesian Airlines to Bali. We had heard a good deal about Bali, and
read about it and although it was becoming a centre for tourists,
especially downmarket Australians, we felt we should go before it
became ruined. We had heard about its beauty and about Balinese
culture and had seen some of the art. Bali, situated just off the eastern
tip of Java, seemed so insignificant on the map compared with the
enormous islands of Sumatra and Java in this vast archipelago. We
had been told by an acquaintance in Gloucestershire, who was an
importer of Balinese art, that Bali had breathtaking beauty, gentle
people, music, dance and colourful festivals, and as our plane
descended on Denpasar Airport, we could hardly wait to sample all
this.

We stayed in the Bali Hyatt Hotel, one of several luxury hotels on
Sanur Beach, which was built, furnished and decorated in pure
Indonesian style. As you enter you go up some steps into a large
foyer, which is like a huge straw-covered barn; all the furniture is of
bamboo, and by the entrance there was a gamelan band. The lovely
tinkling sound of gamelan music seemed to haunt us wherever we
went on the island; it was a type of music we had never heard before,
peaceful and relaxing and unique. The accommodation in the hotel
was around three large courtyards, connected by a wide open passage,
lined by fascinating terracotta figures about two feet high, in the top of
which at night they put large candles and flowers. The courtyards are
named after these flowers, bougainvillaea, hibiscus and frangipani; we
were in a first floor room in frangipani court with a balcony
overlooking a beautiful tropical garden, and some seventy yards away,
the Indian Ocean.

The male hotel staff were dressed in white shirts and shorts with long white stockings to the knee and white shoes, all very smart: they did everything for you, and on the first morning two of them brought two sun-loungers and put them under a coconut palm just in front of our room. Esmé said that as she watched them carrying the sunbeds across the gardens, with myself following behind and carrying nothing, I looked like a White Sultan lording it over his native servants. We felt that this was a life we could get used to and we had better enjoy it, because things would be very different back home in Cheltenham.

After recharging our batteries for a couple of days, we set about seeing the rest of the island. Esmé as usual had worked out what we should see; she had become very interested in comparative religion, and when she heard that Bali was known as "the island of a thousand temples", she wanted to visit some of these; the other description of Bali by Pandit Nehru, 'the morning of the world', led us to get up on the second morning to witness the dawn. Apart from the temples, we hoped to attend a cremation, which in Indonesia and in Bali particularly is an all-day affair, attended by the whole village and ending with the ashes ceremoniously tipped into the sea, but this proved impossible. We went up to the Mount Agung volcano and saw the most sacred temple on the top of it; Mount Agung last erupted in March 1963 and destroyed the temple, but by the time we were there in 1979, it had been fully restored. We saw a performance of the kekac monkey dance performed by hundreds of young villagers; this dance depicts some of the Ramayana story, and the locals were very keen that we should know all about it. It was largely about one king killing another king to get his wife back, assisted by apes and monkey-soldiers. We saw a barong dance, the barong being a legendary animal with a very frightening facial mask, a huge mythical lion who represents the good spending most of the dance struggling against a long-nailed witch named Rangda, who represents the evil; it all goes on for a very long time and merges into the legong dance, danced by two beautiful girls in ornate dresses and headpieces, fingers bending, eyes flashing to the insistent beat of the music. The whole thing ends eventually with a trance dance, where everybody seems to kill everybody else with daggers, which is probably just as well. Esmé was very glad to spend one afternoon in a Hindu temple and chatted at length with a priest, and felt she had learned a lot about Hinduism.

We were so taken with the terracotta figures lining the passages in the hotel, that before we left for home we asked where we could buy two of these. The hotel arranged for them to be delivered to us and also to box them in plywood boxes with handles, so that we could take them on the plane with us. Esmé christened them the Garuda brothers after the airline: one has a very sad face, closed eyes, fat cheeks and is holding a cockerel under his right arm, the other has a cheerful look about him, is wearing a round hat and carries a drum in front of him, which he is beating. When we got them home we put them on our patio, where they have been ever since; Esmé's favourite was the sad one with the cockerel and she called him Lal; when we had parties on summer nights we put candles in them and also flowers, though our roses were a poor substitute for bougainvillaea and frangipani.

We returned to the Bali Hyatt Hotel in 1981 on our way back from Hong Kong and Bangkok. This was a shorter visit and we could see that more and more hotels were going up along Sanur Beach, though it was encouraging to hear that there was a limit of two stories on all future hotels. We also noticed that there was a considerable increase in lager louts from Australia, and the Australian lager lout is no improvement on the British one.

Nearly ten years on we returned to Indonesia. Esmé's grandfather, who was a colliery manager in Loughor near Swansea at the turn of the century, gave up his job and sailed to Sumatra for a new life as a mining engineer in the tin and copper mining industry. Esmé always said that the reason he did this was not only to make more money, but to get away from his wife and ten children; she was told all through her childhood how much she loved her grandmother, but she said that in truth her grandmother was the most selfish old woman she ever met. Her grandfather used to send the money home to Loughor, and Esmé's mother who was the eldest of the ten children would put it in the post office bank. Esmé found it extraordinary that her grandfather should have the courage to go almost to the other end of the world, in days when sailing a hundred miles could be hazardous.

We discovered when preparing for this holiday that books on Sumatra were difficult to find; it was not an island that was yet on the tourist route, but eventually we found a Post Guide which told us enough. We wanted to start with Sumatra, then go down to Java and finally northward to Sulawesi, an island of extraordinary shape and, as we would find, extraordinary in many other ways.

We flew from Gatwick with Garuda Airlines to Medan, the capital of Sumatra. In those days the jumbo jets had to go down in the Gulf to refuel and there were many delays; we lost seven hours in this flight so that when we finally got to Medan we were totally exhausted. The people were welcoming in immigration and customs, and Esmé asked why were they all so nice and smiling all the time, she felt that they even seemed glad to see us.

When we got to the hotel and lurched into the bar, we found that we were the only people there. The barman shook us warmly by the hand and brought our drinks and sat with us at the table: his English was pretty poor, but his need to be friendly was delightful. I told him what we were proposing to do in Indonesia, and that we had stopped short of going to Irian Jaya because we would not have time; when I mentioned Irian Jaya he fell about laughing, and said that they were so backward in that part of Indonesia that they made the people in Papua New Guinea seem modern. The next year we were going to Papua New Guinea from Australia, and thinking about it now, I am not quite sure that he was right. In Sumatra eight-five per cent of the people are Muslim and we were alerted to the fact that Ramadan had started the very day that we arrived. A year before we had gone to Egypt in Ramadan and to get a beer was a major operation, though Esmé was always all right with her duty-free. The next day we had a look around Medan, which seemed very much like other eastern cities, all bustling humanity, thousands of becaks, strange vehicles which were really tricycles with a sidecar, and many multi-coloured minibuses packed with people. The houses built by the Dutch gave the city an air of prosperity, and the people seemed so happy and contented going about their business, compared with what we had seen in Manila in the Philippines.

After a fairly brief tour around the city we set off on the one hundred and ten mile drive to Lake Toba in the mountains in the north with Anthony, our guide, who spoke good English. We passed through miles and miles of rubber, palm oil, and cocoa plantations, and we stopped in a rubber plantation, and had a demonstration of the way in which they collect latex. Anthony told us that the main reason most tourists visit north Sumatra is to visit Lake Toba, which is nine hundred metres above sea level, the largest lake in South-East Asia, all of eighty kilometres long. We drove round the lake and ended up in Prapat and stayed at the Danau Toba Hotel. We realised that this was mainly a resort for Sumatrans, there were very few European visitors which eminently suited us. We arrived on a Saturday, and judging by the number of Sumatrans there, Sumatra had discovered *le weekend*.

We wanted to explore the lake, and we did that on the following day on a double-deck boat and had it all to ourselves with Anthony, who took us to a Batak village where civilisation was recent, and we were told that cannibalism was still practised at the turn of the century; Esmé observed that her grandfather could very possibly have ended up in a stew. The Batak houses are unique to Sumatra, they have curious saddle-shaped roofs and are on stilts, they consist of one huge room in which everybody lives, up to eight families, and underneath are the pigs and the chickens.

In the centre of the village in an open space there was some Batak ceremonial dancing, which was interesting, but less artistic and colourful than on Bali. At the end of the dance they brought on a buffalo, and it was of great importance to the villagers with regard to good crops and prosperity, that the buffalo should have a "good action" rather than a "bad action". As the buffalo was tethered with the southern end directly in front of us, we were in a good position to assess the outcome. After a few minutes the buffalo duly performed, and it was led away while the important men in the village inspected the result, and after much deliberation, they announced a "good action". Esmé asked Anthony what would happen if the buffalo failed to perform, he said that they give the buffalo "what you call enema, before they bring him out"; she felt that the buffalo might be better off being slaughtered at a funeral feast than have to suffer these indignities. The boat took us to Samosir Island in the centre of Lake Toba where we had lunch, and I remember very well that there were large trees of bougainvillaea more than thirty feet high, which were simply stunning.

On the way back Anthony told us about Sumatran funerals. In Indonesia, as in the far east generally, there was a totally different attitude to death from European thinking. When somebody dies in Sumatra, they bury the body close to the home to prevent the corpse being abducted by people intent on practising black magic. After maybe some years the family will gather from all corners of the earth,

52

and when they are all together the bones are removed to a permanent grave and a gravestone is erected. Anthony told us that if families cannot produce the money to have a proper funeral, the bones are left where they were originally buried, and if there is a family dispute at the start the body does not get buried at all and is kept in a wooden box until the problem is resolved, and "body get to smell very bad". On the way back to Medan from Prapat we had a comfort stop and were amazed when a young man appeared with a white bag and said that he was a member of the Salvation Army. We felt we must contribute.

The next morning in Medan we went to the Mosque, which was certainly the most impressive building in Medan. It was called The Sultan's Mosque, and at the gate Esmé was taken to one side and issued with a "sarong" which was nothing more than a skirt a few inches longer than her own skirt, and she was given a wisp of something to put on her head. Before we went in she had seen to it that her arms were covered, and she knew that she must not be unclean by menstruating, and there was certainly no problem about that. Inside the Mosque there were many people at their devotions on their mats, and Esmé asked me why were they were so worried about women being unclean for physiological reasons, when all the men she saw in there were absolutely filthy because they did not wash.

Before we left we visited the Sultan's Palace. The Sultan surrendered power after the end of the Japanese occupation in 1945, and there was then a bitter war which eventually led to Indonesian independence from the Dutch in 1949. Esmé discussed the approach to religion in Sumatra with Anthony, and wrote in the journal that in Sumatra religion is regarded as a totally private affair between the individual and his god, and nothing whatever to do with another individual; she found this refreshing and I had to say that this was all very well, but before she went into the Mosque, they did ask her if she was menstruating, which can hardly be called minding your own business. We gathered from Anthony that the important thing for Sumatrans was to have plenty of sons, as it is a strongly patrilinear society, and daughters really do not count. When asked how many children he has, a Sumatran man will merely give the number of his sons. Esmé was never a feminist, but there was no way that she could accept this, and asked how could I ever face Cathy and Emma if I subscribed to it.

We flew to Jakarta and the approach to the airport was very striking; as you looked out of the window you could see ten thousand feet below, the "Thousand Islands" just off the north coast an extraordinary sight, with each tiny island covered with vegetation, and you felt from ten thousand feet that you could step from one to another without getting your feet wet. We walked across the tarmac from the plane into a pleasant building in classical Javanese style, the large arrival hall overhung by a broad roof, the whole thing open at the sides and the roof supported on thick red wooden pillars. We caught another plane to Yogyakarta, flying south-east, and we found our way to the Ambarrukmo Palace Hotel. I was by now seriously afflicted by what is known in Mexico as the Aztec Two-step, in Egypt as Tutankhamen's Revenge and in India as Delhi Belly. I felt that I was in the last stages of cholera, and when we got to the hotel I lay on the bed and told Esmé how much I loved her, and that I almost certainly was not going to survive; I suggested that she should kiss me and hold me, because by tomorrow morning I would be in a box in a corner of the room, awaiting some sort of Indonesian burial arrangement. She was quite unconcerned and simply told me to take more immodium, and that she was going down to investigate the bar and the restaurant. I felt that on occasions like this, however much you love somebody and however long you have been married to them, it is still possible to go off them.

The next morning, when I realised I might live, I suggested we should plan the day. The Indonesian Times was pushed under the door and Esmé fell upon it; she loved these newspapers, and keeping abreast of the news wherever in the world she happened to be. She discovered that this particular hotel specialised in an eastern breakfast, and she said that we must partake. I told her that there was no way that I could partake, but that if I could retrieve my bowels I would come and support her as an observer. In the journal of Wednesday 12 April, she wrote that at breakfast everything was on offer, all juices, fruit, cereals, eggs cooked in front of you how you want them, ham, bacon, cold meat, rice, various eastern dishes, rolls, croissants and cakes. I remember just watching all this, and wondering if I could keep down a cup of coffee.

Our guide in Yogyakarta was Budi, a very educated man who was anxious to tell us everything he could about Indonesia; he was born locally and Esmé quickly established a rapport with him over the next three days. First he took us to the Sultan's Palace and delivered us to an official Palace guide who was slightly younger than Esmé. She explained that the Palace was still occupied, but the Sultan's and the female quarters were only a small part of the whole complex; it appeared that all the Sultan's sons and daughters were employed in the factories and hotels that he owned; although wielding no power, he had enormous wealth. The Palace buildings were of painted wood and we were shown instruments of the Sultan's gamelan orchestra, but on the whole one got the impression that everything was out of time. Esmé raised the question of female circumcision, and the guide told us that every Muslim girl should be circumcised as a baby, not by a doctor but by someone designated for the purpose and it was carried out using a sterile bamboo stick. We discussed this later with Budi, and he said that this was really only for the Palace children, elsewhere in Java female circumcision was on the wane.

We went to a batik factory and a small silver factory, the batik made by covering certain parts of the design with wax which remains impervious to the dyes. We felt that batik colours were rather unexciting, though the patterns were attractive.

We were treated in the evening to yet another Ramayana epic classical ballet in the open air: most of its symbolism passed over us and we felt that the female dance had much to do with posture, particularly hand and foot, and wondered how the joints were made so supple and how could the digits of hands and feet point in such unnatural directions. The ligaments must be stretched very early in growth, each curve of the finger has a special meaning; the girls were incredibly attractive and beautifully made up and dressed.

When we drove the next day to Borobudur, we told each other that this day we were going to see and hear about Buddhism at first hand, a religion to which both of us were attracted. The drive took us past mountains on each side, one of them a huge smoking volcano, rice paddies, sugar cane, banana and palm trees everywhere, and we were impressed by the lushness of this land. On the way Budi discussed the problem of crime in Indonesia and it appeared that there was plenty of street crime until 1982, when it suddenly stopped, not because of police action, but because the people themselves took things into their own hands, and they pursued and often killed the muggers; the death penalty in Indonesia is very rarely used.

Borobudur is the biggest Buddhist temple in the world, built between the eighth and ninth centuries, before Islam really took root in Java. It is a huge mass of volcanic stone, seven tiers in all, and depicts the life of Prince Siddartha of Nepal, who renounced all in 500 BC in search of perfection, or Nirvana, which would release the soul from the perpetual threat of reincarnation into a higher or lower form of species.

The temple was abandoned when the Hindus and Buddhists quarrelled and departed in opposite directions, and was not rediscovered until early in the nineteenth century. Governor Raffles heard about Borobudur, and sent a delegate to investigate the area before he went off to found Singapore; Raffles was Governor in Java from 1811 to 1816 at a time when Holland was allied with France. The reconstruction of Borobudur has continued, and was only finally completed in 1972. It stands high on a hill in the middle of a plain between faraway mountains on each side, and there was an extraordinary peace about this huge building in spite of the many tourists. Esmé thought that the bas-reliefs were exquisite, and unlike those around Hindu temples, they showed no obvious sexual connotation. We moved leisurely among the fine carvings and stupas on an afternoon of brilliant southern sunshine beating down from a vapourless sky, and felt entirely at one with our world.

We dined in the roof restaurant of the Ambarrukmo, my cholera having departed and my intestinal tract having been returned to me. After dinner we went out on to the roof balcony, and Esmé pointed out to me the Southern Cross; we had looked for this in the South Pacific without success, and since my childhood, when I read books about the South Seas, and Kingsford Smith first flew from England to Australia in a small aeroplane of that name, I had a strong wish to see the Southern Cross before I died.

The following day we had an early start for the Prambanan Temples, the only Hindu temples in the area; they were close to Borobudur and were superb. There were three of them, enormous buildings, the third was under active reconstruction; one temple dedicated to Brahma, one to Siva and one to Vishnu, and surrounding them there were no less than two hundred smaller temples, many yet to be fully excavated. There had to be so many peripheral temples, because under the Hindu caste system, many Hindus would not have been allowed into the main temples, and the untouchables were not allowed into any at all. It was rather strange to be talking to Budi, our educated guide, about other religions, he a devout Muslim but completely open-minded; he told us that while there may be an untouchable caste in India, this was always present in Indonesia under early Dutch rule, when the Dutch alone had the use of the highway and the locals were forced to walk at the side.

The bas-relief carvings around the main temple illustrated the continuing epic of Ramayana, the everlasting struggle between good and evil, and there were small temples, Buddhist and Hindu, nearby; we bought a stone Buddha head about four inches high to add to our collection on the window-sill of the dining-room.

Before we left Yogyakarta to fly to Sulawesi we just had time to see the University campus and the medical school, and we felt that Yogyakarta was very much the cultural centre of Java.

We flew into Ujung Pandang, Makassar of old. If either of us had read more of Joseph Conrad, and later the book by Gavin Young *In Search of Conrad*, we would have appreciated the importance of Makassar on the old shipping routes at the turn of the century. At Ujung Pandang we were met by Nathan who told us that his parents had been converted to Christianity, and that was why he had the name of Nathan. He spoke very good English and had spent three months in England in 1987 attached to the Toraja exhibition at the British Museum. The hotel was comfortable and friendly and we had a room overlooking the Flores Sea; the dining room was on piles over the sea and the food was pure Indonesian, which suited us.

The next day dawned beautiful and sunny, warm and perfect for sightseeing as we boarded our minibus, headed north and first stop was a village called Palawo. As we entered the village there was a funeral procession forming in the road and the bereaved relatives were in black, standing round a van with the coffin inside. Nathan was keen to show us the genuine Torajan houses in the villages, which were rather like the Sumatran houses with the extraordinary roofs sticking up towards the heaven at each end. They were high up on wooden pillars and entered via a long ladder, and opposite each house was a rice barn. We climbed the ladder into one of the houses and Esmé hoped that as she went up the ladder the locals would not be looking up her skirt; they were but I did not tell her. We entered a house and it consisted of one long room which accommodated six families, there were two huge beds on the floor and several mattresses, they cooked on the same floor and there was no privacy at all. We lunched on Chinese-style soup, shrimps fried in oil, pork and ginger and rice; the temperature was 100°F and we were glad of the cold beer which they produced for us.

After lunch we went to see the cliff graves. Wealthy people are placed in caves carved high up in the sides of cliffs, and covering the entrance to the graves are life-like figures of the deceased, effigies known as Tautau; we hoped to witness a funeral but nobody had died recently. Funerals in Torajaland are joyous occasions, they are celebrations of the soul of the departed being freed in the hereafter, and they are held well after the actual death, with dancing, excitement, music and colourful dress, and, according to the wealth and class of the family of the dearly departed, many buffaloes and pigs are sacrificed during the ceremonies by having their throats cut. The major religions in Indonesia, Islam, Buddhism and Hinduism, are often overlaid with animism and ancestor-worship, and Indonesians have a special awareness of the mystical forces that surround them. We did, at a village called Marente, come upon the end stages of a funeral, some men were squatting on their haunches dividing up buffalo meat. This was a small funeral, only three buffaloes had been killed, with five pigs, and the buffalo skins were stretched out to dry on wooden stakes.

We stayed at a small hotel in Torajaland, Toraja Cottages, which was full of French tourists. Esmé loved this place, there was a little balcony where we could sit and write the journal and have evening drinks, and she practised her French on the neighbours. Next morning we went to Lemo, where were the best of the cliffside graves and effigies, but thieves had removed many of them; those left were thought to be between seven and eight hundred years old, and we looked up at them standing in a rice field. Next was a market which had the air of medieval barter, as money did not seem to change hands; there was a pig corner where small pigs, forelegs and hind legs tied together were sold. We saw eels being killed and sold, killed by pressing a thumb just below the head. We saw a blacksmith whose fire was kept going by an extraordinary Heath Robinson system of bellows; there were two long lengths of wide-bore bamboo side by side and upright and connected at the bottom, and the blast of air for the furnace was provided by an elderly man sitting high up pushing two plungers down the bamboo tubes. There was an area covered by a tarpaulin under which an evil looking man pranced around singing and intoning, the while dispensing patent medicines which were eagerly snapped up by the populace. We had seen markets in places like Pizac in Peru and also in La Paz, but they were nothing like this. Nathan took us into a cave near here, the burial place of a nobleman, and there were skulls and bones on the floor, but they seemed to have been arranged with care to impress tourists. To get into this cave was quite a problem because it was under a huge rock, and to get in was a feat worthy of a West Indian limbo dancer. This day had been an extraordinary experience, and reading the journal now seven years on, I still cannot quite believe what we saw, but tomorrow was to be even stranger.

When he met us after breakfast, Nathan told us that he had had news of a house-warming which would go on for two days with only pigs being slaughtered, the buffaloes having a few days' grace. We went along an endless bumpy road, and eventually in the distance we could hear the noise of what sounded like cannibal drums. We got out of the van, walked through a jungle until we came to a clearing, as we did this there were many people coming in the opposite direction carrying pieces of pig meat on bamboo sticks, and some carrying long pieces of bamboo which were containers for palm wine, long since drunk. In the open space in the trees there were literally hundreds of people sitting around as if in a theatre; the smell was awful, there were people dancing around a large black pig and to one side there was a lot of pig meat on poles, as yet unclaimed, from the last pig to die. It worried Esmé that on the way into the clearing there were ten other fully-grown pigs tied up to a fence by a back leg, awaiting their turn for the knife.

We were invited to join the dance, to do which you had to fix a five hundred rupiah note to a bamboo stick, venture into the centre of the dance and stick it in a girl's hair, and if she liked the look of you she allowed you to dance with her. It was rather like the Hammersmith Palais of old under very different rules. The man whose house was being warmed sat on a bamboo platform slightly above the proceedings. Fortunately, a pig had been killed just before we arrived, and we were able to depart before the next one was slaughtered. As we walked out past a line of old people sitting on their haunches chewing betel nuts, and spitting red fluid all over the place, there were people leaving the scene carrying packets, made by tying up large green leaves containing pig's blood, which they were taking home to make into puddings. I asked how they kept the meat in this very hot climate, and was told that they dry it in the sun or they smoke it.

On the way back to the hotel we passed the site of a big Torajan funeral of a nobleman which had taken place a week earlier; special bamboo buildings had been built, and the corpse was still there. The whole funeral cost sixty million rupiah, about twenty thousand pounds: one hundred buffaloes had been slaughtered and two hundred pigs, and the meat distributed throughout the community. This day was one of the strangest of our lives.

We returned to Ujung Pandang next day and put up again at the Makassar Golden Hotel; it was pouring with rain and we could not swim. The clothes in the suitcases had become creased in spite of Esmé's usually infallible packing system of rolling up and placing in plastic bags; she did however work wonders with the small travelling iron plugged into a power socket for the TV. We had arranged to fly back to Bali on the morrow and then on to London. On that last night at Makassar Golden we dressed up in our tropical finery for dinner and were entertained by a jazz group, with a male and a female singer who fancied they were Billy Eckstein and Sarah Vaughan.

We needed to go home to try to assimilate all that we had seen in Indonesia, with the help of photographs and the journal. Sumatra, Java and Sulawesi are quite different and Bali, colourful and beautiful though it is, has given itself over to the tourists. In Java we realised how hated were the Dutch, and how badly at the end of the war the Indonesians desired independence; they even aided and abetted the Japanese invaders, cruel though they were, as happened in North India.

The flight from Bali was overbooked and we were put into the business class cabin which was fatal, because as she sipped the first glass of free champagne, Esmé decided firmly that hereafter it would be business class all the way for us, and so it was.

Chapter Six

Seychelles

When we saw a tropical island for the first time, Barbados in 1978, we became very hungry to see more. In the bar at the Coconut Creek Hotel we got into conversation with a very pleasant elderly couple who told us that if we liked what we were seeing in the Caribbean, we should go to the Seychelles. We did so four years later in 1982, and over all the world that we saw, for sheer beauty, nothing surpassed the Seychelles. It is an archipelago of small islands in the middle of the Indian Ocean a thousand miles from any other land. When General Charles George Gordon took time off from keeping the British flag flying in South Africa, and went to the Seychelles, he is on record as saying "I think any requirement is fulfilled for deciding that... Eden is near the Seychelles". They will tell you on the island of Praslin that Vallée de Mai is the original Garden of Eden; the climate is tropical but the heat is tempered by soft south-east trade winds, and when rain comes you have a warm shower.

On our way by taxi to Fisherman's Cove Hotel at the far end of Beau Vallon Beach, Esmé said that even the sparrows were bright red, but she was looking at red cardinals, which are as common as sparrows in the Seychelles. The years of French colonisation have left behind a mainly Creole cuisine, the people speak a strange French dialect and Esmé, whose French was good, found it difficult to understand them. Since the British took these islands from the French, the English language was imposed, and now both languages are spoken by everybody.

We were tired when we arrived in the Seychelles and spent most of the first week soaking up the sun, reading our books, Esmé at the rate of one every two days or so, and marvelling at the birds above and around us, and the fish on the coral reefs below us. At Fisherman's Cove we discovered the delights of many kinds of tropical fruit for the first time, and breakfast each day started with passion fruit and mangosteen.

During that first week on Mahé, the largest and central island of the group, we did summon the energy to go into the capital Victoria and spent a day on a boat visiting two smaller islands, Moyenne and Round. Victoria is a surprisingly large port for such a small island, but the isolation of the Seychelles and their distance from any other port of call explains this. There were many ships, mainly cargo boats carrying containers, tied up at the quayside or anchored further out awaiting their turn; we saw that several were flying the flag of the Peoples' Republic of China and on the way to the port in the minibus we had passed a small tin shack which was flying the same flag, and had a sign outside on which was written 'Embassy of the Peoples' Republic of China'. There had been a strong left-wing influence here since President Jimmy Manchin had come to power, but on a recent visit to London he was deposed in his absence, and we were told that big changes were afoot; we hoped that there would not be a full revolution while we were in the islands.

We dismissed politics from our minds and our boat left the port and headed for the two islands of Moyenne and Round. Before we reached Moyenne, we sailed across a large marine park, and from the side of the boat we saw fish and turtles. Moyenne Island, where we had lunch, is privately owned by an Englishman who met us on the beach, showed us turtle tracks and took us on an informative guided tour of his little island of which he was very proud. We had lunch in a straw-covered hovel, hot, spicy and Creole, and while we were having lunch a flock of red cardinals flew into the bush just a few yards away; our host told us that their correct name was Madagascan "fody" and that only the males were this brilliant red colour, which they lost completely immediately after mating. After lunch we went across to Round Island opposite. Ten years later, although we did not know it at the time, we were going to have the chance to show all this to our son Bill and his family. After a week at Fisherman's Cove we caught a small inter-island plane to Praslin, and stayed at Côte d'Or where there was a long beach of fine sand, and we occupied a wooden rondavel just a few yards from it. This was quite idyllic until, when we got into bed on the first night, we found that we were sharing with a rat the size of a puppy in the roof. It spent much of the night scampering across on a rafter, and Esmé asked me how could I be sure that it would stay on the rafter and not join us in the bed, and I could not. We always had two or three mosquito coils burning throughout the night to protect us from whatever winged beasts were indigenous, and Esmé said that perhaps these were anti-rat as well as being anti-mosquito, but that if I really loved her I would get out of bed and fight the rat. We got quite used to this rat and we called it Samuel Whiskers in memory of Beatrix Potter. There was a daily ferry boat plying between Praslin and the neighbouring island of La Digue, and we spent a day on La Digue. We were transported by ox-cart from the jetty to a small hotel on an almost deserted beach, there were no motors cars, and the alternative transport to ox-cart was bicycle. We enjoyed a lazy lunch and swam off Grand Anse Beach.

We were keen to visit the reef some distance from Praslin, and we found a man with a motorboat who took us several miles out to a tiny palm-covered island which had a very small beach, strewn with enormous granite boulders, known locally as Cocos Island. He showed us where we should go to see the best fish, so we donned our snorkels, waded into the sea and as soon as we put our faces under the water we thought we must be in paradise. In all our travels subsequently, in which we swam over and around many coral reefs, we never again saw the quantity and quality of fish that we saw here; there was no need to swim, you just floated and watched. Having shown us this, on the way back to Praslin the boatman told us that as a result of hoards of Italian tourists coming here with sacks and taking away as much coral as they could carry, the Government had decided that Cocos Island and the sea around it was to become a prohibited area, and we found that it had remained so when we came back ten years later with the family.

After leaving Cocos Island we chugged to another small island where a fish was barbecued on the beach for us, and during the whole of this day we saw no other human being until we returned to Praslin.

We were anxious to sample another island of the Seychelles group, and we flew back to the main island of Mahé, changed planes and flew to Bird Island, which is on the periphery of the group and a very small speck in the Indian Ocean. The landing strip was an elongated lawn, the airport terminal was a little straw hut, and we met the manager and his wife, Georges and Margaret. Georges was a Seychellois and Margaret was the daughter of a general practitioner in Devon; they were young and energetic and they gave the impression that they would do anything to help us enjoy our short stay. We slept in another straw roofed rondavel just off the beach, and for anyone who wishes to drop out of civilisation, Bird Island is the place; there is literally nothing to do except enjoy the sea and the birds. Here is a famous nesting place for the Sooty tern, and during the breeding season, at the north end of the island are thousands upon thousands of these small seabirds; they sit on one egg until it hatches, and when the time is right and the birds are sufficiently grown, they fly away. Georges told us that each bird will spend the next two to three years winging over the sea without stopping, and eventually will come back to Bird Island to nest; when we walked round the island we saw long-tailed tropic birds, and in the evenings we watched frigates circling high above us before coming down to roost.

A day or two before we were due to end our holiday, Esmé was standing in the surf; the sea was rough, and a piece of boat hit her left shin causing two nasty deep cuts; something had to be done and we sought the help of Georges and Margaret. A German surgeon had visited Bird six months previously, had left behind a surgical kit with needles and sutures, and I prepared to operate. Esmé sat in the shower basin, she said that if I was going to stitch her up there could be a sizeable blood loss; both of us now faced a daunting task because I was totally miscast as a surgeon. I asked Margaret to fetch a large glass of brandy, which she did, and handed to Esmé. I took it quickly and drained it, so Margaret had to go and get another for the patient! Five stitches were required, the operation was successfully completed, and Esmé was marvellous.

Before I describe the rest of our experiences in the Seychelles I have to say here that a month after we returned home Esmé complained of pain in the scar, and I could see that something was about to come out; with forceps I withdrew a piece of wood half an inch long, and I could not deny that it was a piece of the boat because on one side it was painted green. Esmé said that if I really loved her I would not have sewn pieces of boat into her legs; it took several gin and tonics, followed by a slap-up dinner at a very expensive restaurant in Cheltenham, to get things back on an even keel. I tried to excuse myself by saying that I was a wise physician and not a surgeon, and that the whole business had hurt me as much as it had hurt her; I told her that I loved her and I kissed her, but I got the feeling that I still had some way to go. When she first suffered the injury she said that it had ruined her beautiful legs, but no thanks to my surgery this was most certainly not so. When we flew from the island she was very sad because the second half of our week there had been ruined for her. We promised each other that we would come back and we did, twice.

We were back in the Seychelles three years later in 1985 and stayed at Northolme Hotel on Mahé, La Reserve on Praslin, and the last two nights back on Bird Island; this was our only holiday that year: I was about to retire from the National Health Service and Esmé had just retired from the Social Services. We simply drank in the beauty of the place and read our books.

In 1990 we had planned a safari in East Africa and arranged to meet our son Bill and family in the Seychelles at the end of the safari. They had never seen the tropics and they were dumbstruck by the beauty. I had booked us all in at the Sheraton Hotel because I thought that there would be more going on for the young folk and we spent our days across the water on Ìsle Thérèse. The grandchildren had rudimentary lessons in scuba-diving and everybody stocked up on sun; they had their first parasail experience on Beau Vallon beach and at the end of the first week we all went to Praslin. Bill and Sue had seen a television programme about the bird life on Cousin Island which was some miles off Praslin, and we arranged to go across before the end of the holiday. Our eldest grandson, Barney, made friends with a Rastafarian who had a boat, and he took us a mile or so out to a tiny island named St Pierre where the coral reef and the fish were almost as brilliant and plentiful as off Cocos Island. The family spent all day with their faces in the water in wonderment, and we persuaded Basil the Rastafarian to take us out again the next day.

Esmé and I had been to Vallée de Mai and we felt that the rest of them ought to go there to see the birds and where the famous coco de mer grew. The Seychellois are very proud of their coco de mer, an extraordinary double coconut with a hairy husk and shaped liked the private parts of a woman. They take many years to grow and if you want to take one home you have to get an export licence. The theory of their origin is that they came across the sea from India, hence their name. On our first visit we bought a small replica, intended as a key-ring, and we adapted it for Esmé's tropical necklace. The Vallée de Mai is also famous as the sole home of the black parrot, but we never saw one on our visit and neither did the rest of the family, and I have never met anybody who has seen it. They saw many other birds, bulbul, fruit pigeon and heard the whirr of humming-birds, and they felt that it was a morning very well spent.

The boat which took us to Cousin Island was a powerful fishing boat powered by two large Yamaha outboard engines. The sea was choppy and we all got very wet, but the main worry was that Esmé and I might get swept off the boat into the sea. When we reached Cousin we had to get out of this boat into a smaller boat in two groups, and the only way they could get us to the beach at Cousin was to wait until a large wave came, go in on the crest of it and get us out very quickly before the next big wave. Four strong natives lifted Esmé bodily onto the beach, and she asked what this would do to her neck and her back; but there was really no time for any musculo-skeletal considerations, we were in a survival situation.

We saw much on our tour of this little island: there were tortoises, which they call land turtles, copulating under a bush; we saw large lizards called Seychelles and Wright skinks, and many sticky Pisonia trees which kill birds with their sticky seeds which get among the feathers. There were white Fairy terns sitting on branches and making love, and long-tailed tropic birds nesting on the ground in hollows; they have to do this because their feet are placed too far back on their bodies and they are unstable if they sit on branches. We saw the rare Brush warbler and little yellow sunbirds; Bill took the glamour out of the warblers by saying there were plenty at home and we called them chiffchaffs. There were shearwater chicks in nests under tree roots.

We crossed the water to Curieuse twenty minutes away, and had lunch in a clearing in a wood; it was extremely hot and we were grateful for the shade of two enormous takamaka trees. There was salad, barbecued dorado fish and kebabs washed down by plenty of bottles of cold Seybrew beer. After lunch we walked across the island with an American guide who pointed out an Indian almond tree with white bark, mango trees and cinnamon bushes, also a vanilla creeper, which has to be artificially pollinated because the island lacks the bee which normally does this elsewhere in the world. We saw coco plum bushes from Venezuela and we came to a mangrove swamp and walked across a very narrow swaying wooden bridge. The guide told us that mangrove acts as a filter, holding up soil and preventing coral reefs offshore from getting silted up. Turtles are protected here, both Hawksbill and Green; they were decimated years ago, the former for tortoiseshell and the latter for soup and food. There had been so much to take in today, but the children all loved it; every experience in these islands enthralled them.

We got back to the Paradise Beach Hotel on Praslin in the same uncomfortable way. We all had tea, consisting of coffee and banana cake on the balcony of the restaurant, and the cake was shared with red cardinals, doves and mynah birds. We had supper at the beach bar, and the locals entertained us by dancing on the beach to Sega rhythms. This holiday for Bill and the family was unique. Esmé and I had seen two more islands we had never seen before, Cousin an international nature reserve and Curieuse, an old leper colony, with the doctor's house still standing. We doubted if we would come back again because time marched on, and there was still more of the world to see.

Reflecting on this holiday Esmé said that it was a great privilege for us to be in a position to introduce Bill and family to the tropics; they really got the best out of it all and we were proud of them. Esmé always believed firmly that it was very important to avoid broadcasting family successes, exam results, jobs whatever they might be, not to say boast about them too loudly; she felt that this was both unkind and unwise, because success may be just the transit zone to failure, to borrow an apt phrase from Peter Preston, editor of *The Guardian*; unkind because there might well be somebody within earshot who had not been so fortunate, unwise because failure may well follow success, and friends could have long memories. I agreed with her philosophy absolutely. Modern-day triumphalism so often shows a total lack of humility among winners, and this can only deny dignity to losers.

Chapter Seven
Mauritius

After our first visit to the Seychelles in 1982, we felt that we should also take a look at Mauritius. Situated just above the Tropic of Capricorn, Mauritius is thirty-six miles by twenty miles and has several very good hotels. We stayed at Le Saint Géran on the southern end of the island, ideally placed with the Indian Ocean and the reef half a mile out on one side of it, and a lagoon on the other. We were lucky to get a room right at the end of the beach, and at beach level. Saint Géran was the name of a sailing ship which long ago was wrecked where the hotel now stands; this inspired a French love story and the name is now bequeathed to this hotel, which is reckoned as five star and can compete with any hotel the world over. It was filled with wealthy South African and German tourists and the men competed with each other from dawn until dusk. They were out very early doing gymnastics and jogging, and later in the morning they fought each other at water polo; they had an international tennis match every day and Esmé and I simply watched them in wonder.

We had planned to do nothing on this holiday and brought out a whole pack of paperbacks. There was good swimming in the sea right opposite us, and we used the tennis club run by the hotel with a professional coach. We played regularly and it not only worked wonders for Esmé's backhand, it helped us work up a man-sized thirst.

I felt that I knew the man in the next door room, and when I realised eventually who he was, I went up to him and said, "You are Dennis Haynes and you and I batted together for St Catharine's College in Cambridge forty years ago." He nearly fell off his sunbed and we all had a drink together; he told us that he was a retired champagne importer, and that he had to retire early because he developed an alcohol problem. Esmé, large rum daiquiri in hand, said that I had an alcohol problem too, without the help of being in the champagne trade, and I wondered where was wifely loyalty; I certainly drank plenty of alcohol; my only problem was ensuring that there was enough cold beer in the fridge, because it was a very small one.

We felt we had to pay a visit to the capital, Curepipe. We drove across the island, with sugar cane on either side of us and every field was littered with black boulders. Curepipe has nothing to offer, but we found a shop where there was a marvellous collection of pretty sea shells of every shape, size and colour, and we bought some of these to put on a plate of white sand from the Seychelles, in the corner cupboard in the living-room at home. If your palate is tempted by food prepared in Creole, Indian or Chinese style, or by mouth-watering beach barbecues and buffets in the evening you should go to Le Saint Géran.

A few miles up the road northward along the coast there is another hotel, Le Tousserok, owned by the same company, and they provide a complimentary shuttle service; Le Tousserok had become famous just before, because it was where the Duke and Duchess of York spent their honeymoon. It is attractive, and there is a long drive to it between huge bushes of bougainvillaea; it consists of tasteful chalets around a small beach, there is a stone jetty and a small harbour from which we took a boat through large mangrove swamps to Île aux Cerfs. We had lunch here and walked round this little island in intense heat and Esmé bought two colourful pareos on the beach. There were many shops in Saint Géran, obviously catering for the very wealthy; it was like strolling through Mayfair in the tropics, and people were spending money without a second thought. We showed immense self-control because we knew that the bank manager had been getting very restive before we left home.

On Mauritius we were in our early sixties and there did not seem to be any demonstrable reason why this life of ours should not continue until further notice; we loved each other and until some disaster occurred there seemed no reason to alter what we were enjoying so much together. Thinking my sad thoughts now, I feel strongly that if you have to lose a lover before you realise to the full how much you loved her, you probably did not tell her often enough. Tacit assumption of love is not enough, because love needs to be refreshed and renewed like a fragrant flower; you cannot buy back the past, and posthumous regrets must be quite unbearable. I trust that if our positions were reversed Esmé would have no regrets. I do not think that she would. We were sure of our love and we enjoyed telling each other, and I do not think that either of us would need to buy back the past for reassurance. I need the past now because I cannot live with the present and I cannot see any future. I wish that I could control my thinking and banish from my mind the awfulness of Esmé's ending. I need to stay back in the past when we loved so eagerly and refill my mind with the anticipation and excitement of the prospect of my flavoursome wholesome Welsh girl, with the heart bursting heights of feeling which we climbed together, ledge by ledge till we danced on the pinnacles in pirouettes of pleasure, before we surrendered in the thrall of it and were lost in the exquisite throes of the depth of our passion. I need to remember how the light of the sun and the moon and the stars became her. I need to recall the music of her laughter and the lilt of her voice with its delicate hint of Welsh song, and the soft light of love and promise in her eyes when she looked at me. Byron so beautifully described friendship as love without its wings and I need also to dwell upon our decades of close friendship, mutual understanding and trust, and then upon our companionship and contentment in the gloaming of our life together, and the wit and the humour which was the running theme of our whole relationship. I must weigh all this as profit against the unbearable loss and manner of her going, until I can go myself and be sad no more. I need to reopen a million capsules of stored memories of happenings and happinesses, but I cannot find them. I know they are there because together we put them there.

Chapter Eight

India

I retired from the National Health Service in March 1986 and, as we had promised ourselves, in April we went to India. Esmé had learned much about India by then; she had read VS Naipaul, RK Naryan, MM Mehta, A Desai, Mark Tully and MM Kaye, and persuaded me to read as much as I could before we went to India for the first time.

We landed in Delhi at 4 a.m. and as the taxi drove out of the airport towards the centre of Delhi, the roads were already busy with people and traffic. Esmé saw a camel drawing a ramshackle cart with several Indians sitting on it, which amazed her, because she had not realised that in India camels were used in this way and neither had I. Delhi had been the capital of an empire for five hundred years and it was difficult to imagine that when Bombay and Madras were merely trading posts, and Calcutta a village of mudflats, Delhi was the capital of the country and already an important city. Hindu and Muslim dynasties ruled from here, then the Moguls, and finally the British; this was the seat of British government from 1911 until Indian independence in 1947. The capital of New Delhi was finally completed just in time to turn it over to the new nation of India.

We stayed at the Taj Mahal Hotel which is very grand and conjures up visions of the days of the British Raj. For the Taj Mahal Hotel Esmé wore a pretty silk dress, pink and mauve with a lowish neck, and she had found shoes to match. I wore a grey tropical suit which I had bought just before the holiday in Piccadilly, and we felt right royal. Esmé never took her best jewellery abroad, not that she had all that much of it; she always relied on costume jewellery, and I remember she looked very good when we went into dinner that first night. I never ceased to marvel that she was mine, and although we had been married for forty-one years, the sight sound and smell of her continued to thrill me all my waking hours. I never remotely considered losing her and what that might do to my life; now I know.

As we had only a few days in Delhi, we had to use them to best advantage, and Esmé had done her preparation for this. First, we had to see the Red Fort, the symbol of Mogul power and elegance, built as long ago as 1648, and we did this on the second morning; it is of red sandstone, and you could imagine elephants decorated and swaying past, covered with a cloth of gold and probably a Mogul prince riding on top in a silver houdah. The Fort was built by Emperor Shahjahan and our guide told us as we entered it that we were in fact entering the seventh city of Delhi. There was marble everywhere; especially impressive was the Hall of Public Audience, and we pictured the Emperor sitting high up on a raised dais and holding court, with everybody below bowing and scraping. The guide told us that they could never meet the eye of the Grand Mogul, because if they did and he thought that they were being irreverent he would frown, which meant immediate execution.

We walked along the Rajpath and looked back at the Presidential Palace, the centre of the Government of modern India which was built in the twentieth century and designed by Sir Edwin Lutyens.

We were there in spring and the colour of flaming gulmohur and yellow laburnum trees was brilliant. Lutyens had great difficulty in persuading the Viceroy at the time to agree to his plans, but ultimately he had his way, and the result is a benefit to all who are lucky enough to see it.

We were anxious to see the Rajghat where Gandhi was cremated; he was assassinated on a Friday, and every Friday they hold a ceremony here in memory of the father of modern India, as Sun Yat Sen was to China. The ghat is on a gentle slope, grass covered, simple and unpretentious like the man himself. We saw Qutb Minar, an enormous tower of the Afghan period, which was eighty-seven feet high and intended to be much higher, but the designer died and it was abandoned; it was galleried and pointed to heaven like a giant's ridged phallus. We were taken out of the city to see Humayun's Tomb, a mausoleum for Emperor Humayun built by his grieving widow; in India all these magnificent tombs and memorials are built either by grieving wives or grieving husbands. We had time in Delhi only to see a few of the main sights before getting on the road to Agra.

On our last evening in Delhi we went to see India Gate floodlit; this was modelled on Menin Gate in Belgium; it commemorates the Indian dead of World War I. We ended our last evening with Son et Lumière in the Red Fort which was memorable, a marvellous illustration in sound and light of the lives of the Mogul Emperors, one after another. The mosquitoes were working overtime, we had prepared ourselves with various ointments and sprays and were wearing long-sleeved shirts and trousers, but a couple sitting next to us were unprepared and were bitten to death. Esmé gave them our Autun spray and they emptied it in no time; it was a pity for them because they were unable properly to appreciate a quite remarkable show of history.

In Delhi we missed the Great Mosque because it was Ramadan and the Mosque is closed to visitors then, but as Esmé said we had seen the Red Fort with its Hall of Public Audience and its Hall of Private Audience with the world famous Peacock Throne, we had seen the Rajpath of Sir Edwin Lutyens, we had seen the Narayan Hindu Temple and we had seen where arguably India's greatest citizen was cremated.

It was to be Agra next and Esmé could hardly wait for it, she said that all her life she had wanted to see the Taj Mahal, if not by moonlight then by any light. Agra is only one hundred and twenty-four miles by road from Delhi, one hundred and twenty-four miles from the capital of modern India to the former seat of the Mogul Empire, the royal road of the Mogul Emperors. Apart from the Taj Mahal we were to see the Agra Fort, and we were to go to Fatehpur Sikri, the extraordinary ghost city which was the capital of Akbar the Great for such a short time.

When we arrived at the Mogul Sheraton Hotel we were offered the choice of a western or Indian style room and Esmé chose Indian, she said that it would be nice to lie again on the floor with me. There was a good swimming pool in this hotel and as the thermometer was above 100°F we used it much, when we were not sightseeing. For dinner in Agra Esmé brought out a simple white frock with which she wore gold earrings, a cultivated pearl necklace and gold shoes. For many years her perfume had been Femme, but for India she decided to change to Cinnabar, and I remember that as she went down a circular white marble staircase in this hotel to the dining-room, she left a cloud of Cinnabar in her wake; it is strange how scents may live longer and more powerfully in the memory than sights and sounds. Wherever we went in India we were very aware of the special scent of the subcontinent, a mixture of the pleasant and the unpleasant, but wholly and utterly India's scent.

Although the golden age of Agra was surprisingly short and finished with Shahjahan in the seventeenth century, it had to show for it the two shrines of the Agra Fort and the Taj Mahal. The Agra Fort is an impressive building with lovely red rust-coloured sandstone walls, and inside it there are white marble palaces, in some of which the marble lattice work is exquisite. We were shown, as in Delhi, halls of public and private audience, and Esmé asked why did I not wave peacock tails over her to keep away the flies as the eunuchs did for Shahjahan; I felt that Autun was good enough. There was an octagonal tower with a courtyard paved with octagonal marble slabs, and we were told that in this tower Shahjahan used to sit and look through the marble lattice across the river at the Taj Mahal, and he died at one of these windows during his imprisonment by his son Aurangzeb. Our guide said that when his beloved Mumtaz died he vowed to build as her memorial the biggest and most beautiful building in the world at that time on the banks of the Jumna River. Esmé felt that he would have had Mumtaz for much longer if he had not impregnated her so many times; as she had fourteen children, and died in childbirth, Esmé probably had a point.

When we stood in Shahjahan's palace and looked across the river through the lattice-work at the Taj Mahal it was mid-afternoon, the sun was still high and the Taj Mahal was brilliantly white, and by the time we had crossed the river and entered it the sun was setting and the colour had changed to a lovely mellow orange-yellow. As you walk towards the Taj Mahal across a walled garden along the side of a rectangular pool, with cypresses standing to attention on each side, you are amazed at such perfection of rhythm and proportion. The tomb of Mumtaz and Shahjahan lies under the big central dome; you enter through an archway more than ninety feet high, and everywhere you look you see marble inlaid with millions and millions of precious stones. In the centre is the tomb of Mumtaz, but both Mumtaz and Shahjahan are actually buried in a crypt underneath to which we descended; it was small, and the overpowering smell of unwashed humanity soon drove us out. When you look up into the great dome from inside you see a marble heaven eighty feet above you, stars and all.

The abiding memory of the Taj Mahal is the beautiful shape and proportions of it from a distance, the extraordinary mogul pietra-dura inlay work on the marble, and the colour change as the sun kisses it and leaves it with such reluctance. As we were walking back down the avenue of cypresses, our guide rather took the shine off it all by telling us that every man who worked on the building of the Taj Mahal had his hands cut off, so that he would never be able to do work of such quality for anybody other than Shahjahan himself.

We had only two full days in Agra and on the second day we went to the ghost city of Fatehpur Sikri, which in some ways was more remarkable than the Taj Mahal. It was twenty-four miles west of Agra by road, and when it was built in 1583 by the Emperor Akbar it was bigger than the London of that time, both in population and in the grandness of it. Akbar, because he had no heir, decided to visit a holy man who blessed him. He immediately sired a son, and this decided him to move his capital to the village where the holy man lived, so he built this city with a circumference of seven miles, it has been aptly described as an epic poem in red sandstone. There were many interesting buildings, we saw halls and temples with columns elaborately decorated, there were courtyards and cloisters, there was a play area which Akbar shared with his harem, and our guide told us that he sat on a throne flanked by marble screens and played chess, with slave girls as living pieces, on the courtyard behind. Akbar was so interested in astrology after the holy man got him an heir, that he built here an Astrologer's Seat, where the astrologer would determine each day what colour the Emperor would wear and there was a choice of yellow, purple or violet. In 1584, which was only fourteen years after the city was completed and Akbar moved into it, he abandoned it, probably because the water supply failed. On the way back to Agra we really felt that Akbar should have been able to make up his own mind what colour to wear each day, and we also wondered what happened to the architects when the water supply ran out.

From Agra we went through Rajasthan, which includes the Great Indian Desert and is very sparsely populated. The women wear brilliantly coloured saris, they are covered with jewellery from the top of their heads to their ankles, and most of them were very beautiful with wonderful features and slender figures. The Rajputs during their history have been very warlike people, the men were great horsemen and this lives on today, because Rajasthan is really the centre of polo in India.

Our first stop in Rajasthan was Jaipur, and during this journey through northern India by road we were driven in a private car, the driver of which asked us to address him as "Mr Virk". He was a very pleasant man, so keen that we should appreciate India, and went to great lengths to show us as much as possible. He spoke reasonable English in a very high squeaky voice which surprised us, because he was a big muscular man. When he dropped us off at the Rambagh Palace Hotel, which was once the Maharajah's residence, he was very proud and behaved as if he half-owned the place. This was unlike any other hotel we had ever been in and it retained fully the atmosphere of a Maharajah's palace, with one hundred and five rooms and a beautiful garden and swimming-pool. They claimed that each room was air-conditioned, and there was an ancient unit fitted to the window, but the air that came out of it was if anything hotter than the air that went in. Esmé rather fancied herself here, imagining that it was still the British Raj as she sat on a long verandah on bamboo furniture enjoying her sundowners and being waited on by uniformed servants. As an alternative to the verandah we could drink in the Polo Lounge with its pictures of famous international polo players covering the walls, and we visualised VIPs such as Nehru and the Mountbattens and their friends sitting there drinking their tall gins.

The main reason for going to Jaipur was to see the Amber Palace up on a hill outside the city, and the Palace of Winds in the centre of it. We saw the Palace of Winds first, built in the same pink sandstone which early writers have described as the 'tone of the Autumn sunset', and it seems to be all windows. We entered and climbed up to the top floor where we looked out through small open windows to the street below and our guide told us that this was where the women would congregate, and from here they could watch life going on below in the city without being seen. We paid a brief visit to the City Palace which is a museum. In the grounds there was a monument to a large dog and we learned that the Rajah, in high summer when the palace was too hot, would go out into the garden to sit, and he used the dog to take messages in its mouth to the harem, when he felt the need for entertainment.

We drove out to the Amber Palace which is high up on Kalikhoh Hill to the left above the green waters of Moata Lake, and we climbed to the Palace on the back of a tired and overworked elephant. This palace has the world's best Chamber of Mirrors with countless pieces of coloured glass, and there are many panels of alabaster with frescoes and extraordinarily attractive inlay work; the palace has a huge courtyard which you enter under a high arch.

The drive across Rajasthan Desert from Jaipur to Udaipur was long and hot and in India there are no pubs to stop at. Mr Virk was anxious to get us to Udaipur by lunch-time, which he managed, and took us straight to the Lake Palace situated in the middle of Pichola Lake. When we came round a bend and descended towards the city, Esmé thought that the view of the Palace from above, shining white like an ocean liner in the centre of this shimmering blue lake was breathtaking. It looked so small from the top of the hill, but later when the boat took us out to the Palace we realised that it was really a large building with eighty-five guest rooms. It was built two hundred years ago by the Maharani of Udaipur for summer residence, and Esmé thought it was not at all bad for a summerhouse.

There was little to see in Udaipur and the main reason for coming here was to stay in the Lake Palace Hotel. There was a small swimming-pool and we caught up with our reading here; we had been so busy sightseeing during the early part of the holiday that we were behind with the books. Esmé got through nine hundred pages of Jilly Cooper's *Riders*, and insisted on reading out loud to me the more juicy bits, much to the amusement of the guests around us. I endeavoured to be more dignified with Noël Barber and *Woman of Cairo* in which there were plenty of juicy bits, but I kept them to myself. We saw the Maharani's Palace on the crest of a ridge which looked over Lake Pichola, a very large building luxuriously decorated with mosaics, mirrors and paintings and relics of historic Udaipur. We went up to the roof garden and had a marvellous view.

On the way back to the Lake Palace we bought our memory of India for the dining-room window-sill; Esmé wanted a Ganesh, she was fascinated by this half elephant, half man and the stories surrounding it. She picked one made of sweet smelling sandalwood and was delighted with it.

Late on the afternoon of that same day we paddled in a little boat to the side of the lake, the sun had finished with the day and there was a soft and fragrant night wind; Esmé was standing in an archway looking back across the lake at the palace deep in thought; her thoughts must have been pleasant because she was smiling to herself; she was in her beloved India. She was wearing a dress with pink and white hoops which she loved, we did not speak and everything was quite quiet; watching her and loving her then with all my heart, I knew that here was a moment of the purest magic, a moment poised in time and captured for ever in memory. I loved her so much at that moment, I knew that one day this would all have to end, and I just hoped that she would go first so that she would never have to endure the pain of losing me. Writing this now in my grief and desolation, with the longing and the aching for her which never leaves me, more than ever do I feel the same. After a year I have strong feelings from time to time that Esmé will appear in the doorway and that this is all part of some cruel charade, some obscene misunderstanding, a malign design upon our happiness successfully thwarted. I have regular vivid dreams that we are together again, but in bizarre, grotesque and always stressful circumstances, and these fantasies only add to my pain as I remember so vividly her absolute stillness and coldness and smallness when I touched her, kissed her and held her for the last time; her fear of being cold in life amounted almost to terror. If dream I must then let my dreams be pleasurable, that I am in gardens bedecked with houris and every houri is my darling come back to me, and we make love for ever in a boundless paradise where the flowers never die and the birds never mute their gladsome song, and where time stood still so long long ago.

Soon after Esmé died I went back to Gower, I went back to the house above lovely Caswell Bay where she took me to meet her mother and father, and I stood for a while with my thoughts of such happiness there. I walked again the cliffs and bays of the south Gower coast, past Brandy Cove of smugglers fame to Pwlldu Bay, where the dominant dune of large grey pebbles is more than a match for the sea; onward westward past blue borage vetch and campion to Pobbles, Three Cliffs, Great Tor and Oxwich, magical names of the magical places of her childhood and our loving. I stood on her favourite Mewslade Bay; the tide was low and I was quite alone. The sea birds wheeled above me and their screams echoed from the towering walls of cliff and crag around me. I was in one of nature's most magnificent cathedrals, with the birds my choir, the sea my music, and my prayers were to my love. I walked across Fall Bay to Worms Head and I talked to her all the way. I stood on the high point overlooking Rhossili Bay and far below me the parallel lines of white-plumed Atlantic rollers looked like the ripples on a pond, as they rumbled toward the four mile beach where they vented their fury at the way she suffered in clouds of spume and spray. I remembered the first time she took me there on an afternoon of burnished gold so many Octobers ago. I remembered the coat she wore and the way the friendly fingers of the cliff-top breeze riffled her raven hair, my heart heaving within me, my giddy senses reeling and spinning out of control, doubt, care and caution in glorious rapturous free fall, because I knew that she was all mine.

Perish the waiting game, let aching love and throbbing desire be blissfully requited. We wrote such a love-song that wonderful bygone day, one which would echo and resound without cease through the galleries, labyrinths and tunnels of time, until we both were dead. Here was my miracle marvellously performed, here was my true beginning; now was life's happiness bestowed upon me, draped like a cloth of gold in panoply unique: farewell to worry, there was nothing that we could not achieve together, Esmé and I, nothing would be beyond us. The infinite magic and enchantment that the world had to offer was suddenly, awesomely, ours: we were in love.

Love brings such strength, such conviction and confidence as nothing else in human experience, so much the more when you are blessedly young at heart, with all that precious optimism endemic to youth.

Love is the finest of the fine wines of life, quaffed so avidly and with such urgency when you are young, and everlastingly to be sipped and savoured in the timeless pleasure of growing old together.

Each year will I make this pilgrimage to Gower until I can think no more; I have just two consolations: Esmé never had to feel this pain, and with every dragging day, week and month that passes I get ever closer to the oblivion I crave.

We had been strongly advised back in England that we should be sure not to miss the Ajanta and Ellora caves; this meant flying down to Aurangabad in the Province of Maharashtra. The caves illustrate the development of religion in India, Buddhism, Hinduism and Jainism and they represent a span of six hundred years. The sites are remote, and they were lost until their rediscovery during the nineteenth century. The temples and the caves themselves were man-made by monks and artists hammering the buildings out of solid rock, starting at the top and working downwards, a technique which eliminated the need to erect scaffolding. There now remain thirty-four temples at Ellora and twenty-nine at Ajanta and it takes two days to see them.

We flew to Bombay and, as in Delhi, we stayed at the Taj Mahal Hotel; even more than its namesake in Delhi the Taj Mahal in Bombay exuded Victorian opulence. It had been completely renovated and it was a pleasure to stay there; the standards of service remained as good as ever and the Taj Mahal in Bombay was always famous for this. We had a west-facing room looking out over the Arabian Sea and below us to the left was the Gateway of India, an enormous arch built to commemorate the visit of King George V before the First World War in 1911.

We had little time in Bombay but were determined to see the Elephanta Caves which involved crossing Bombay Harbour, and we embarked just beside the Gateway of India. While we were waiting for our boat to come a man fell into the sea, there was a big swell going and it was quite obvious that he was unable to get out, and one could not be certain that he could swim. A large crowd gathered, viewed the scene with the usual eastern lack of urgency, and he was eventually pulled out with ropes. As we crossed Bombay Harbour we saw many different boats, fishing boats, flatboats for tending nets in the harbour, and just off Elephanta Island there were tankers and liners moored.

The Elephanta Caves illustrate Hindu mythology and the carvings were beautiful. We had a very knowledgeable woman as a guide, who was the wife of a solicitor, and Esmé listened to her intently as she talked about the figures shown in the sculptures, emphasising the peace and the love and the strength that they showed. The Hindu god most prominent in these sculptures was Siva, but in a central recess in the main hall of the main cave there was a triple sculpture, showing the three faces of the Hindu Trinity, Brahma the creator, Siva the destroyer, and in the middle Vishnu the preserver. When our guide told us that Siva was responsible for bringing the River Ganges down to earth by letting it trickle down through his hair as a filter to remove impurities, Esmé said that he would probably be sorry to let it trickle through his hair as it was now; we had hoped to see the Ganges at Benares when we were in the north, but we did not have the time.

When we arrived in Bombay from Aurangabad Esmé found that the duty-free was running dangerously low, and I went out to replenish it. I was told at reception where I could find a liquor store, and I walked out of the front door and round the corner and immediately was accosted by a man without legs and with some sort of congenital abnormality of his face, which made it appear that he had only one centrally placed eye; his method of transport was a trolley propelled by his hands on the road. He suggested that I would like a little boy or a little girl, and when I said that I was not interested he suggested I should try the two together. He went on offering all sorts of delights and I remembered the taxi driver in front of the Oriental Hotel in Bangkok nearly ten years before, who suggested at least half a dozen options for me and some for Esmé. I ran down the road heading for the liquor store but he was much faster, and the way he went in and out of the traffic on his trolley was quite extraordinary. I reached the safety of the liquor store but this was only temporary. I bought a bottle of "Lundon Gin" and ran down the road back to the hotel, hotly pursued by the legless terror. When I got to our room I told Esmé that for the sake of keeping her duty-free at a reasonable level, I had been exposed to and terrorised by a legless man with an appallingly ugly face. I got little sympathy, and when she poured herself a gin and tonic and tasted it, she said that it was foul.

We had five days to go and knew that if we did not go up to Kashmir on this trip we would probably never go. We flew from Bombay to Srinagar, where the airport buildings were made entirely of wood, and we had a houseboat reservation on Lake Nagin. We had aimed for Lake Dal because we knew about it from *The Jewel in the Crown*, and Esmé really fancied being waited on like a Maharani in the luxury of these houseboats. We were taken to the lake, which involved going up a mountain through dense fir trees, and eventually we were deposited on our houseboat. There were many of these boats moored some fifty yards apart all round the edge of the lake; Lake Dal and Lake Nagin are connected by a wide channel and the total area of the two lakes is about twelve square miles. It was a very tranquil scene, standing on the stern of this large houseboat and looking across the lake at the other houseboats and shikaras, graceful little boats with curtains and canopies, paddling around and going from houseboat to houseboat. Our boat was carpeted with a crimson carpet, and it had a large sleeping area and a spacious dining/sitting area; we were waited on by a young man who arrived early in the morning, asked us our requirements for the day and saw to it that they were met, and he told us that these houseboats were developed by the English because the Maharajah put out an edict prohibiting them from owning any land, and so the boats were their floating homes.

We arranged to have a day trip round both lakes in a shikara and also to visit Srinagar at the side of Lake Dal. Our shikara had a straw canopy and silk curtains and we lay on a pile of silk-covered cushions. Esmé was wearing her white towelling hat with the buckle on the front and a striped green, blue and white shirt; she wore white trousers rather than shorts or a skirt because she did not want to have the boatman looking up her legs. The boatman was quite a character and chatted now and then, but he respected the need for quiet; periodically he stopped to relight his hookah. We disembarked for a while at a small island in the middle of Lake Nagin, where we sat under lotus blossoms, and we went from here round Lake Dal and then on to Srinagar. Water pedlars in their shikaras full of things to sell approached us several times, but our boatman shooed them away. We found Srinagar unattractive, and were glad to return to our houseboat.

On the final day we sat on the roof of the houseboat and read our books, and were happy with our world. Before flying from Srinagar to Delhi to go home we took a coach trip to Gulmarg, higher up the mountain where it was cold and wet, and we found that the contrast with the heat and dust and the colour of Rajasthan was immense. The people were certainly colourless, they were tall, dark and wore fur hats and dark brown cloaks, looking more like Afghans than Indians. Up to the north-east of us lay China, over to the north-west was Afghanistan, and we felt that we were just under the roof of the world.

We were glad that we had been to Kashmir and seen the lakes and the life on them; not only were there the houseboats, but there were narrow channels going everywhere through dense trees, and there were villages on the water where people were trading, shops, barges full of merchandise, corn, wood, everything imaginable, a complete waterworld.

For many the poverty and the begging throughout the Indian subcontinent is a deterrent. In every city we visited we were met by an army of beggars, many crippled and repulsive, the more repulsive the better when it came to getting money from tourists; more profitable for them and for the pimps who run and exploit them; but this is only a small facet of India, albeit at times an irritating one. A major problem is the inevitable "Delhi Belly", and I was afflicted in Delhi at the start, Esmé suffering the Agra variant. It tends to last no more than two days and, as in Egypt, it is impossible to avoid it. When I developed the disease in Delhi, I told Esmé that I thought I was going to die, and that she would have to carry on the tour without me. She told me that I should pull myself together and that it was all in the mind, but when she got to Agra she thought differently.

North and south India are so different that it is quite essential to visit both, and in the spring of 1987 we flew back to Bombay where we joined a group for the tour of South India. After one night in Bombay in a second-rate hotel we flew to Bangalore in the province of Karnataka, a huge garden city with few ancient sites to see. We were taken to the Westend Hotel, and standing outside the main door I saw a coach with 'Pakistan Test Team' written on it and parked on the other side of the roadway was another coach with 'Indian Test Team' displayed. I realised that there was a test match being played here between these two mortal enemies, and that both teams were staying in this hotel. I recognised a few faces and when we went out to the poolside to have drinks before dinner, I said to Esmé that she was surrounded by Pakistani and Indian cricketers and they were even talking to each other. She asked me which one was Imran Khan, and a man sitting just behind her turned round and wished her a very good evening. We had no time to watch the cricket, which was a pity because that next day was the final day of the final test match of the series, and Pakistan won on Indian soil for the first time ever, thanks largely to the bowling of Imran Khan.

Before getting on the road for Mysore the next day, we were taken to the large botanical Lal Bagh Garden where there were trees and fountains, lotus pools, and many tropical bushes; but most of all I remember the jacaranda trees, a glorious mass of the most lovely blue colour. It seemed as if heaven had come right down to us and was just above our heads. There was an eighty-five mile drive to Mysore, where we put up at the magnificent Lalitha Mahal Palace. As you entered the front door between large pillars, in front of you was a very wide straight white marble staircase leading up to a half landing, where it split and went on up to the first floor. It is all beautifully balustraded and we got a member of the staff the next evening to take a photograph of us standing on this staircase, Esmé in a pure white shirt with a long skirt of brilliant checks and white shoes, and myself wearing my Thai silk shirt and white trousers and shoes. The photographer said that it was the Maharajah and Maharani come back to Mysore. The Lalitha Mahal Palace was built by a Maharajah to house his foreign guests who were sufficiently distinguished, and apart from this magnificent Italian marble staircase there was a lofty dining-hall with a dome of stained glass, where we dined accompanied by three men playing Indian music. All this appealed very much to Esmé's vivid imagination which was extremely infectious.

The most important building in Mysore was the Maharajah's Palace. This was a vast building, by far and away the biggest palace we saw throughout India, almost as big as the Government Buildings in Delhi. There was much oriental decoration with turrets, arches, rows of columns and sculptures. We saw Durbar Hall where the Maharajahs received the public, and there was a great court with an awning which looked like the roof of the new Mound Stand at Lord's cricket ground. We took a trip out of Mysore to the summer palace of the Tipu Sultan, a famous Mysore Rajah of the sixteenth century, a large square wooden building with a wide verandah all round. We were conned into making a very long trip by road to Ootacamunda, a famous hill station during the time of the British Raj, and during the hot summers the Indian army and civil service used it greatly to escape from the heat of the plains. It was four hours away in an uncomfortable coach, and had we known this we probably would have opted out, because the road was endless and there was little to see.

In Ootacamunda we went to "the club" and were served with drinks by a very elderly man, who told us that he was there during the days long before Independence; we got back late in the night to Mysore, totally exhausted. In the days of the British Raj, Ootacamunda was to British in the south what Simla was in the north.

On the last morning before we flew to Madras we saw the Nandi Bull on a hill just out of town, a statue sixteen feet high carved out of a single boulder, and said to belong to Siva; we stopped at a coffee plantation and saw how the coffee beans were dried and packed for export, and since then we have always rotated Mysore and Mocha, mixed with other coffees.

Madras is the capital of the state of Tamil Nadu, we were given a morning tour of the city and we visited an enormous market where beggars and rotting vegetables seemed to occupy most of the pathways. It was on this trip to south India that we met Tim and Valerie Ashby with whom we became very good friends; we had much in common, and spent most of our time with them. At the market Valerie was approached by a man, half of whose face was missing. He had saliva and nasal secretions flowing freely, and made Charles Laughton in *The Hunchback of Notre Dame* look pretty. Valerie stood transfixed murmuring, "Dear God".

Madras has beautiful beaches south of it on the Bay of Bengal, and fifty-seven miles south-west were Mahabalipuram and Kanchipuram, the famous Beach Temples with the Bay of Bengal only a few feet away, Hindu and magnificently carved; Mahabalipuram is known as the City of the Seven Pagodas and was built in the seventh century AD. We walked around and among these beautiful temples in blistering sun. Kanchipuram, the Golden City of a Thousand Temples, actually contains one hundred and twenty-four separate shrines.

The next day we were taken down the coast road to Covelong Beach, where we swam in the Bay of Bengal. We liked it so much here, and the small hotel on the beach where we had lunch, that Esmé and I decided to come back for the day the next day rather than do any more sightseeing. I remember both of us standing on the beach, having just come out of the sea, and I said to Esmé that far away beyond the horizon looking due east were the Andaman and Nicobar islands which played quite a part when the Chinese Opium Wars took place, and I suggested to her that one day we might even get there. She merely said that my travel bug had caused terminal disease and she was right, there was no stopping now; but we never got to these islands, although we were closer to them when we were on Phuket. Esmé asked me to take a picture of her on the beach, which I did, there was something romantic for her about the Bay of Bengal.

We were to fly from Madras to Madurai but the flights were cancelled for some reason, and we had to go in four cars; we went with the Ashbys and the guide, and it was one of the longest, hottest and dustiest drives of our lives to the border of the state of Kerala. When we finally got to Madurai we were in the deep south of India, and the whole countryside was green and tropical and so very different from the north. The reason for going to Madurai was to see the temple, the Meenakshi Temple which honours the god Siva and his wife. We had to take off our shoes to enter this place, the floors were absolutely filthy, and we had no idea what we were walking on or in; Esmé asked what diseases of the feet we might pick up and I told her to wait and see.

The temples of Madurai were packed with people and at Meenakshi they were all bathing in a vast pool in the centre; the carving in these temples was particularly massive and detailed. When we had seen Madurai, Esmé and I felt a little punch-drunk and certainly intoxicated by the sights of south India, and we were ready to drop out on the beach in Goa; but before this we were to go to Cochin, one of the three most important ports on the west coast of India. Here was a true port of the east, outside the port itself there were lagoons, islands which were wooded, and waterways where we passed many houses on stilts, and on our motorboat we spent a pleasant three hours puttering down these canals. Cochin shows evidence of Portuguese, Dutch, Jewish, Muslim, Hindu and Chinese influence, the Chinese influence limited now to their characteristic wide fishing nets. We went to a synagogue in the centre of Cochin; the first emigration of the Jews to India was to Kerala in the sixth century BC, and many more came in the first century AD, fleeing the Roman persecution in Jerusalem. Esmé, the daughter of her father, lapped up all this history.

In Goa we stayed at the Fort Aguada Beach Resort, where the accommodation was in little bungalows. There was a long beach with the Arabian Sea pounding on it with unexpectedly large waves, a paradise for surfers. I asked Esmé if she would like to surf in the Arabian Sea before she died and she said that she would certainly die if she did. We spent three days lying in the sun, made one trip to the centre of Goa where we went into a church and were fanned by large fans in the ceiling worked by a punkah wallah, and outside there were gravestones with Portuguese and English names. Our next door neighbours in our bungalow were on their honeymoon, and day and night we heard loud evidence of their sexual delights which appeared to be almost non-stop. When I asked Tim Ashby what we should do about this interminable conjugal concert next door, he suggested that at the end of each performance we should clap loudly. This worked a treat, from then on whatever they did was soundless and we felt we were a couple of geriatric spoilsports. Esmé said that if I really loved her we could be doing what they were doing all the time, and I had no satisfactory answer to that which would have given any comfort to either of us. I asked her did it not bring back wonderful memories of those heady days when I would run up her ramparts and storm the very citadel of her love. Her reply was short, two-worded, and depressingly unromantic.

We did not go back to India, although Esmé would dearly have liked to do so. Now that she has gone away from me, I wonder if perhaps she has gone to those *Far Pavilions* of MM Kaye, and perhaps I may soon be able to join her there, and we can sit together and look out over the India of her dreams and her delight, her India where you address the mysteries only if you wish, her meditative brooding India, bewitching and beguiling with its poetic grandeur of mien, its hint of wistfulness and pervading sense of irony; and perhaps there may be an end to this yearning and sorrow, this grief and this pain, and perhaps there may be final and absolute peace for both of us.

Perhaps.

Thailand: Chaio Phraya River from the Oriental Hotel, Bangkok.

Thailand: The beach on Phi Phi Island, Phuket.

Hong Kong: Typhoon shelter, now no longer.

Indonesia: Typical Batak houses, Sumatra.

Indonesia: The huge stupas on the top of the Buddhist temple of Borobudur, Java.

Indonesia: Effigies outside the cliff graves, Sulawesi.

India: The Taj Mahal in the late afternoon sun, Agra.

India: At the side of Lake Pichola in the early evening, Udaipur.

The Philippines: Dinner with the Third Baron Moynihan and
Edithe his fourth wife, Manila.

South Pacific: Lagoon at Beachcomber Hotel, Tahiti.

South Pacific: The dancers, Tahiti.

South Pacific: The mysterious Moai, Easter Island.

South Pacific: Blue Marlin for supper, Bora Bora.

Egypt: Camel train setting out from the base of the Great
Pyramid, Giza.

Egypt: The felucca on the Nile, Aswan.

South America: Writing the journal at the lodge on the Amazon, Peru.

South America: Llama on the mountain above Cuzco, Peru.

South America: Macchu Picchu from Inti Punea, Peru.

South America: Magnificent Iguacu Falls, Argentina.

Australia: Circular Quay and the Opera House, Sydney.

Chapter Nine
The Philippines

Toward the end of 1986 I was invited by the insurance company to whom I was Consultant Medical Officer, Mercantile and General Reinsurance, to attend the fifteenth International Congress of Life Assurance Medicine in Tokyo. Esmé bubbled with excitement when she heard this; the company would pay for me, but we would have to pay for Esmé. We had been to these congresses before, but never out of Europe, and when we knew that we were going to Japan for a week, we had to decide where we would go after the congress; looking at the map the Philippines seemed reasonably near to Japan, and we decided that this was where we would spend the second half of our holiday.

As usual we read it all up and when I told Douglas Barrington, who at that time owned the Lygon Arms in Broadway, that we were thinking of going to the Philippines, he said that he would arrange for us to be looked after there by Lord Tony Moynihan. Douglas had met Tony's mother on a world cruise and they had become firm friends. Tony had left UK in a great hurry in 1970 because he was facing fifty-seven charges of criminal fraud, had jumped bail, had gone to the Philippines where there was no extradition treaty with UK, and set up house, and brothels in Manila. The first Lord Moynihan, Tony's grandfather, had been so honoured for his surgical prowess; he was famous for designing forceps for biliary surgery, which remained in use until the latter-day development of keyhole surgery. The second Lord Moynihan, Tony's father, had physiological needs which were not acceptable in his generation, or any other for that matter, and it seemed that Tony had truly inherited his father's genes. After we left the Philippines I asked Esmé whether Tony's problem was that he did not know the difference between right and wrong, or that he did know this difference and found that 'wrong' was more convenient and profitable. She was sure that it was the latter, but she did think that from birth he had been overindulged and hence deprived. He tried very hard to look after us because he knew that Douglas Barrington was a good friend of his mother's, and in many ways it was our association with him that made this visit to the Philippines so remarkable and enjoyable.

We flew from Osaka in Japan to Manila where Tony Moynihan met us. Our first impression of him was of a tall man, well over six feet with a large head, close set eyes and a long nose. Bejowled, pink-complexioned and pinguid of belly, he looked the picture of cheerful self-indulgence. He appeared to have the run of the airport and had no problem with getting right to the arrival gate, and he led us through immigration and customs with scarcely a sideways look; we later found that in the Philippines, wherever Lord Moynihan wanted to go, nobody got in his way. He had been a close friend of that infamous plunderer Marcos and his wife Imelda and he told us that since the fall of Marcos he was finding that "doing business" was much more difficult.

Awaiting us outside the airport was a large air-conditioned car. Esmé got into the back with me, and Tony got into the front; also in the back was a diminutive woman whom Tony called Lennie who was his housekeeper. When we got to the Manila Hotel, Tony made arrangements for us to go to dinner at The Sheraton, which was further down the road, and Lennie told us to wait downstairs in the bar while she went upstairs and unpacked. Esmé said that this was the first time anybody had ever unpacked for us; when we went to our room Lennie had gone, but all our clothes were beautifully hung up, our drawers filled and our toiletries arrayed in the bathroom. The Manila Hotel is very impressive: it is not a Hilton, a Holiday Inn, or a Sheraton, it is an old dignified and gracious place with real history. You enter through a large doorway and the foyer leads into a huge lounge with a very high roof, and there are galleries all around on two levels. During World War II the Manila Hotel was successively the headquarters of General McArthur, then when the Japanese took the Philippines of Admiral Yammamoto, and finally McArthur again when the Americans returned. Our room overlooked a wide park and beyond that there was the harbour, and in the far distance at the mouth of the harbour we could just see the island of Corregidor.

At dinner at The Sheraton we were introduced to Tony's fourth wife, a pretty little Filipino girl named Edithe who looked about seventeen but must have been in her early twenties. We got to know each other at this first dinner, and Tony spent the next two days showing us round Manila. I wanted to go to Bataan, where the Americans held out against enormous odds before surrendering to the Japanese, and where the infamous Death March took place on which hundreds of American soldiers died. I also wanted, if possible, to take the hydrofoil to Corregidor which was also the scene of tremendous American resistance, and I wanted to see the tunnels and gun emplacements there. Tony showed us a medieval dungeon by the harbour which was built in the middle ages to hold fifty prisoners and into which the Japanese crammed hundreds of American soldiers; many died of suffocation and dehydration and it was one of the worst massacres of the Pacific war, for which Yammamoto was eventually hanged. We saw the American War Cemetery high up on a hill above Manila, an enormous green park with the grass closely cropped and the edges sharp and hundreds upon hundreds of small white crosses in curved lines with names on them. They stretched away into the distance, almost as far as the eye could see. Esmé looked at these and she said that each one must represent so much sorrow and pain to mothers, fathers, brothers, sisters, wives and girlfriends, and this mass of white crosses made you realise how great was the American contribution toward the ending of tyranny in the Pacific; we tended in Britain to be obsessed with the European and Desert wars.

The Spanish ruled the Philippines from 1655 until 1898 when the Americans helped to create a Republic, and there is evidence of Spanish influence everywhere in names and in buildings.

Tony pointed out a medium-sized hotel which he had just bought, which was obviously a new brothel. Whenever we went to a bar to have a drink, shifty-looking men would sidle up to him and there would be short, over-the-shoulder conversations; not only was he into prostitution but into drug smuggling too. Esmé said that it felt strange to be associating with a major criminal; I think she found it rather diverting. Edithe was anxious to go to Paris and London on a shopping spree, and Tony said that she would have to go on her own because it would be too risky for him to accompany her; we did not blame her for wanting to stock up as much as she could, because Tony's wives tended to have a pretty short innings.

On the second night we invited them to have dinner with us in The Manila and we had a very good evening. To dine there men have to wear a barong Tagalog, a thin long-sleeved white shirt worn outside the trousers, with lace panels with holes both for decoration and for ventilation and pearl buttons on the sleeves. I did not have one of these, but the hotel supplied me with one and when we left the Philippines finally I bought a barong, and it was much admired when I wore it elsewhere in the world. Esmé really dolled up for this dinner. She wore a dress with bright blue, orange, yellow and red stripes, and I asked her if she was trying to get Tony interested in order to become the fifth Lady Moynihan. She said that that might be an idea because her chances of being Lady Ellis were non-existent; she always wanted a title simply because it got you to places in comfort.

The latter part of our holiday in the Philippines was spent on the island of Cebu and we stayed on the beach in a little hotel called The Tambuli Beach Resort. On arrival Esmé was bitten badly by mosquitoes while waiting to check in. When we got to our little wooden bungalow we lit five mosquito coils but it was too late, and she asked me how long would it take for malaria to kill her, I reassured her that there was no malaria on Cebu, which was an outrageous lie, and I prayed that we had the right antimalarial pills.

We had a young Japanese couple on honeymoon next to us and Esmé said that we always seemed to end up next door to honeymooners; she asked why these Japs were so quiet, compared with honeymooners of other nationalities with whom we had been cheek by jowl. She thought they must make love in a different way. I was not quite sure what she meant and I did not like to ask them what they were doing or how they were doing it.

The young hotel staff held what they called the Tambuli Olympics while we were there, and they did me the honour of asking me to be the sole referee, judge, umpire and scorer, such power that I had rarely experienced previously. They sat me at a trestle table under some coconut palms with pencil and paper and they then ran through a series of games which took several hours, volleyball, tug-of-war, long jump, high jump and much more. They were in three teams red, yellow and blue and I had to judge each event and decide first, second and third. Looking on from our balcony twenty yards away, Esmé said that wearing my panama with the MCC ribbon I looked like Graham Greene.

In the restaurant there was an extremely pretty girl who was in charge of food and beverage; she had a badge on her chest denoting this and we got to know her very well. She wanted some day to come to England; all the young people seemed to want to get away from the Philippines if they could because there was so much unemployment and the pay in any job was very low. She showed us a small shop on the beach where we bought two shark's teeth on little silver mounts for the tropical necklace.

At the end of our week on Cebu, Tony and Edithe arrived with Lennie and quite an entourage. They had arranged for us to go for the day on a catamaran to a small outlying island and roast a suckling pig on the beach for lunch. The catamaran was owned by a friend of Tony's named Bobby, a very wealthy man who owned both the university and the hospital in Cebu City. He was extremely generous to us and plied us all day on his catamaran with food and cold beer: San Miguel, the best beer in the South Pacific. Tony spent the latter part of this lovely day in a semi-drunken stupor with Edithe fussing around and trying to look after all of us, and we felt a little sorry for her. I disgraced myself on the way home by putting my foot through a plastic window in the deck, my leg was quite badly lacerated and Bobby was very worried about this. When we got back to Cebu City he insisted that I go to his hospital where he summoned three casualty officers. I was afraid that in their zeal and wish to please Bobby they would get out the curved needles and the catgut and start sewing me up. The cuts were very superficial, although numerous, and they cleaned my leg up and bandaged it and I was able to tell Esmé that I thought I might live. We thanked Bobby for a marvellous day, said goodbye to him and made arrangements to meet Tony in Manila in a couple of days' time to do some shopping. Douglas Barrington had asked us to bring back for him some white silk shirts, and Tony took us to a shop in Manila where we bought these shirts, and also some salad bowls for ourselves shaped like mangoes. Tony arranged for Lennie to pick us up from the Manila Hotel and take us to the airport and see us safely through to the departure lounge; Esmé was very glad about this because she was worried about the hustlers and muggers who thronged the approaches to the airport. In the event Lennie was very impressive; she was a tiny woman but she waded through all these men and made quite sure that we had no problems. It is now apparent that at the time we were in the Philippines, Tony was a pimping partner of Howard Marks and had shared interests with him in the drug trade. Marks at that time was the leading light in the distribution of cannabis world-wide, but it was rumoured that Tony in addition was involved in the onward passage of heroin from the Philippines to Sydney. In his recent autobiography written since his release from jail in 1995, Marks has denied any activity in the heroin trade, but undoubtedly they shared brothels in the Philippines.

Three years after we were in the Philippines at the end of 1989, Tony, in exchange for the dropping of the fraud charges against him in England, went to America and furnished evidence including taped telephone conversations, which helped to put Marks in jail with a sentence of twenty-five years; after this he had the brass neck to throw a big party at the Savoy Hotel in London for the police. He fabricated a divorce from Edithe by forging her signature, and bigamously married a belly dancer, Jinna as his fifth wife; he had a son by Edithe and another son by Jinna, but claimed that Edithe's son was not fathered by him.

There has been much in the press recently because after Tony died of a stroke aged fifty-five in 1991, the inheritance of his title had to be decided, and also the inheritance of his money: three million pounds in the Philippines earned as a brothel-keeper, pimp and drug trafficker. To die of a stroke at the age of fifty-five is not common, and one is bound to wonder whether revenge could have contributed to Tony's demise, for he must have had many enemies. Cheat, liar, fraudster, swindler, user and discarder of women, bigamist, brothel-keeper, pimp, drug trafficker, police informer, the third Baron Moynihan was most certainly all of these, and considered loathsome by many; but he went out of his way to make our stay in the Philippines enjoyable and we were grateful to him for that.

We talked much of this trip to the Philippines and of the people we met. It is a land where it is as natural for folk to be happy and friendly as it is for the sun to shine, but the corruption in Government has led to such exploitation of the people that it is difficult to believe they can ever recover. Esmé felt so very strongly that it was only the accident of birth that gave us the life we had, and this should never be accepted as of right; all the time that I knew her she had this overriding concern for the underprivileged and that was why she became such a dedicated social worker; her heart was full of humility and compassion, never for her the assumption that she was born better than others, and this was one of many reasons why I loved her so very much. She tried to store her mind and heart with good things, and I am grateful that she had the time to explore and savour such harvests to the full, and that I could share it all with her.

The more we saw of the peoples of the world, the more we felt that bigotry, prejudice and the assumption of superiority by birth were the refuge of the unconfident, the unsure and the afraid. Often did I hear Esmé, ever chary of confrontation, say quietly in the social circles in which we moved, that she was so glad that she was not born a black in South Africa, a Jew in pre-war Europe, an untouchable in India or an Indian under the British Raj; she asked how could anybody accept that they were born second class whatever their god, and how could anybody with any intelligence expect them to.

There must be no prerogative by birthright for any race, colour or creed, when it comes to fulfilment of hopes and wishes, dreams and desires.

Chapter Ten

South Pacific

The first experience can never be repeated, the first love, the first sunrise, the first South Sea Island are memories apart; these are not my words but those of Robert Louis Stevenson in 1889, one hundred years before Esmé and I first set foot on Tahiti. A later opinion on French Polynesia was that of Rupert Brooke who in 1913 felt that in the South Seas the Creator 'seems to have laid himself out to show what he can do'. Somerset Maugham tried to describe adequately all this beauty, and of course Gauguin painted most of his famous pictures here; both he and Stevenson died and were buried in the South Pacific. In our ignorance we thought that in the Gauguin museum on Tahiti we would see many of his paintings. We had both read Stevenson and Somerset Maugham, Esmé more than I, but when it came to Gauguin we were beginners, and we had not realised before we came to Tahiti that all his important paintings had been removed to Paris.

I was very excited to think that I was going to see something of the South Seas, having read as a boy of those famous sailors, Cook, Bougainville and Bligh. The South Pacific seemed so far away and inaccessible and we never believed that we could ever travel that far, but here we were on Tahiti greeted at the airport by Tahitians playing ukuleles and singing, wearing grass skirts and garlanded with white flowers. After the long flight across the Pacific from Los Angeles we were exhausted, but however tired you were, this reception could not fail to make you feel that life was worth living. When you travel far and wide there are inevitably times when the going seems hard, but there was never long between sparks of humour and sharps of wit in the company of my mirth-loving Welsh woman, whose whole body vibrated when she laughed.

We drove to the Beachcomber Hotel, and arriving at 3 a.m. before we could take possession of our overwater wooden bungalow we had to wait for two hours in the bar where we met Ernest, obviously gay and wearing an extraordinary headpiece made up of dozens of white tiare flowers. He was quite delightful, but when we went back two years later he was absent; we tried to find out what had happened to him but we failed and we missed him. While we were sitting in the bar a busload of Americans arrived worrying, grumbling and complaining, and their main desire seemed to be to get to bed before breakfast time which by then was not far away.

Before setting out we had read a good deal of the history of French Polynesia, so we knew that Tahiti almost brought England and France to war, and we knew that the French had conned Queen Pomare into signing documents giving Polynesia to France; we also knew that Queen Pomare had previously written to Queen Victoria asking to become an English protectorate, and that Victoria had declined, and thus in 1880 Tahiti became a fully-fledged French colony. Later in 1903 it became a Territory, and at that point the name French Polynesia was coined. It seemed such a pity that after Samuel Wallace of the British Navy, who first went there in 1767, after Captain Cook who came in 1769, and after Captain Bligh, who had been with Cook, returned in 1788, this beautiful part of the world had been rejected by Queen Victoria at a time when other European countries were staking their claims throughout the world.

We spent three days on Tahiti, and went into Papeete on the local bus, Le Truck. Coming out of the hotel you had to walk up an incline to the road above, the bus stop was a little way down the road, and if the driver saw you he would not leave the bus stop until he was sure whether you wanted to catch the bus or not, which rarely happens in the UK. We liked the Port of Papeete, important geographically because there was a lot of ocean between French Polynesia and other Pacific islands. There were many ships including a French cruiser and a destroyer, and we saw the *Windsong*, a large four-masted schooner which plied between the islands laden with American tourists. In the main street overlooking the port we found a kiosk selling painted shirts, run by an Italian woman who painted the shirts herself according to your requirement; Esmé chose a white shirt and had some large blue and green flowers painted on it. She was so pleased with it and she wore it in the evening, the bottom tied round the front in a large bow and she looked lovely in it. We got to know this woman quite well, and we told her that if we came back to Tahiti we would be sure to come and get another shirt, little thinking that she would still be there, but when we came back two years later she was, and Esmé bought more shirts.

Downtown Papeete is very civilised, with French ambience everywhere. There are good shops and on the small waterfront we found a shop where we bought two slender pieces of pink coral for Esmé's tropical necklace. These were added to the black coral from Tobago and the small coco de mer from Praslin in the Seychelles, and we hoped that we could travel for years and continue to build up this necklace, which was going to mean so much to both of us. The Gauguin Museum was a waste of time, but in the Maritime Museum we learned many things and especially in detail how Pacific atolls were formed.

As we sat on the balcony of our overwater bungalow there was the wide Pacific Ocean to our left and to our right the large island of Moorea, which seemed close to Tahiti; we found that there were daily ferries and we went across to investigate, taking the local bus to a hotel where we spent the day. There was good snorkelling and we had a pleasant lunch beside an enormous anchor, very rusty, which they claimed to be the anchor of Captain de Bougainville. There was a large lagoon and beyond it the sun torched down from a cloudless azure sky, the ocean pounded on the reef, and we did not wish to leave this place.

Back at the Beachcomber the evening entertainment during and after dinner was breathtaking. Esmé discovered on our first night that there was a pre-dinner pareo exhibition in the bar. I felt I would rather stay with Jeffrey Archer in the overwater bungalow, but I went down with her and I was glad that I did. A very graceful and beautiful girl was dancing to Tahitian music supplied by three men in the background, and she was putting on and taking off dozens of pareos of different colours and tying them in different ways, a memorable exhibition of graceful rhythmic movement.

The Tahitian dancing during dinner started with six men beating drums of different shapes and made of wood. The rhythm rose to a crescendo and then on came a dozen pretty barefoot girls with brilliantly coloured pareos tied round their hips, they wore head-dresses of brightly coloured flowers, their breasts were covered with black cups and they wore garlands of tiares round their necks. They danced and sang, and the emphasis was on gentle movement and sweet melody, very pretty and colourful, and you felt that you wanted it never to stop.

The men came on and the whole mood changed, the emphasis was highly sexual, they were powerfully built, with legs like tree-trunks and buttocks like pumpkins and they made forceful coital movements at the girls giving loud triumphant shouts; we waited for their floral head-dresses to fall off. The dance ended with a final violent thrust accompanied by a bellow of exultation. Esmé asked was it like the bee, one first and last glorious thrust followed by sudden death. I said that from the look of them this was not the first and was most certainly not going to be the last, and they looked far from dead. At the end of the dance they came among the tables inviting us to join in, I was all for it, although I did not particularly want to dance with the men. Esmé had reservations, I think she felt that she might get hurt; she said that she had not had enough practice recently at that sort of thing at home, and I was not at all sure how I should take that remark.

We had arranged to fly to Bora Bora, an hour away, spend three nights there and then board a small cruise ship and return to Tahiti by sea. On arrival at the pretty little airport on the reef we were taken across the lagoon in a motor launch to the village of Vaitape, and thence by road to the Hotel Bora Bora, which is considered one of the best hotels in the world. We occupied an overwater bungalow and we found that when we went down the steps from the jetty into the lagoon beside the bungalow, the fish were so plentiful that all we had to do was to put on a snorkel mask and put our faces in the sea, there did not appear to be any need to go out to the reef to see the fish. Bora Bora is very mountainous, and surrounding it are dozens of tiny islets called motus. We were here only for a short time and we simply lay on our balcony and luxuriated in the sun with the huge Pacific skies all around us.

We boarded the cruise ship Majestic Explorer and quickly realised that we were the only non-Americans on the boat, two among seventy. When we went into dinner the first night somebody shouted, "Take a bow Bob and Esmé Ellis." I was completely nonplussed by this, and I did not know quite what to do; Esmé suggested a little brief shadow boxing. I went up to the cabin after dinner to read, Esmé investigated the notice board and she told me that the next day would be spent decorating dinghies in competition, and the day after would be spent playing horseshoes in the morning and crab racing in the afternoon. I suggested that perhaps we could still jump over the stern and escape back to Bora Bora, but Esmé felt that dinghy decorating might just be better than death by drowning. Americans have to be organised and entertained every hour of their day and here we were absolute prisoners among them. We refused to decorate dinghies, but we did take part in throwing horseshoes at poles on the beach of a tiny island, and we did have a bet or two at the crab races.

At breakfast during this dreadful cruise we were exposed for the first time to the blini. I might have managed the fried food and the sweet food on the same plate, but it was the maple syrup poured over everything, including the sausages and bacon, which defeated me. Esmé looked out of the porthole and tried to pretend that she was not there. There were some American travel writers on this cruise, a couple of whom were very pleasant; they asked Esmé where she would like to live if she did not live in the United Kingdom, and she told them it would be the South of France. Americans always expect you to want to live in America, and when Esmé told them that it would have to be the South of France, they accused us of being civilised snobs, which of course was true.

On the way back we stopped at two pretty islands, Huahine and Raiatea, the second biggest island in the group of Society Islands, and we were shown where the original Maoris embarked for New Zealand.

The next part of our holiday was on Rarotonga in the Cook Islands, far to the west and much nearer to New Zealand. Immediately on arrival at the Rarotongan Resort Hotel I walked out of our ground floor room to look at the beach and I saw, about fifty yards away, Robert Bent, whom we knew well and played tennis with in Cheltenham. I rushed back and told Esmé that I had just seen Robert and she told me that the cruise with the Americans had turned my mind. I went out again and stalked Robert through some bushes and I went back to Esmé and repeated what I had seen but she still did not believe me. At dinner that night in the upstairs restaurant, Robert and Megan Bent walked in and sat down at a table across the room. We greeted them and they looked as if they had been shot; Megan said that they had come to the bottom of the world to get away from their friends in Gloucestershire and here we were. We had a super time together during the following two days, we played tennis and met for dinner at night which cemented a friendship which was to be important for us all back home. Looking at photographs now of the four of us on Rarotonga I am filled with consuming sadness, because two have now gone. Robert died in August 1993 quite suddenly, and my own love only six months ago. We looked so happy in these photographs with Megan and myself having not the slightest premonition of the sorrow and the loneliness that lay ahead for us.

Fifteen or twenty years before we went there, the Cook Islands were virtually undiscovered by tourists who went mainly to Fiji and Hawaii, but by the time we arrived they were very popular for package tours from New Zealand, and this started when New Zealand built an international airport on Rarotonga.

With the Bents we went to the main town of Avarua where we did some shopping, and then made a round tour of the island in a hired moke. In Avarua we bought a Rarotongan Fisherman's God, a painted image eighteen inches high and carved in ironwood. He adorned the prow of all the fishing boats, had a prominent belly and belly-button and a large penis pointing downwards, not erect like the devil god in metal we had bought on the island of Hydra in the Aegean many years before. Esmé noted that the penis was circumcised, and told me to go and find out if this was so on all the men in the Cook Islands; I told her that as there were nine thousand of them, a population survey would take rather a long time, and anyway I would probably get hurt. We had some cold beer in the famous Banana Court Bar on the little waterfront, which was run by a former heavyweight boxing champion of the Pacific named Apiro Brown; he was very large and friendly and we reckoned that he had no need to employ a chucker-out when there was trouble.

Robert and Megan had arranged to spend two nights on Aitutaki, a tiny northern atoll and we decided to join them. We flew in a small four-seater plane, and after forty-five minutes flying time we saw below us a ring of islands, and we realised that Aitutaki was part of the crater rim of a huge volcano. A small bus took us to the edge of a lagoon and we went across to the Aitutaki Resort Hotel in a flat-bottomed canopied boat. They told us with pride that we were to occupy a bungalow which Prince Edward had slept in the month before; this did not impress us, being a strong republicans, but what did impress us was the quiet beauty of this place. Our bungalow was surrounded by "walking" pandanus trees, and it was arched by bougainvillaea.

We went in a motorboat with Robert across the lagoon to a tiny island called One Foot, no more than a hundred yards across. As we approached the beach there were palm trees growing out of it, and they seemed to be standing in line waiting to welcome us, their thin trunks angled towards us and leaning elegantly, their tousled heads over the lip of the lagoon with the fronds waving gently in the soft southern trades; we told each other that we had glimpsed eternity, the perfect peace of this place was palpable, we had touched the end of time. We swam and snorkelled while they caught some fish for lunch, and we ate this barbecued in a little spinney of coconut palms in the centre of the island. When we got into the boat to go back we were given a large clam shell, and whenever I hold it in my hand now I have the most vivid recollection of this southern November Sunday in 1987. We were together discovering the South Seas, utterly contented, in total harmony with our perfect surroundings and with each other. When I look at two of the photographs which I took on One Foot, one of Esmé sitting in her swimsuit on an almost horizontal palm trunk, and one of her with Robert standing on the beach with their arms around each other and laughing happily, I simply want to cry.

We had the best part of the next day on Aitutaki and met a delightful local woman, big in mind and heart and body. She was built like an All Black prop forward and when she came to swim in the lagoon with us we admired her haughty nipples, proud and upstanding as guardsmen on parade, biceps like rugby balls and thighs that could crush an ox. Esmé discovered that she had something going with an airline pilot; we hoped that he would survive, but we could think of many worse deaths. On our second night on Aitutaki we went on a land crab hunt with long sticks. We caught twelve crabs in pitch darkness by torchlight, and the owner of the hotel took the crabs to cook them for supper. The next day we returned to Rarotonga, bade farewell to Robert and Megan and headed back to Tahiti for just one night and then home. We saw the dancing that night, and because they knew that we were going the next day those lovely girls sang us their goodbye song, a soft and haunting melody in which they asked us not to go, but if we must then please come back again soon; as we turned to go Esmé and I looked at each other and we could barely tear ourselves away.

Like Captain Bligh we had to return, though not to collect breadfruit trees for transplantation in the West Indies, but to go to Easter Island to see the fascinating stone statues; apart from that we had to see those lovely people again, who would greet us off the plane with leis of Tiare Tahiti gardenias, and we wanted to smell again the heady scent of sweet tropical blossoms which fills the air wherever you go in those islands. I was anxious to find Quinn's Bar, the most famous in all the South Pacific, and Esmé could not wait to get into to Papeete to buy some more painted shirts from her Italian friend in the kiosk on the waterfront.

This time, in 1989, we had an overwater bungalow facing due west with the port and the airport in the distance. This was a good position for myself because I could sit on the wooden balcony with my book and my binoculars, and intersperse reading with watching the varied shipping and the different planes heading to and from Papeete. One afternoon as we sat there Esmé suggested that I was using the binoculars solely in the hope of seeing demonstrations of the famed Tahitian promiscuity. I denied this with dignity and force, but I did not tell her that I had great hopes of a couple who were in sole occupation of a raft way out towards Moorea; unfortunately these hopes were not fulfilled, it must have been too long a swim for them to get out there. I saw the ancient Lan Chile Boeing 707 come in from Easter Island and we were highly excited to think that in another two days we would be on it flying back there. Each evening when the sun was low on the horizon we watched from our balcony crews of local men race each other in long canoes, ten to a canoe. They shouted in rhythm with the paddle stroke, they would paddle three strokes on one side of the boat, change over and paddle three strokes on the other. We thought of these people paddling about the Pacific in ancient times and Esmé said that when she got home she would like to read Thor Heyerdal's *Kontiki Expedition* again. We had with us his authoritative book on Easter Island, *Aku Aku*.

Before flying east to Easter Island we had a final dinner. Esmé wearing one of her painted shirts with bright pink trousers and gold shoes, and she always wore her tropical necklace which was by now becoming very attractive. A waitress spotted my barong, the white decorated evening shirt which is obligatory when you dine in the

Manila Hotel in the Philippines; she was born in the Philippines and I think very much wanted to go back, but there is little or no work there for anybody, and that's why you find Filipinos all over the world, mostly doing the menial tasks; they are sweet people who deserve much better.

While in our bungalow we had been invaded by an army of cockroaches and Esmé felt that we had lost the war with them. I thought that a draw was a fairer result because early on the last morning before going off to Easter Island I went to the loo where I killed the biggest cockroach of all with Esmé's sponge bag. When I got back into bed I told her what I had achieved, that with no thought for my own safety I had gone into battle and that I should be cited for a decoration. She said that I had made an awful noise and had woken her up much too early, and told me to go and wash the sponge bag. Interestingly enough it brought back memories of biology at school when we dissected out the mouth parts of a cockroach, I remember being rather good at this, and made a little pocket money by doing the dissections for my more ham-fisted mates.

The flight to Easter Island in the geriatric Boeing took five hours; there was not enough room and Esmé had a painful back. We arrived at the little airport in teeming rain and were very worried that if it rained like that all the time we were there, which was only a day and a half, we would not be able to see the moai. The locals told us that it often rained on Easter Island and our chances were slim; it is below the Tropic of Capricorn and on about the same latitude as Brisbane.

There is only one small "town" called Hanga Roa with only one possible hotel, and when we arrived Esmé licked her wounds incurred during the flight. She has written in the journal that she had an acute low back pain, acute right elbow pain, pain in the neck and a sore knee as well. I was very loving, considerate and solicitous about her many discomforts; I had to be because I had left all the painkillers back on Tahiti. Luckily there was a well-stocked bar and after several pisco sours she stopped talking about her skeletal problems. We met our guide whose name was Dina, a pleasant fat Italian girl who took us under her ample wing like a hen partridge with her chicks. She had come out to see the island two years before, met an Easter Islander and married him. Esmé said that this was probably the last place she herself would want to end up, the most isolated island in the world, and although it had been called by the early natives Te Pito o

Te Atnua, the navel of the world, Esmé suggested another name would be more apt and what she suggested was an orifice rather than a mere depression. Even the Polynesians who lived here abandoned the island ahead of the arrival of the first Europeans, who were the mutineers from the Bounty in 1790. Pitcairn Island, which was the final home of the majority of the mutineers, is all of two thousand kilometres to the west. It is not known who were the first Easter Islanders who built these fantastic statues, but the original settlers must surely have come either from South America in the east or Polynesia in the west. If you read the legends about the beginnings of Easter Island, the first era was ruled by King Hotu Matua, after this there was a long period of strife between the Long Ears and the Short Ears, and the Short Ears eventually defeated the Long Ears. Dina told us that Hotu Matua was probably a Polynesian, and arrived there between four and five hundred AD.

After completion in the quarry at the foot of Rano Raraku Volcano, the moai were all somehow transported to the periphery of the island and were erected with their backs to the sea. You could not come to Easter Island and fail to be enthralled by the haunting mystery of the place and by the huge monoliths weighing up to eighty tons, unique in the world, and they are on this tiny bleak volcanic island, less than one hundred and twenty square kilometres in area and two thousand kilometres from any other land. They are an endless enigma, a riddle never to be solved.

The rain mercifully stopped and during the only full day that we had on Easter Island we were able to see all that we needed to see with the help of fat Dina and a minibus. All the moai were felled as part of some unexplained cataclysm and considerable attention has been paid to this quite recently. The conclusion is that an earthquake occurred, and the fact that eighty per cent of moai had fallen in a westward direction and were lying on their faces suggested that there must have been a seismic force from the east. Many moai have been re-erected around the coast, and they stand singly or in rows with their grey bodies and carved faces and their red topknots. The most fascinating site on the island was the quarry at the foot of the volcano where there were moai in all stages of completion, there were huge blocks of stone lying horizontally and with the features yet to be chiselled, there were part finished statues lying on the ground and others, some fully erect and some leaning, scattered all over the grass foothills. Many of them seemed to be just heads but in fact they are whole statues buried nearly to the neck in the earth. It seemed that the workers had suddenly downed tools as if for a tea break. The biggest statue was twenty metres high and his face was nine metres long. We loved these pensive faces with their heavy brows and prominent noses, large dilated nostrils, prominent chins and large long ears; some show hands and breasts and navels, some have carved backs and originally they had eyes of white inlaid coral. We wandered around among these tight-lipped, sunken-eyed giants and we went up round the volcano to the crater where there was a lake. Dina told us that there are sixty statues around this crater and one hundred and sixty unfinished statues in the quarry below; she said that the total number of statues made at the Rano Raraku Quarry must have been between five and six hundred. It is known that the carving was done with basalt tools called toki, and thousands of them were found lying around in the quarry. I took a picture of Esmé standing in front of one of the moai with his huge nostrils seven metres above her head. The statues were probably transported using tree-trunks as rollers and large tripods and ropes. According to Dina the reason that Easter Island is so barren and treeless is because all the trees were cut down in order to transport the moai; that there were many trees on the island is confirmed by the finding of pollens in the sediment of the lake from palm trees which have been extinct for two thousand years.

We had this one day to look round and at the end of it we retired to the hotel bar and wrote furiously in the journal; in all our travels we tried to write up the day's experiences at the end of it, rather than put it off until later and rely on the memory. In the bar here we met two Australian archaeologists who told us a lot about Easter Island, and we drank pisco sours with them, which reminded us of the bar in Cuzco where Esmé got the recipe for the drink; it has a rather strange but pleasant taste and you can get through several without ill effects the next day. After this amazing day we went to bed early with our books, Esmé was reading *Love in the Time of Cholera* by Gabriel García Márquez which she was very much enjoying, and I reread *Aku Aku*.

Because of the dull weather and virtual absence of sun the photographs really did not do justice, but I filmed many of the moai, some in the quarry and quite a lot round the coast, and I also had pictures of the aku, the altars on which the moai stood. The coastline itself is very rocky with big Pacific breakers thundering on the shores, and if you could move Easter Island up into the tropics it really would become a tourist trap, but because of its inaccessibility the number of tourists were very few at the time we were there. Before we left the island we went to a small shop and bought ourselves a statue carved in stone with his red topknot, about nine inches high, for the window-sill in our dining-room where he would stand next to a smaller wooden statue of a Tahitian warrior with a spear, whom we brought back two years previously.

You get the impression on Easter Island that Chile, which owns it, is somewhat disinterested and very little money is being spent there. The hotel bedrooms are basic, and one of the archaeologists described them as little better than rugby changing rooms. What soil there is on the island is untilled, and they do not even seem to fish very much; Dina said that the Pinochet Government in Santiago was bankrupt, and they had no expectation on Easter Island of any further development in the foreseeable future. I should imagine that now, six years later, tourism will have increased, but they will have to improve upon that clapped-out old Boeing 707.

Katherine Whitehorn has recently written in *The Observer* about the importance to men of the size of their penis and the ways to increase this, and she states that the early Easter Islanders based their alphabet upon it. She also wrote that Sibelius attributed the enormous scope of his music to the size of his member; Esmé was always much less impressed by size than by performance; she was concerned with what it could do rather than how big it was, and she might have suggested that some of the often mournful and depressing nature of what Sibelius wrote suggested that he had serious doubts and worries about his potency.

In Polynesian and Melanesian art the penis and its size was paramount, but this was not apparent on the moai of Easter Island, though many were buried up to their waist in earth; only in Papua New Guinea did we see any attention paid to the female vulva.

The primacy of the pillicock has existed throughout the ages and even in modern times when a Pope is elected in Rome it is not only the smoke which comes out of the chimney which tells the waiting masses that a decision has been made, but the triumphant shouts of "Habeat" by the Cardinals, in their pathetic fear of selecting another Pope Joan.

As far as the Cardinals can know their God may be a woman and the Virgin Mary, who in their belief achieved the messianic zygote, her ovum unsullied by the sperm of man, should qualify. An independent, intelligent and enquiring woman, Esmé was unconcerned by male chauvinism and simply wondered why men who resorted to it were so frightened of women, and she rather pitied them. She was never anti-establishment nor even anti-privilege so long as it was earned and never abused; she often said that with the father and husband that she had she never needed to worry about male chauvinism, and I loved her for that. We often talked about Freemasonry, and I always felt that if I could not get to where I wanted to be on my professional ladder without having to join secret cliques and gang-ups, and I had plenty of overtures, I was probably on the wrong ladder anyway. Esmé could not understand why some men needed to play charades behind closed doors in order to boost their self-respect, and she felt rather sorry for their wives. As far as she was concerned the only association worth joining was the Human Association without any exclusions whatever.

We had one night back at the Beachcomber Hotel on Tahiti and then flew to Bora Bora for two nights at the Bora Bora Hotel. We went on a catamaran to one of the little motus surrounding Bora Bora and had a gorgeous lunch of barbecued fish. The next day we went on the same catamaran out to the reef, a submarine wall of coral twenty feet in height with magnificent colours where we saw many of the fish we had seen in the Seychelles, but here in addition we watched the shark feeding; we had thought that we would be watching this event from inside the boat, but we were told to get into the water and swim some twenty yards behind the boat, where just under the surface there was a long rope. The captain of the boat told us that the sharks would come and eat the meat which they threw out beyond the rope, and would not be interested in us. We had to take his word for it, and we just hoped that the sharks knew that our side of the rope was off limits; they looked pretty formidable from ten yards away, some of them eight feet long. The catamaran took us gently back to the hotel and we lay on the deck as we sailed, looking up into a cloudless blue sky with frigates hovering high above us. When we got back to the hotel jetty there was an enormous blue marlin hanging from a gallows; it had been brought in an hour previously and I took a picture of Esmé looking quite small beside it.

This happy day had to end, and we went down to the beach bar for drinks before dinner, where Esmé was persuaded to try the drink of the month, which they called Barracuda. I took a picture of her sitting at the bar Barracuda in hand, tiare gardenias in her hair and leis of the same round her neck; she was wearing her light pink linen trouser suit and she looked utterly gorgeous. An enlargement of this photograph is now on my desk as I write this, and it will surely accompany me if and when I ever travel again on my own. We got the barman to take another photograph of both of us sitting on a wooden pole, Esmé had her second Barracuda in her hand and I was holding a pint of cold draught lager; when I look at photographs like this, and I have looked at hundreds taken on our various trips abroad, I try to remember the happiness we had in those long past days, all the laughter and the way we loved each other. I am told, but I am unconvinced, that it will become easier to do this, and memories will become clearer and stronger and perhaps the writing of this book will help me to relive the past and retrieve the good times, because the present is intolerable, and the future without her I simply cannot contemplate.

The next night was our last, and we felt that we could not leave Bora Bora for the last time without eating, at Bloody Mary's. This was about half a mile down the road from the Bora Bora Hotel, a large straw-covered barn-like place, overhung by trees, casuarina and takamaka, and the floor was of sand. It was much frequented by American visitors, but fortunately the schooner *Windsong* was elsewhere. Bloody Mary's is a famous bar in the Pacific, like Aggie Grey's on Western Samoa and Quinn's on Tahiti. Bloody Mary's has a radio telephone link with fishing boats out to sea and they give their orders in this way, I asked the manager if he took credit cards and he said that he would take anything that was not actually screwed down, and he told us that if we could not pay we would have to wash up or clean the carpet, the carpet being the sandy floor. The fish were enticingly laid out in a bed of ice; Esmé had marlin and I had jackfish, all quite delicious.

On a board outside Bloody Mary's there is a list of famous people who have eaten there and we saw names of many celebrities, among them Nelson Rockefeller, Jane Fonda, Dudley Moore and Julio Iglesias. Esmé said that we did not need any of them because we had each other, and how could I be interested in Jane Fonda when I had her? I let this pass because I did not wish to ruin a perfect evening, but we agreed that it would have been rather nice to have had Julio 'beginning the beguine' in the background.

We boarded the little plane at the airport, which taxied between palm and casuarina trees and fifteen-feet-high oleanders. Back on Tahiti we went into Papeete on Le Truck to do some business. Esmé wanted to pick up some painted shirts, especially a turquoise one which she had ordered for our daughter Emma, but unfortunately Madama Italiano had been unable to finish it because it had been raining and she could not dry it. She promised to post it to us in England, and this she did. When we took off from the airport, climbed high in the sky and banked westward toward Sydney, Esmé turned to me and said that this time we had left French Polynesia forever, we would not return; I could go back now alone, but as with half the globe, it would strike chords in my memory which would escalate into such a symphony of sadness as even Sibelius himself had never contemplated. The next year, 1990, we had planned Jordan and Jerusalem in the earlier part of the year and Fiji, Australia and Papua New Guinea later. Papua New Guinea should be part of our experience of the South Pacific, but it was so different that I have decided to give it a chapter of its own.

In the early part of November 1990 we flew on another round the world ticket to Los Angeles where I wanted to see the Queen Mary which was now moored permanently in the dock and was an entertainment centre. We had five hours' wait in Los Angeles, and we boarded a bus to take us to where the Queen Mary was docked, but the bus took so long that we got frightened, and about three quarters of the way to the harbour we got off and headed back because we were afraid we would miss our plane, and we never saw the Queen Mary.

We landed on Fiji via Honolulu and went to the Regent of Fiji Hotel. We were shown a cottage somewhat back from the beach which Esmé rejected, and she cajoled the management into giving us a room right on the beach; she was a girl who never liked to accept second best if she could help it. Fiji was the first stop on what was to be a long journey, taking in Papua New Guinea which I shall describe in a later chapter, and cricket in Australia.

The Regent of Fiji is an excellent hotel and it has a tennis club attached, owned by Australian former Wimbledon champion John Newcombe, which we used a lot. Lying on sunbeds outside our cottage we read our books, Esmé had Evelyn Anthony and John Le Carré, those few books of his that she had not already read. I had John Pilger and *The Pacific War* by John Costello; in reserve we had PD James and Robert Ludlum. When I realised what she had brought to read, I suggested that the sexual gymnastics in the books of Jilly Cooper and others seemed to have palled. We had a serious discussion about this under those coconut palms outside our room, and we agreed that men who expected their partners always to respond to their lovemaking with orgasms that could be registered on the Richter Scale were not making love, but merely seeking reassurance for themselves. It was the pressure that men put upon women to achieve orgasm that made them fake it fifty per cent of the time. We felt that our generation should take responsibility for many of the problems of the next generation. The fact that they expected more from relationships, sexual or otherwise, had to come from what they believed were the possibilities, and they could only have learned about these from us; we both suspected that they were looking for something that really was not there.

We knew that a love that passeth all understanding, if it existed at all, must be the stuff only of others and their gods. We accepted that a lasting love between human beings required a want and an ability to work to preserve it, the resistance of outside options and temptations, and the repudiation of them for the impostors they are.

It seemed to us that having sex, to use that hackneyed modern idiom, when it did not involve the making of love, risked relegation of what could be a consummately beautiful shared experience to a mere physiological release, albeit pleasurable – a much needed elimination perhaps, the scoring of yet another orgasmic goal no doubt, but loveless, it would always proscribe perfection.

Interviewed recently by Harriet Griffey of the Guardian, Joan Plowright, whose marriage to Lawrence Olivier lasted twenty-eight years to his death, quoted Rainer Maria Rilke, who considered that idealistically marriage should be the 'nurturing and guarding of two solitudes'. Esmé and I preferred more mutual involvement; our separate working lives provided enough space for us in our marriage, and apart from this we needed always to be close.

Esmé announced one morning that she was going parasailing: they strapped on a life-jacket and the parachute harness, the boat revved up, and before I knew where I was my darling old puss was high up in the sky waving her legs and heading fast toward New Zealand. I wondered how she would land, usually it was into the sea but here it was on to the beach, she descended most elegantly, four large men caught her and removed all the straps and she ran towards me excited like a child; she said that never before had she been in the grip of four gorillas and she might have another go. I could not let this go unchallenged and I allowed the gorillas to strap me up. Unfortunately the boat started prematurely, I was not ready and I was dragged at high speed feet first into the Pacific, quite a lot of which entered my stomach. I also had my camera round my neck for the taking of aerial photographs and the camera and the film inside it were completely ruined. Descending to the beach at the end of my flight I looked down and I saw four black faces and row upon row of shining white teeth grinning up at me. When they got me down and unstrapped me one of the gorillas said, "Lady very good, you very bad." I had to accept that he had a point.

The day after this we took a boat called the Island Express, a large catamaran of some two hundred tons with the upper deck part covered and a lower air-conditioned cabin with a well-stocked bar, to Mana Island. We were accompanied by a very noisy group of Italians who sang all the way to Mana to guitar accompaniment, and we belted out 'Volare' with them. We had barbecued steaks under the trees on Mana and boarded a Yellow Submarine, a semi-submersible, and went out to the reef, we had never been on one of these vessels before, and as we boarded it Esmé said that within the last forty-eight hours and at the age of sixty-nine, she had flown high in the sky with the birds under a parachute and had gone deep under the sea with the fish in a submarine, both for the first time.

There was a renowned gourmet restaurant at the Regent of Fiji and we had a memorable meal there, starting with crisp chapati to dip into liver pate and garlic cream, followed by an extraordinary oyster soup, followed by the chef's compliment, an eggshell filled with chicken and mushroom and topped with a little cap of puff pastry. The main dish was orange and roughy, a local fish, with Chinese cabbage and black bean sauce. We had wine, coffee and chocolates and the whole meal cost just £37. We felt that we would come back to reality in Sydney on the morrow.

After French Polynesia the Islands of Fiji seemed different. The Polynesians are slim, brown people, especially the women, while on

Fiji they are Melanesians of much heavier build, and there seems to be a premium on obesity. Before we left for Australia we took a bus to Suva, which has a pleasant harbour. I bought a souvenir in the form of a carved wooden figure of two lovers, and we had a good lunch in a Chinese restaurant. We just had time to go to the museum, where the most interesting relic was the rudder of the Bounty, recovered from the lagoon off Pitcairn Island, where the mutineers ended their journey and burned the Bounty.

Fiji is so readily accessible for New Zealanders and Australians, prices are so much cheaper than in French Polynesia, and the tourist trade was booming when we were there. It is a group of some three hundred islands lying one thousand one hundred miles south of the Equator; one hundred and five of the islands are inhabited, and it is a very handy stopover for people on round the world flights. There had been big political troubles on Fiji just before we went there, the Fijians objecting to the Indians whose forbears had been exported there at the end of the nineteenth century to do the work, and the number of Indians equalled the number of Fijians in 1990.

We were treated to an exhibition of fire-walking, and Esmé suggested that I ought to have a go because she was sick of having my cold feet on her in bed; and we tried kava drinking, which I would not particularly recommend. As you go across the South Pacific east to west, apart from Easter Island, there is a good deal of similarity between Polynesia, the Cook Islands and Fiji as far as topography and the way of life of the people is concerned. We were going on from Fiji to Australia and then up to Papua New Guinea, which we knew would be very different. Easter Island apart, the abiding memory of all our experiences in the whole of the South Pacific was the singing and dancing on Tahiti, and I remember as we watched the girls dancing our minds became concentrated on the umbilicus, that blind little vestige of our maternal attachment, it became a live thing, a wild thing spinning in front of us like a Catherine wheel; we never saw dancing like it before or after anywhere else in the world.

So often did we stand together on balconies of hotel rooms and watch glorious tropical sunsets of astounding beauty, lay together in the heady scents of the deep mazarine midnight, and wake to the songs of birds as they beseeched us to come and greet the dawn of another wonderful day; now as I lie in my lonely bed thoughts of this fill me only with sorrow, because I have lost for ever my nearness in the night and my touch in the morning.

I had always believed that absence was a negative state offering no positive assertion whatever, but Esmé's absence shouts at me when I enter the house, heckles hectors and harangues me by day, is there when I wake in the night, and mocks my every dreaded dawn; it fills my existence, seeps into every sulcus of my brain, permeates every pore of my skin. No spectre, no wraith, her absence is tangible, I not only touch it, I inhale it and I ingest it, so that it is absorbed into my being like some poisonous mutagen for which there will never be an antidote, until I can escape this life; what daunts me is the sheer dimension of my task, to live without her until the bell tolls for me also and I have to think no more.

Chapter Eleven

Egypt

By the time we fitted Egypt into our scheme of travel most of our friends had already been there before us and none of them spoke about Egypt in other than superlative terms. It was Kipling who said that 'going down the Nile is like running a gauntlet before eternity' and we were absolutely delighted when we knew that our very old friends Willy and Osyth Juckes would join us. Willy and I had pursued parallel medical careers since we first met fifty years before, and Osyth and Esmé had shared a flat in London just after we all got married; Willy and I had had a professional relationship for the past thirty years.

At check-in at Heathrow Esmé and I arrived first and joined a small queue. Willy arrived a little later, thought he recognised Esmé from behind and hugged her, only to realise that he was hugging the wife of a complete stranger; she did not object and said that it was a pleasant surprise.

Esmé realised in the departure lounge that we would be in Egypt during Ramadan, and she said that if I really loved her I would not take her to countries where the pubs were shut, so we boarded the plane pregnant with duty-free, rather more so than usual. We had been airborne no more than half an hour when a woman near the front of the cabin showed signs of distress, and with the Hippocratic Oath ringing in our ears Willy and I were at the ready to assist, but we were beaten to it by an Egyptian doctor, and it appeared that a miscarriage was imminent. She had brought the child who was with her to London for a specialist opinion, abdominal pains had started in the departure lounge and we could not blame her for trying to get back to Cairo. The captain had to land in Rome and an ambulance was waiting, Esmé was very worried about her and wondered what would happen to the child who was with her. Because of this we were delayed two hours, it was dark when we arrived in Cairo and we got to sleep at 2 a.m. in the Mena House Oberoi Hotel. We woke to see the pyramids virtually in the next door garden. We spent the first day exploring Cairo and later in the afternoon we went to the pyramids. First stop was the Egyptian Antiquities Museum, which contains the most important collection of Egyptian antiquities and relics spanning the period from three thousand BC to the sixth century AD. There are statues, paintings, jewels, implements and your mind is a whirl as you walk along the four sides of this rectangular building, which is built on two floors. After taking in as much as we could of the contents of the first floor, we climbed to the second where is the Tutankhamen collection. All the many pieces removed from this tomb were dug out by Howard Carter between 1922 and 1932 and it is the only significant tomb in the Valley of Kings which escaped the robbers. We saw the magnificent pharaoh's throne, made of wood wonderfully carved and coated with gold, and there were inlays of glass, coloured stones and silver; the legs were those of a lion. We saw the famous mask of Tutankhamen which is breathtaking, made of solid gold inlaid with blue glass, and it was placed over the head of the mummy, the richly bejewelled gold dagger which was found lying beside the mummy and an ornate crown are in the same case as the mask; we were very struck by the coloured glass inlays everywhere which were as remarkable as the solid gold itself. The granite sarcophagus of Tutankhamen is preserved in the tomb in the Valley of Kings, but here in the museum we saw his inner, middle and outer coffins, the inner made of solid gold and the middle and outer of wood, fitted one inside the other. There are over three thousand pieces from the tomb and you would have to spend more than a day to take them all in.

The message of all this was that the ancient Egyptians tried still to serve their relatives after death, and they believed that their eternal life depended on the descendants supplying them from earth. Esmé was a humanist who believed that birth and death were simply biological events, you had a beginning and you had an end, in the beginning you were born and in the end you died and that was that. We were both of the opinion that as rules for good human relationships the first five of the Ten Commandments were totally irrelevant, and if only Moses had appreciated this and dropped the stones on which they were written by the wayside he would have had a much easier walk. Robert Ashby, Director of the British Humanist

Society has suggested that if the Society had to have a commandment it would be "think for yourself and act for others" and Esmé would most certainly have agreed with that. All over the world in all the cultures that we saw there was obsession about death and the need for something thereafter, and this was never more apparent than in ancient Egypt.

After a short tour of the rest of Cairo the 'City of a Thousand Years' we went out to Memphis, the City of the Living and Sakkara, the City of the Dead. There is little remaining of Memphis which was for centuries the capital of all Egypt; there is a recumbent figure of Ramses II in alabaster and a sphinx, also in alabaster. Sakkara is one large necropolis and we saw here the Step Pyramid, the oldest of all the pyramids, the forerunner of Giza. Our guide here and for the rest of our tour in Egypt was Dina, the daughter of a high-ranking Civil Servant. She was a history student and very knowledgeable, with a great need to impart her knowledge. She was black-haired, slim, very attractive and a very devout Muslim, so very different from fat happy Italian Dina on Easter Island. She let it be known that she abhorred the decadent habits of the West, she held rigidly to the rules of Ramadan and not a drop of water passed her lips from sunrise until sunset, though she talked all day. I knew about Ramadan, because when I was a medical student at St Bartholomews Hospital I had a cheerful, rotund Egyptian colleague, named Rassim, and he told me that from sunrise to sunset there were no drinks, no food, no smokes and no fuk-fuk. I had ample evidence that he did not observe the first three, and had a pretty good idea that he did not observe the fourth either.

By the time we had seen Memphis and Sakkara and returned to Cairo it was late afternoon, and we went to the pyramids and mounted camels. Esmé was worried that she might slide forwards down the neck and end up in the sand when it got up hind legs first; she managed to hold on and we all rode in dignified procession around the base of the Great Pyramid. Esmé loved the camels because they had such dignity and disdain for the awful human beings all around them. They were led by fellahin and when we dismounted I took a photograph of Willy in deep discussion. He seemed to be telling them that they should not try to make money out of the tourists all the time, and discussing the ethics of the situation, but for all I know he might have bought something and refused to pay the going rate; I would not put it past him. In the evening we had Son et Lumière at the Sphinx with the three great pyramids behind, floodlights played on the Sphinx and the pyramids, while recorded sounds and voices seemed to come from the mouth of the Sphinx. In floodlight the pyramids seemed larger than ever, and we could well believe it when Dina told us that the base of the Great Pyramid could accommodate St Paul's Cathedral, Westminster Abbey, St Peter's and the Cathedrals of Florence and Milan. She also told us that it consisted of two and a half million tons of stone, each stone weighing an average of two and a half tons. In Egypt you have to try to maintain the proportion of things in the timechart of your mind. As we walked back to the hotel, Willy asked Dina if she had a boyfriend and she said that she had, he then asked her if she was engaged to be married and she said that she was; Osyth and I waited in fear and trepidation for what was Willy's normal next question, but he did not ask it and we thought he was rather daunted by perfervid Dina.

The next morning we flew to Luxor and checked in at the Etap Hotel, which was pleasant. It had a large swimming-pool of which we made full use and we looked forward to spending the next day at the temples of Luxor and Karnak. At this point the Nile is widely cultivated on both banks, there is desert in the distance to the east and low hills to the west, beyond which begins the desert of Libya.

Outside these two most important temples in the whole of Egypt there are hundreds of beggars demanding backsheesh, and we simply had to wade through them to get to the temples. The temple of Luxor is very well preserved, having been dug out from under a huge mound of earth, stone and sand which was covered with buildings for many centuries. The temple was built in the reign of Amenophis III, who also built the Colossi of Memnon which we were to see later. Ramses II added on to the temple and built the pylon, and in front of it six statues of himself; apart from being a supreme egotist he was a great builder, and we had evidence of this when we saw Abu Simbel later. He built two obelisks in Luxor, one of which is now in the centre of the Place de la Concorde in Paris. We walked through the temple out of the North Gate and along an avenue of ram-headed sphinxes with many now missing, which brought us to the gates of Karnak. We entered the South Gate of Karnak and this breathtaking temple revealed itself before us. In ancient times ceremonial processions took place in the opposite direction, starting in Karnak and ending in Luxor, and the temple of Karnak was built for the worship of the god Amun Re, the patron of Thebes. It was the hundred or more vast columns which originally supported the roof of the Hypostyle Hall, that stunned us, and this Hall must have been one of the biggest enclosed spaces in ancient times. Outside the Hall there is an obelisk of Queen Hatshepsut, almost one hundred feet tall and hewn from a single piece of pink Aswan granite. In the afternoon sun the colour of all this ancient stone around us was so deep and rich, and standing at Karnak and trying to absorb herself in the feeling of the place, Esmé said that she felt so humble; our senses had lost their moorings and were adrift in a scene without time. That evening we returned to Karnak for Son et Lumière and walked the whole length of the temple complex while our eyes and ears were filled with five thousand years of history.

When we boarded the cruiser Nile Dream the next morning, I suffered an acute attack of fulminating arrival angst which was new for me, for although a martyr during most of our years of travel to departure angst I have never before been attacked on arrival. It made me pour the greater part of the duty-free into the wash basin thinking that it was stale drinking water; I always decanted the duty-free from the glass bottles into plastic bottles to lighten the carrying load. At this point I knew that I was close to divorce, but fortunately I managed to buy some gin from an Indian in a small shop in the Suk, who was unconcerned by the restrictions of Ramadan.

The Nile Dream first took us north down river to Denderah on the west bank which had been a district capital under the Ptolemies, and this was the first of several Ptolemaic cult temples which we were to visit on either side of the Nile. It was the temple of the cow-headed goddess Hathor, goddess of all things good and beautiful, of love, heaven and joy; it took more than one hundred years to build, starting in the first century BC, and it was never finished. There were many well-preserved wall paintings, many depicting Hathor with her cow's head entertaining other gods and goddesses, and these paintings were especially striking in the Hall of Appearances. Dina told us that it was the belief of the ancient Egyptians that Hathor paid annual conjugal visits to the falcon-headed god Horus at Edfu. I asked Esmé, had she been the goddess Hathor, would one dirty weekend a year up river at Horus' place have been enough for her; she said that as I had been married to her for forty years, I should know that that was a stupid question. Austere Dina overheard us and gave us a very severe disapproving glare; she could not have been more cross with us had we farted in the mosque. Before we left Denderah we went up to the roof of the temple and had a marvellous view of the Nile Valley, curling and twisting to the north like a green-coated snake. Back on the boat Willy had by now become the ship's doctor, and so many and varied were the complaints of our fellow passengers that he had to hold a morning surgery by the funnel. Most of the complaints were of colicky pain and diarrhoea, but there were others for the treatment of which we did not have the right pills. I became involved when I was asked to visit a very fat woman in her cabin whose husband was convinced that she was dying from a growth in her abdomen; although it was like looking for a pea in a bolster, I palpated her and reassured her husband that I could feel nothing wrong; my main concern was to retrieve my right hand. Willy was very good in the way that he tried to help these people, dispensing not only his own pills but mine as well, and he was rather upset when one of the men complained to him that the pills that he had given to his wife could have been out of date because she was no better. Esmé said that a couple of beers would have been more in order than complaint, because after all we were not employees of the boat company, and were on holiday like the rest of them. Because we all of us at one time or another suffered from Tutankhamen's Revenge, I took the matter up with hotel managers who all told me that stringent precautions were taken among the staff, and suggested that the paper money which we all handled could be the source of infection. I brought a banknote home, took it to a bacteriologist colleague and suggested that he should take cultures from it, but he was rather disinterested and asked me to what use I had put the note, which was the end of that scientific experiment.

We left Denderah and cruised south to the Valley of the Kings on the west bank. After the boat was moored we first went on a detour to see the Colossi of Memnon, two enormous seated figures, twin statues representing the Pharaoh Amenhotep III, over sixty feet in height and sitting in splendid isolation. They probably guarded the entrance to a large temple which has long since completely disappeared; badly damaged by Greek and Roman soldiers, in ancient times the statues were said to emit sounds of song at the dawn, which ceased when a crack was discovered in the statue on the right and repaired in one hundred and ninety-nine AD. At the Valley of the

Kings, Osyth unfortunately was stricken with the dreaded 'gippy tummy' and could not come with us to the tombs. Dysentery and cholera were amongst us: when we got to the entrance to the tomb of Tutankhamen Willy had to set up an emergency first-aid post, and at one point he had to carry one of the women some distance back to the bus. It was very hot hereabouts and we were quite glad to spend time in the cool of these wonderful burial places which have yielded such a plethora of treasures, many of which we had seen in the museum in Cairo. In this Valley of the Kings and Queens there are over sixty pharaohs' tombs, but only a few are open to the public, and the important ones are Seti's where the decorations cover the whole of the inside of the tomb, marvellously preserved, and the equally impressive tomb of Ramses VI. Before we left the Valley of the Kings and Queens we visited the mortuary temple of Queen Hatshepsut, a large colonnaded building with wide terraces leading to it. It is built at the foot of cliffs which tower hundreds and hundreds of feet above it but still do not seem to dwarf it. After the fierce unrelenting sun of this day, during which we had seen so much, it was pleasant to be back on the cruiser in the cool of the evening, sitting at the stern in wicker chairs with our friends and enjoying pre-dinner drinks. As the boat moved slowly upstream we got the impression somehow that it was not really the boat that was moving but the banks on either side that passed before our eyes, presenting us with such a delectable diorama of the life and the events of this river unique in the world. At one point as we cruised towards Esna, Willy decided that he would go to the bridge and see how the captain was coping. He came back rather quickly and said that when he went onto the bridge he could not see the captain, but eventually found him lying on the floor and praying to Allah, and that as far as navigation was concerned we were now in the hands of Allah.

Esna was a relatively small site, but was unusual in that the temple of Khnum was in a pit in the centre of the town with a market just beside it. In ancient times this was a stopping place for caravans wending their way across the desert and attention was drawn to it in the last century by Flaubert, the French writer, who also appeared to have plenty of time to sample the brothels, and this upset his mistress in France when she learned of it. The temple, which is all of ten metres below ground, was built by the Roman Emperor Claudius in the first century AD and is relatively unremarkable.

120

Edfu was forty miles further up-river, and when we moored we were taken to the temple of Horus in black horse-drawn carriages. Esmé enjoyed this, but she said that if I really loved her I would have chosen a less flatulent horse. The temple is almost complete and is probably the largest in the whole of Egypt after Karnak; building was started in two hundred AD in the reign of Ptolemy III and was never completed. The god Horus appears everywhere in paintings and carvings with the head of hawk or a falcon, and the wall paintings illustrate his dirty weekends with the goddess Hathor, and also his regular bouts of fisticuffs with the god Seth, which he usually won. Looking at these wall paintings, Esmé said that had she been the goddess Hathor she could never have had the hots for Horus, but she was careful to say it out of earshot of devout Dina.

When we reached Kom Ombo we had covered over one hundred miles from Luxor, and we were within thirty miles of Aswan, and approaching Kom Ombo we saw the green and the cultivation on the east bank merging into the Arabian desert, arid, rocky and forbidding. The river was narrow and we saw the temple standing at the riverside with its feet in the water, consisting of two parts, originally identical and separated by sanctuaries. In the chapel of Hathor we peered through iron gratings at piles of crocodile mummies thrown there by workmen through the ages; a few columns remain and, unlike anywhere else along the Nile, they had ornate floral capitals, Corinthian in style. Before we left Kom Ombo we looked down into two very large Roman wells, so deep that we could not see the bottom, where sacred crocodiles were kept in ancient times. We eventually reached Aswan which is five hundred miles south of Cairo and was an important gateway on the southern trade route to the centre of Africa; as a result there is much about it that is Oriental and African. It was the furthest point south reached by the Romans, and it is where Egypt ends and the Sudan and Nubia begin; the people are different, darker of skin, taller and supple of body and they exude a tranquillity in keeping with the remoteness of this place, surrounded on all sides by endless desert with the fierce fire of the sun by day and the cooling breeze of the river in the deepening blue-violet as the night falls. Aswan is very much larger since they built the new dam and it had grown to a population of half a million by the time we were there.

After disembarking and checking in at the Aswan Oberoi Hotel on Elephantine Island, so named because of its importance in the ivory trade from the south in olden days, Esmé and I spent the afternoon and early evening sailing in a felucca around the islands, one of which was called Kitchener's because it had been given to Lord Kitchen when he was Consul General, and there were lovely botanical gardens through which we walked. We saw the Age Khan's mausoleum and felt that he had chosen a perfect place in which to spend eternity. The sunscorch of the day was relenting, there was just enough river zephyr to keep us moving very slowly, and in the distance there were many other feluccas, their little white sails looking like moths on the surface of a pond in summer. Esmé relaxed in the total peace of this living moment, her happiness seemed as always to flow into me, to invade and possess my senses, so that no other feeling, no other mood or emotion than our pure shared contentment was imaginable. That afternoon burns bright in my memory now, and since I lost her I feel that every pleasurable afferent impulse that ever targeted my brain originated with her, with our life together and the children we created and loved from the day they were born.

In 1964 the course of the Nile was changed; although the building of the High Dam has produced more power and more agricultural land it has created problems such as the erosion of the banks, the undermining of the buildings and a reduction in silt deposition. It is a very impressive structure, an immense engineering feat, and as we stood on the top of it we had the enormous newly created Lake Nasser to the south of us which seemed to stretch to the horizon, while immediately below our feet there were huge jets of water of immense power and velocity. The dam was nearly two miles across, and by building it the Egyptians have tamed the river and made it predictable. Between the old and the new dams there is a lake of water four miles long, and in the middle of it we went to an island whereon was the Temple of Philae. Before the building of the new dam Philae was almost entirely under water during the flood months when the old dam was open. When they built the new dam they moved this temple piecemeal in crates to another island, re-erected it so that it was permanently above water, and the whole operation took three years.

Esmé and I felt that we could not go home without flying to Abu Simbel, there had been much in the national press about Abu Simbel for years when discussions were taking place about the building of the new dam, and with world-wide support the Egyptians moved not only this colossal Temple of Ramses II but also the cliff which was behind it to a point beyond the danger of flooding. It was a blisteringly hot day when we went to Abu Simbel, and we stood in awe in front of the four colossal statues at the entrance to the temple. They are of Ramses and his wives with his favourite Nefertiti on his right hand, seventy feet high; and as we stood in front of them, in sunshine of unbelievable brilliance which lit up the sandstone so that it seemed incandescent, Esmé said that they made her feel so insignificant, so unimportant and petty in her transitory life. There was a Hypostyle Hall inside the temple behind the statues which contained more figures of Ramses and Nefertiti, and also many wall paintings. We tried to take in the magnitude of this whole edifice of stone and realise that it had been completely re-sited, and we had to accept that the Egyptians were probably right when they said that with all the help that they had they had achieved one of the greatest engineering feats ever. Future generations must thank not only Egypt, but more than forty other nations for this heritage.

Before we left Aswan and on the last night on the boat, there was a traditional fancy dress party. We wore djellabas and Esmé and Osyth had head-dresses and we all felt absolute fools. After dinner there was a dumb crambo game, and for me the star of the party was a rather droll Englishman, who refused to dress up at all and merely put a handkerchief over his head, knotted at four corners, and said that he was a 'typical English tourist'.

On the runway at the airport at Aswan as we sat awaiting take off, a member of the cabin staff turned a handle on one of the doors, and the escape chute shot out and down onto the tarmac. There followed much discussion among the staff about this, and eventually they simply cut it off from the plane and we flew back to Cairo without means of escape. Back at the Mena House Oberoi we relaxed by the pool and then went again to the pyramids. Esmé and I entered the Great Pyramid through a hole at the base like a couple of rabbits, and we walked, stooped, clambered and crawled our way up into the centre of it for what seemed an eternity until we reached our goal which was the funeral chamber of Cheops, a surprisingly simple, plain, half dark and empty room except for an elongated stone box along one side, which was the sarcophagus of Cheops. We felt that we had seen more interesting rackets courts. After the pyramids, Willy Osyth and Esmé went to see Cheops' boat in a museum next to the pyramids, which was discovered with another boat in 1954, a finding that much interested archaeologists world-wide. The boat was thought to have carried Cheops' body from Memphis to Giza after his death. I was unable to accompany them because I had finally succumbed to what had afflicted everybody else in the group, and retired to bed with diarrhoea of such severity that I was quite sure I would return to England without any gut at all. We brought back with us from Egypt a small head of Queen Nefertiti in black stone and a gold cartouche for Esmé with her name engraved in Egyptian letters, which she loved and wore often, and when I open her jewel box now and see it, my heart breaks.

My abiding memory of Egypt is not of the temples and tombs but of that afternoon on the felucca at Aswan, when the soft warm wind caressed our faces, and time paused like a patient lover while we pleasured to fulfilment in the tranquillity of that most serene episode in our lives. We might have second thoughts now about touring Egypt, but they would only be about postponement in view of the political troubles and the current danger to tourists. Anyone with the slightest interest in ancient history surely should not die without making the ultimate journey in time along this green river valley, with cliff-high sand-dunes poised over it like tidal waves about to break, and bury and obliterate again those wondrous relics, so lovingly and painstakingly excavated for the benefit of all mankind.

Chapter Twelve

South America

Having corrected our earlier omission and seen ancient Egypt in the spring of 1988 and having heard that an extended tour of South America was hard work, we felt that we ought to do this before we were any older. Esmé was ever ready to tap the rich veins of experience of others, but although some of our friends had been to Rio, none of them had attempted what we were proposing to do. I had read *Conquest of Peru* many long years ago but we were going to have to rely on guidebooks. Our journey was to cover a large swathe of the continent, starting above the equator in Colombia at Bogota, going down to Lima and Cuzco, a double back on our tracks to Iquitos for a trip down the Amazon, along the top of the Andes across the Bolivian altiplano to La Paz; then to São Paulo to see the Iguaçu Falls, up to Brasilia, and finally finishing in Rio de Janeiro, it would take just over three weeks.

Esmé became very excited at the prospect of seeing all this, and a little earlier than usual I had the onset of my departure angst. It seemed that if anything would go wrong, it would do so on an ambitious journey like this; we also knew that crime and violence abounded in the countries through which we were to pass, and that the law was applied with malleability and venality. We would not see beauty such as had kissed our eyes in the tropical islands of the Indian and Pacific Oceans, but that enchantment and mystery awaited us we were assured.

For South America Esmé decided to return to L'Air du Temps. She had worn this perfume years before and asked me did I not remember how it made me want to jump on her; I pointed out that I was always ready to do that, never mind the perfume. She felt that L'Air du Temps would suit the mountain scene and make the best of her. She often said that she liked to change fragrances from time to time, so that I could imagine that I was taking a new mistress on holiday. I remember thinking that with a new mistress I would not only get a new fragrance but also a new woman underneath, but I banished those thoughts instantly from my mind, because in a love like ours there was no place for such treachery.

In the middle of October 1988 we joined a group in Terminal 4 at Heathrow. We found ourselves sitting in the bar next to an elderly Welsh couple who had travelled the world, and were also on their way to South America with a different tour company. Esmé told them that they were very courageous to do all this travelling, and especially to brave South America at all at their time of life, before she discovered that they were the same age as herself!

We landed in Bogota and were allotted a room on the thirty-first floor of the Bogota Hilton Hotel. We got to bed at 5 a.m. and at 7.30 we experienced our first earthquake, low on the Richter Scale, but enough to wake us up and rattle the windows and the bottles on the dressing-table. Our Colombian guide warned us of the street crime and to keep any valuables firmly protected; I wore a bodybelt for the money, but as the tour progressed Esmé stuffed more and more into it, so that by the time we got to Peru I looked and felt like a gravid woman. Bags disappeared from shoulders throughout South America within minutes, and several of our party had things stolen before the tour ended in Rio.

Bogota is at an altitude of nearly nine thousand feet, and we noticed immediately that even slight exertion caused breathlessness and were warned that this would increase when we reached Bolivia. Colombia is the only South American country which has a Pacific and a Caribbean coastline, but we saw little of the country, and were limited to sight-seeing in and around Bogota.

On the first day we got to know Terry Jones, our Kuoni tour manager. He had run a tourist agency in Tokyo for several years before joining Kuoni, had been all over the world many times and was to take a tour to China as soon as we had finished this one; he was a very kind and helpful man, never less than interesting, and he had a knowledge of the world which we envied. Dinner on the first night was at a restaurant in the centre of Bogota and we discovered that there were fourteen of us in the group and they seemed pleasant people; after our unfortunate experience in South India one year before, we had become nervous of groups: it is a matter of chance.

At this first dinner Esmé noted that we had a Professor of Mathematics from Edinburgh and she was pleased to see that he had some trouble with converting sterling into local currency, which had been no problem for her.

Fiercely Spanish, there are nearly thirty million Colombians and there is a powerful Indian mestizo streak; the people seemed dark and serious looking.

We started our tour in Simon Bolivar Square in pouring rain and went to a Gold Museum which houses exquisite authentic work of the original Indians, dating back to the time of Christ, and also visited an emerald factory; Esmé fancied a pair of emerald earrings which were priced in English money at around one thousand pounds. She said that they would make a nice change from her jade earrings at home, but after a brief discussion she agreed that perhaps they were rather too expensive, and I got her out of that place as quickly as I could. The house of Simon Bolivar was attractive in the colonial style and as a revolutionary he seemed to have done pretty well for himself; having liberated Colombia, Venezuela, Peru, Ecuador and Bolivia, he apparently fell into disfavour and had to do a runner. Esmé noted that his bed was very small and concluded that he must have been a very short man; she wondered how he made the most of his many mistresses in a bed like that, even one at a time. We visited a disused salt mine a little way out of the city which had been turned into a cathedral, an original concept; it was dark, cold and forbidding.

Colombia has been called the "Emerald of the Spanish Main", but limited to Bogota as we were, we did not see enough of the country to subscribe to that.

We flew Aero Peru to Lima, a crowded and uncomfortable flight and on the plane Esmé noted that the Professor of Mathematics was having more trouble with local currency, this time converting the erstwhile sol into the inti, which was apparently in free fall against the dollar, and inflation had soared to two hundred per cent in the previous few weeks. Terry Jones told us firmly that if we went outside the hotel in Lima we should turn left at all costs, if we turned right by mistake we might never been seen again. He repeatedly warned us about pickpockets, and the women were advised strongly not to wear any jewellery at all.

We walked out of the hotel and came to a plaza after twenty minutes, where there were stalls, one of which was occupied by a local doctor who was selling vaccination for children, and he had a long queue. We went into the cathedral to see Pizzarro's remains, but they had been removed and he is now devalued, which is just as well, because what he did to the Incas is almost beyond belief. The Museum of Archaeology and Anthropology was fascinating; there was a huge chart showing the epochs of the various world civilisations and much unbroken Inca pottery, which is still being excavated from tombs; as in Egypt the worldly effects were buried with the dead.

We had by now become friendly with another couple in the group, Leo and Marian, who owned a vineyard in Kent. One evening we had a drink with them in a rooftop bar, and they told us that an Australian friend, a catholic priest, had taken them on an instructive tour of a shanty township that afternoon, and the abject poverty was very reminiscent of Soweto in South Africa; the townships spring up almost overnight and have little in the way of running water or sewers. As we were talking that evening I remember looking out over the Pacific at the sunset; Esmé remarked that it seemed to have an unusual pink-peach colour, which was reflected on a monastery across the square from us, a pleasant and peaceful scene from our high vantage point up and away from the crowds and the crime in the city streets below. Lima is a drab city and not helped by the fact that it is so often enshrouded in fog.

We first heard Andean pipe music in Lima in the hotel restaurant. The pipes are small instruments made by sticking different lengths of bamboo together, and the music they make, combined with guitars, is wistful, melancholic and moving, and we heard much more of it as we went south along the Andes. We made a short flight from Lima to Iquitos, where we boarded a long narrow boat which took us down the Amazon for two and a half hours and brought us to Explorama Lodge, a group of thatched wooden buildings, high on stilts and connected by long walkways. It was primitive, providing only the basic comforts of life, with mosquito nets over the beds and thunderbox loos. We were just below the equator, it was hot and very humid and I said to Esmé that sitting beside this great inland waterway I felt I was Sanders of the River. In spite of its rather crude appearance the lodge had a bar with plenty of cold beer and pisco sour on tap, the windows of the bar and restaurant fenced in by thick wire mesh to keep out the mosquitoes and their allies. Esmé suffered a mosquito attack when she went to relieve herself in the night, which involved walking some distance because there were no loos in the rooms; when she came back she told me that she had been bitten, and when I asked her where, she said it was in a very personal place and she hoped the same thing would happen to me; she seemed quite disappointed when it did not.

We had several jungle walks. The river folk live in thatched dwellings on stilts and they grow sugar cane and bananas. We met the Yagua Indians who are supposedly the earliest settlers here, they wore grass skirts, and some trading was done in goods, because they are not to be corrupted by money. They are dwindling in number because the young leave the jungle to go to Iquitos in search of a better life; they gave us a blowpipe demonstration and we were amazed at the length of the pipes and their accuracy with the darts.

By the time we got into the boat to return to Iquitos we were indescribably dirty shoes, socks and trousers covered with mud, shirts soaked in sweat, and Esmé could not wait to get under a hot shower; the boat took much longer to get back to Iquitos because we were struggling against a strong current. When we got back to Lima we cleaned up, and over a beer and a pisco soup, we relived our Amazon experience. We were glad that we took the chance to do it; apart from the river and the jungle, we enjoyed meeting some American biologists who showed us many animals and plants including a viper, a stick insect and a praying mantis on shrubs close to the Lodge, and also a tapir the size of a fully-grown badger, and known locally as a 'rodent'.

Next day we had a dawn start and the sky over Lima was cold and grey, so very different from the heat and humidity of the Amazon jungle. Esmé found Lima a very depressing city with its rapid, haphazard growth, dreadful slums and unattractive climate. Most people use Lima as a take-off point, a doorway to the Andes, Macchu Picchu, Lake Titicaca and the onward road over the Bolivian altiplano, before the eastward turn to Brazil. Our preferred memory of Lima was of the pink Pacific sunset, and the plaintive music of the Andean pipes.

Before we left by air for Cuzco we had got to know most of the group; I found that one of the men came from my home town of Cambridge. We had played for the same cricket club, Camden, and also for Cambridgeshire, and sitting at supper the first night in Cuzco we talked of people whom we both knew.

As you approach Cuzco it looks as if it has been casually thrown onto the top of the mountain. We were met by our guide who warned us not to let unofficial porters handle any of the baggage, because we would be unlikely to see it again; there were all sorts of men milling around us and it was a situation very like that at Manila airport. The guide was a small woman, attractive and, as Esmé noted, her gorgeous legs were emphasised by her well developed superstructure. She invaded the would-be muggers and pick-pockets who appeared to be frightened of her, and she got us to the coach with all the bags intact in no time at all. Cuzco is at an altitude of eleven thousand feet; I felt quite breathless, but the main problem when you arrive is crushing fatigue.

The foyer of the Libertador Hotel was full of Americans, almost all of whom were panting under oxygen masks, and the whole place was littered with empty oxygen cylinders. The hotel is extremely attractive, an old monastery which has now been added to; apart from the effects of the rarefied atmosphere several of the group had by now developed other problems, and I had to take a physicianly step forward and declare myself. One middle-aged woman had a very painful left elbow, very swollen and red and she could not move the arm at all; she had a septic arthritis and needed antibiotics urgently. Terry Jones the tour manager and I went out into the Sunday night to see if we could find a pharmacy; we must have walked around for forty-five minutes, and I was scared; every doorway seemed to be filled by shady silent men with glowing cigarettes. Eventually we found a pharmacy which was open, and they had some Tetracycline, which was not what I wanted but it had to do; when I got back to the hotel I found that it was over a year out of date. The elbow improved and its owner was soon able to take part in the tour again. As I write this I call still see those sinister, silent men in the dark doorways, and the red points of their cigarettes.

We went by coach around Cuzco and up to Sacsayhuaman, an impressive fortress built from huge boulders, most marvellously fitted together. Further up the hill there were Quechuan Indians who live in adobe huts and breed llamas and alpacas, from which they take the wool and spin it; here was the true life of the Andes. A woman posed holding a llama around the neck and we took photographs for fifty intis a time, and for the same amount they offered to show us their babies; every woman we saw seemed to have a baby on her back. We

understood from Terry that birth control schemes were developing in
Peru but, as Esmé said, this would all come to an end as soon as the
Pope returned to South America. He had visited Peru the year before
but had been laid low by a nasty attack of La Seroche, the disease of
the high altitudes which was obviously no respecter of person; in
Cuzco it even prevented the papal celebration of mass.

We lunched this day at a restaurant overlooking the Plaza das
Armas, and during it there was a brass band marching round and
round, colourful but totally tuneless; I had not heard anything quite
like it since I last heard the Salvation Army band in my home village
in the fen country. Cuzco is a lovely city and well worth a visit in its
own right, without being used as a springboard for Macchu Picchu.
We strolled round the city, the sun was high, the air clean and warm,
and we bought Peruvian turquoise and silver.

In the evening we quaffed pisco sours with the youngest members
of our group, Kate and Kelvin. Kate launched into an horrendous tale
about her childhood in care, even though her father was a Lloyd's
underwriter, and this was right up Esmé's social worker street. In
1970, at the age of fifty, after twenty five-years of supporting me in
my climb up the medical ladder and then establishing myself as a
physician, and bringing up our children until they could fly the nest
and be free of us, Esmé obtained the External Diploma in Social
Studies of London University, working at home on a correspondence
course with the minimum of personal tuition.

As a born student of human nature she found her *métier* in the
Social Services Department in Cheltenham, and for fifteen years she
worked whole time and loved it, specialising much of the time in
helping her "wayward and naughty girls", as she called them. It
enabled her to be her own woman, to gain full recognition and
appreciation quite outside the family, and to be professional and
responsible in her own right at what she did best.

She found that for those in darkness and despair she could light a
flare path to hope. She found that she could shepherd the depressed,
the inadequate, the unfortunate and those who feared their future,
toward summer meadows of self-belief, and persuade them that the
stars in the sky twinkled for them as well as for others.

When she retired from social work she learned sufficient of
Physiological Measurement Technology to be employed by Cotswold
Nuffield Hospital to carry out electrocardiography, lung function

assessments and audiometry in the Health Check Scheme run by the hospital, and to assist me in my practice until I myself retired.

To get to Macchu Picchu, one of the most amazing miracles of human achievement in the world that we saw, a coach took us half way and we then boarded the famous El Treno. At the station the local peasants had all their wares laid out on the tracks; one girl said to Esmé that she was fifteen years old and that her baby was two, and the baby's face was covered with impetigo. At the foot of the mountain below Macchu Picchu little coaches depart every five minutes and the drive up the mountain involves dozens of hairpin bends, not a journey for the nervous. Macchu Picchu is in a basin surrounded by serried ranks of mountains, each higher than the one in front of it, and on arrival as you looked down to the Urubamba River so far below, you felt half way to heaven; the trains at the bottom looked like the Hornby trains of my childhood.

We put up at the Lodge and early the first morning we climbed to the top of the eastern mountain to a point called Inti Punea, where the view was beyond description: below was the lost city of the Incas with its curiously small half-finished buildings, and opposite Huayna Picchu, a towering free standing Sugarloaf peak. The background to all this was formed by high snow-capped mountains, and the early morning sun shone down like a light on a stage. I said to Esmé that it would be worth coming up here just to see the mountains, and never mind the lost city, and she reminded me that at the very time that the Incas were labouring to build these simple houses of stone in this secret mountain hideaway, which they never completed, Hampton Court Palace was already up and occupied; she always liked to maintain historical perspective.

We returned to Cuzco and the next day, Sunday, we went along the Urubamba River to Pizac to see the market; the people are Indian Mestizo and wear the costumes you see in pictures, layers of skirts, shawls on the back carrying everything from babies to sacks of corn and cement, with hats of different shape and colour according to their tribe. The Indian women were small and purposeful, and you were unceremoniously barged out of the way if you were between them and what they wanted.

We visited Ollantaytambo, an Inca settlement with a fortress from which they threw criminals to their death. The Incas managed to support a very top-heavy social structure: the nobles lived up on the mountain while the peasants tolled below and served them, there was a medieval tithe system and they were good at organisation and delegation. They used terracing in their building on every mountain slope available, and built the terraces from the top downwards.

The day-long train journey to Juliaca next day, eleven hours, took us along the spine of the magnificent Andes; single track, thirteen coaches with people hanging on to the outside like leeches for hours as they do in India. We were in the so-called first class section and the doors of the coaches were locked after each stop, if you needed the loo you had to get a key from a steward, if you could find one. The highest point was fifteen thousand feet above sea level, reached with only one engine, where we stopped and got out at the local station; as at each station along the way, it was a passing place and everywhere we were jostled by crowds; several people had their pockets picked. We reached Juliaca in darkness and Terry warned us to stay bunched together going through the barrier for mutual protection, because many tourists had been attacked on this station. We formed a phalanx of which the Romans would have been proud, women in the centre and men on the outside and pushed our way through to the coach, waiting to take us to Puno on the side of Lake Titicaca. I do not know what it is like now when you arrive at Juliaca, but in 1988 it was very intimidating.

From Juliaca to Puno on the lakeside was an hour's coach ride. When we got to the hotel we looked out of the window upon what appeared to be a limitless sea. Titicaca is the highest lake in the world upon which boats can navigate, twelve thousand five hundred feet above sea level, the sky above it and the water are ice blue, and there is a cold remote, almost cruel beauty about this part of the world. There was a full moon and Esmé felt that the view from this window of the altiplano in full moonlight, and the cold white light reflecting on this huge lake was quite unforgettable. Her appreciation and sheer enjoyment of experiences such as this, and her gratitude for the opportunity to witness such natural beauty, so enhanced my own pleasure at seeing these things. I often felt that if I was seeing them without her my own enjoyment would be that much the less; with her small pleasures became joys shared, and thereby she enriched my life.

The next day we took a two-hour boat ride to see the floating islands. These are the homes of Uros-Indians; they are made of totora reeds, and as the reeds beneath rot in the water they lay more on the top and each island is up to eight metres in depth. We visited two of these islands, Tequile and Amantani, where we were shown basket-weaving and embroidery, which are the two industries from which they make their living. Along the whole length of the Andes the bright colours of the clothes of these people and of their embroidery seemed in such contrast to the bleakness of the steppes and the mountains that are all about them. There are some sixty of these reed islands in all, and they have their own small narrow boats, also made of the reeds, which they use for plying between the islands. We felt that there must be incestuous breeding, because several of the children had obvious congenital abnormalities.

The boat took us to a large island called Copacabana for lunch, and we then went on by hydrofoil to the Bolivian side of the lake for the coach to La Paz.

The Bolivian side of the altiplano seemed more prosperous than the Peruvian, and on the way we saw an awe-inspiring storm in the gathering darkness; the effect of the brilliant lightning on the mountain peaks filled us both with reverential wonder, and made us feel so infinitesimal in the whole vast scheme of creation. The guide on this bus was named Jesus, which seemed at this moment very apt, and just before we reached La Paz he asked us to close our eyes and count slowly to ten; as we did this the bus came to a stop, and when we opened our eyes and looked to the right we were on the lip of an enormous bowl, and there below us was the pinpoint light cluster of La Paz at night, the highest capital city in the world but still thousands of feet beneath us. I asked Esmé would we ever become satiated with sights such as this, and I knew what would be her reply.

We had a room in a hotel in the centre of La Paz with an enormous picture window and two double beds; Esmé suggested that we should have one each, but that if I felt friendly in the night she might allow me to pay her a short visit. I said that we had been married for forty years, and I had no intention of returning to the time when I had to get out of her bed to catch the last trolleybus home. After going to bed that first night I experienced a sudden and violent pain in my nasal sinuses, which felt as if they were about to implode. I kissed Esmé gently to wake her up, because I wanted to warn her that I was about to die, I was sinking fast, almost certainly would not make the morning, and she would have to continue the tour alone; she refused to wake up, so I kissed her harder and gave her a prod. She said that in a couple of days we would be descending from La Paz which would cure me, and promptly went back to sleep. In the fastness of that foreign night, under the ceiling of the world, I lay wondering at the scant effect my impending dissolution had upon my ever loving wife, bless her darling little heart. She was, of course quite right, after twenty-four hours you get more used to the altitude. Resurrection was followed by cure, and rehabilitation was well taken care of by those two well tried treatments, cold lager and pisco sour in high regular dosage.

We had a long and interesting conversation in a bar in the centre of the city with Jesus, who was a left-wing lawyer; he was a little nervous to start with because he did not want to be overheard, but he told us about the politics of Bolivia, and although he was against the current Government, he admitted that the peso was now stable, and there was an end to inflation. Because Bolivia is totally landlocked and has no access to the sea, there have been wars from time immemorial with both Peru and Chile. Esmé could not quite make up her mind whether Jesus was an upper-class revolutionary, or just pretending to be one. He told us that Bolivia was about to re-open talks with Chile about creating a corridor to the Pacific, and was hopeful that this might come about when President Pinochet finally departed.

We had only one day for sightseeing in La Paz and we went to the market, where there were many people, the women wearing black bowlers, and we encountered a witch doctor who claimed that he had much to offer ill-humours of the bowels, liver and kidneys, and he told me that he was frequently consulted by the doctors in the hospitals when they did not know what to do. Esmé wanted me to ask him about aphrodisiacs, and I hoped that this was a general question with no personal implications. He showed us some dried llama foetuses, which he said were very efficacious and they smelt awful. We sampled saltenas which are hot, juicy and delicious Brazilian pastries and best swilled down with a can of beer. Jesus was particularly anxious for us to see Moon Valley, so called because it is very like a moonscape, a strange hill of jagged pinnacles of salt and rock the like of which we had never seen before.

We flew from the highest airport in the world, everything in La Paz is the highest in the world, to São Paulo, where we discovered that the currency was in chaos and inflation at one point had risen to fifteen hundred per cent. There are one million Japanese in São

Paulo, fourth generation, who came there originally as landscape and market gardeners, and Brazil is possibly the most multi-racial country in the world, due to immigration from Europe and elsewhere in the early part of the century. During our tour of the city we visited the inevitable market and ended up in a very expensive jeweller's shop; Esmé's eyes glazed over with anticipation, because I had promised that if I came back from the dead in La Paz we would buy some earrings in celebration. She chose some pretty tourmaline drop earrings, a very Brazilian stone resembling emerald though paler, and a silver necklet with a large piece of tourmaline for a pendant. When we came to pay we were told that the best method was to bypass the local currency and use Visa, which would be honoured against the Deutschmark. In this way we would get thirty per cent discount, but we could not quite understand how this arrangement worked.

Esmé and I played truant from the group in the evening and went to the tallest building in São Paulo, at the top of which there was a revolving roof restaurant, and although the night skyline of São Paulo cannot compare with Hong Kong, the view was rewarding and we had a happy meal there together. She wore a multi-coloured blouse with red, green, blue and yellow spots, a white skirt, and, of course the tourmaline earrings and pendant. I cannot remember what we talked about that night, it would have been sufficient for me just to sit and look across the table at that attractive, elegant woman, and marvel that she had loved and wanted me enough to spend her life with me. Esmé and I needed no catalyst for the chemistry of our love, no prop for the perpetuation of it, that lucky were we. Perhaps it was because we never asked too much of each other, there should be no place for 'demand' or 'insist' in love. Throughout our marriage whenever we made love I do not remember the earth actually moving, no rifts or clefts appeared in the garden, cascades and kaleidoscopes of coloured lights of impossible brilliance and mind-blowing music perhaps, but the house still stood and the roof stayed on; Esmé said that she always felt deliciously excited, warm and wanted, and nothing was missing at the end of it, nothing that did not make her want to do it again and the sooner the better.

We flew to the Iguaçu Falls and checked in at the Hotel das Cataratas, a tasteful modern sprawling building. We were given room 3121 and Esmé was convinced that we were in the servants' quarters; we walked endlessly along corridors to find this room, and as we went further and further away from the main concourse, I felt that we should make notches on the wall so that we could find our way back to civilisation. The weather was now really hot and out came a Tahitian shirt for dinner by the pool, the pink one with large blue-green painted flowers, with a pair of pink cotton trousers with thin white stripes and again white sandals; she looked lovely and we felt tropical again.

We were next day to see the Falls from the Argentinean side, which meant crossing the frontier between Brazil and Argentina. Before we did this we were taken to see the Itaipu Dam which was started in 1975 and was to be finished in 1990 and was the largest hydroelectric dam in the world. Standing atop this huge concrete structure, we felt just below our feet the most powerful jets of water that we had ever seen, and the ground rumbled and shook with the sheer force of them; Esmé asked me if I was jealous, and knew that I was.

We crossed the border into Argentina where notices proclaimed that the Falkland Islands still belonged to Argentina. We went to a point above the Piranha River where it was joined by a major tributary, and in the fork thus formed we could see three countries. We were standing in Argentina, to the left was Paraguay and to the right was Brazil. We approached the Falls by walking across the Piranha River on a long, long, rickety walkway. The river seemed so quiet, there was hardly a ripple and we were quite unprepared for the turmoil of water we were about to see, although we could hear the roar. As you get to the Falls you walk down some steps from the walkway and onto a wooden platform, and there, seemingly only feet away, is an abounding wall of angry, brown water cascading down into white clouds below. You cannot hear yourself speak, it is difficult to think and as you stand there you are aghast at this unbridled terrifying force of nature a few feet away from you. There were myriads of the most beautiful butterflies at the top of the Falls, and later we walked down to near the foot of them and viewed this overwhelming cataract from below.

We went to see Brasilia and spent only a morning there; although the guide thought that it was the finest city in the world, it was totally unattractive. It was built in barren desert and every bag of cement and sand was brought by air, as there were no roads and no railways to the site when Brasilia was built. Esmé and I tried to contemplate the unnecessary cost of all this and she said that since they built this ultramodern city there did not seem to have been the necessary influx of foreigners with fresh ideas, and it was a place without warmth, character or heart.

In Rio we were in the Sheraton Hotel for three nights and it rained most of time. Having heard so much about Copacabana and Ipanema beaches, and remembering the music that we used to play endlessly in the sixties, we were disappointed. There were no bossanovas on the beach, Astrud Gilberto not in sight, nor for that matter Ronny Biggs.

There was a strike of cable car staff and we were unable to go up to Christ the Redeemer on the top of Corcovado Mountain, but we did go up Sugar Loaf Mountain, from which there is a marvellous view back towards these huge beaches.

Esmé was delighted when we got to Rio, and she opened the plastic bags with her rolled up clothes in them, and found that they shook out with virtually no creases though we had been on the road for three weeks. She had a marvellous method of packing in this way, and we used it all over the world. They were most anxious to show us the Maracaña football stadium, which was built for the World Cup in 1950 and seated 80,000 people, bigger than modern Twickenham. We had a barbecue, where they came round with two-foot skewers spearing steak inches thick, and we had a floor show with the sort of costumes they use in the Carnival, very colourful, but the music was so loud that we had to make earplugs for ourselves out of paper tissues. The lasting impression was that the magic that we had expected in Rio was not there; the abject poverty in the shanty towns which were without the basic necessities of life, and which clung to the sides of the mountains above Rio like filthy excrescences on vast walls, appalled us. The thousands of homeless children roaming the streets, stealing, begging and the general air of violence, detracted so much from the glamour of Rio. We left thinking that this large country with every conceivable natural resource might be running out of time. All the money from exports and tourism was being channelled into less than twenty per cent of the population, due to graft in high places and human frailty in government. We had seen such wonderful things and had completed our intended journey, but I doubt very much if we would wish to undertake it today. In the past eight years crime and lawlessness has increased to such an extent that we would not care to take the risk; the drug scene in Colombia is out of control, and now in Rio the police are openly shooting the street children on sight.

As a reminder of our journey to South America we brought back from Peru a foot-high statue in basalt; a god standing on the head of a puma with a condor perched on his head, and this was a very important item in our collection on the dining-room window-sill.

Chapter Thirteen
Australia

Largely because of the four-yearly cricket test match series between England and Australia down under, I had always very much wanted to go there, but it was the end of the world and I never thought I would. As a boy I remembered listening to the radio commentaries, starting with the crackling and hissing and almost inaudible broadcasts during the famous bodyline series in 1932. We made the decision to go to Australia in 1989 during our first round-the-world flight, with a stopover on Tahiti on the way, but as I have said previously we could not go beyond Sydney because of a strike of pilots employed by the internal airline Ansett.

We did have a short three day stay in Sydney at the Regent Hotel overlooking the harbour and Circular Quay. The best way to see Sydney Harbour is to take a Captain Cook cruise, these boats leave Circular Quay every hour or so and from the top deck the view of the harbour with all its inlets and creeks is magnificent. We went out past the Opera House on our right and Sydney Harbour Bridge on our left and turned north; we thought the Opera House was extraordinary, with its roof of sails it looked like some gigantic schooner, which was presumably intended by the architect. The harbour cruise takes some three hours and as you cruise round you realise what an enormous natural harbour this is, on a par with Hong Kong; everywhere there were jacarandas, a thousand sunbursts of pure pale blue. We went up to Manly and then turned with the Heads on our left guarding the entrance to the harbour; we wondered how Captain Cook missed this, and Esmé said that perhaps he was in his cabin reading a good book.

That night we went out to dinner with the two nephews of our great friend Robina Jeffreys, whom Esmé had known since 1939, and who was godmother to our daughter Emma. They were sons of Bina's brother Nick who had settled in Australia after earlier years in

Kenya, and we enjoyed the evening greatly. We started off with plenty of South Pacific Export Lager for myself and gins and tonics for Esmé at Clive's flat, and went on to dinner in an Italian restaurant. We had with us Joan, who was Nick's previous wife whom we had met when she came to Cheltenham to visit Bina, and this was all very friendly, and a lovely welcome to Sydney and Australia.

The next day we took the Sydney Explorer bus from Circular Quay and had a very informative tour of the city; the driver kept up a commentary in broad Australian and when he realised that he had a couple of ageing Poms on board he made us the butt of his extensive wit, which we enjoyed and so did the other passengers. We later took another bus out to Watson's Bay because we had been advised by Bina to have lunch at Doyle's there. It was a good lunch of lobster, and afterwards when I went to adjust my fluid balance, Esmé got chatting with a young couple who had a speedboat; they said that they were going straight back to Circular Quay and asked us to come with them. I thought that the bus would probably be more comfortable, but Esmé jumped into the speedboat with alacrity. Ever a game girl she was keen to have a go; I felt it must be the Welsh in her. The seats were hard, the speed was very fast and the water choppy, and half way across the Bay I said to Esmé that I was suffering such trauma to the gonads that I was now effectively a eunuch, but I got an unsympathetic reply.

When we reached Circular Quay the boat rose and fell a good deal, and I was not quite sure how we were going to get onto the jetty. Leonard, whose boat this was, said that we would just have to watch, and when the boat got level with the jetty we should jump, we just had to time it right. The rise and fall was about four feet but eventually we made it to applause from our young hosts; Esmé observed as we walked back to the hotel that Australia was a country for the young.

Before leaving Sydney for Bangkok I felt that I had to see Sydney Cricket Ground. We went there by bus and met the head groundsman, who showed us round with great pride. He took us to the gate which leads from the pavilion onto the field and he asked us to imagine the giants of past Australian cricket walking through that gate. He mentioned Woodfull, Ponsford, Bradman and O'Reilly; I suggested that when they walked through that gate so also did Hobbs, Sutcliffe, Hammond and Larwood. He grinned and took the point.

We had a last lunch at Doyle's, on the harbour, and I took a picture of Esmé sitting in the sun halfway through yet another lobster. I have now had that enlarged and it is on the kitchen table where it helps me to pretend that I am not eating alone. Having had just a taste of Australia it was frustrating that we had to leave so soon. It was like having the foreplay without the act of love, the overture without the symphony: we had the symphony a year later.

In 1990 we flew into Sydney from Fiji and had just one night to meet Bina's brother Nick and his wife Daphne, and they took us out to Sails restaurant just under the bridge. Nick told us to try the fish John Dory which was tasty and nice, but for Esmé all fish had to be compared with the pomfret which we had in Bombay, and John Dory certainly came second or third to this. Nick said that he would like to show us a little of the street life in Sydney and he took us to King's Cross.

Unlike in the UK, prostitutes go about their business entirely unharrassed by the police; the garb seemed to be white frilly shirts and very short leather skirts. Nick told us that in Australia, whether it be Sydney, Melbourne or Brisbane, prostitutes were given an entirely free hand. We ended up in a bar uptown where there was a pianist, and we drank and talked and enjoyed ourselves.

We had an early start next morning for Alice Springs. Our aim was Ayers Rock, but to get there you had first to go to Alice Springs where we had a three-hour wait in the airport, and I had to suffer the indignity of being a Pom in the company of a bunch of Australians while the television showed England being beaten by Western Australia. The flight across the desert of the Northern Territory is interesting, you look out of the window and see red earth and scrub and gum trees for endless miles. You see the Rock in the far distance looking like a gigantic pink nipple, and a little away from it there are the Olgas, similar but more like pointed teeth rising up from the desert. There are several hotels, and it is an extraordinary isolated complex hundreds of miles from anywhere; we checked in at the Sheraton Hotel and went on a sunset tour of the Rock. Here in the centre of Australia the sun beats down mercilessly, and the temperature when we arrived was 96°F. The sunset at the Rock came with cool air after a day of beaten gold, and we just stood and watched the colour change on the rock. We got up early next morning at

4 a.m. to see the sunrise, the streaks of the dawn light pointed straight at this huge monolith and Esmé and I just watched spellbound.

After breakfast in the hotel we went on a tour of the base of the Rock, we decided that this would be preferable at our age to climbing it, although they told us in the hotel that the oldest climber to date was a woman of ninety-six. Around the base of the rock there were caves with very early aboriginal paintings; we thought about the prehistoric paintings of bisons and other animals that we had seen at Lascaux in France, and we were told that this aboriginal work might predate Lascaux and was more than twenty thousand years old.

On the plane back to Alice Springs there was a young man and his girlfriend sitting in front of us wearing tee-shirts on which was written 'We did it on Ayers Rock'. Esmé said that if we had decided to climb the Rock, and if I had not suffered such testicular injury on that boat in Sydney Harbour we just might have been wearing the same tee-shirts, imaginative girl that she was.

We were on our way to Lizard Island at the top of the Great Barrier Reef with an overnight stop in Cairns at The Colonial Club Resort. This was a mistake: the hotel was overcrowded and down-market and no self-respecting hippopotamus would remotely consider going into the swimming-pool at this hotel; the water was cloudy green and there were so many people, it was worse than the Ganges on a Saturday night. Esmé said that if I really loved her I would have taken her to the Trade Winds Hotel, five star, expensive and overlooking the Coral Sea.

While we were in Cairns we took the opportunity to go in a Land Rover to the rain forest in North Queensland, and also on a boat trip on the Daintree River, and this was well worth doing. On the river we saw thousands of fruit-bats hanging in the trees like ripe plums. Every now and then there was a tree completely devoid of them, and this was because there was a python coiled up on a branch. This same day we walked on Cape Tribulation where we met a woman who had been at Cheltenham Ladies' College with our daughters. On another day we went to Port Douglas by bus, a delightful little port with a lovely harbour, and from there we took the Quicksilver, a large catamaran taking up to one hundred people at a time out to the Reef; the coral and the fish were marvellous. After two nights in Cairns we boarded a sixteen-seater Fokker plane for Lizard Island; we flew northwards and landed on the island after a forty minute flight.

Lizard is very expensive, very exclusive and caters for everything you may need, and we dropped out for five lovely days of total relaxation. We went out in a dinghy with outboard and had a picnic lunch on a deserted beach, we raced turtles and we saw the manta rays, huge flat fish, some of them twelve feet across, feeding on the plankton. We also went on a day trip to the outer reef, across the blue lagoon, the same lagoon that Captain Cook looked across from a point high up on the island known as Cook's Look, and from where he saw the gap in the coral which enabled him to get out into the Coral Sea. We got to the outer reef and snorkelled, there were many varieties of reef fish here, most of which we had seen before, but new to us were the enormous cods, potato and flowery cods, very lugubrious-looking, very friendly and some said to be up to one hundred years old. We found great difficulty in getting back to the boat because the current was formidable due to thousands and thousands of gallons of water pouring through the narrow gap between coral walls. We had a sumptuous lunch which included lobster, giant prawns, oysters and various meats, with plenty of cold beer and cold white wine.

The hotel complex on Lizard consists of some twenty-four green painted wooden bungalows, and there is a tennis court behind them which we used early each morning. The dining-room was a long balcony at one end of which was a bar and a lounge. Hanging down from the roof over the balcony there were several nests made by sunbirds, tiny little yellow birds with black heads and long beaks, even more attractive than the banana quits in the Caribbean. We watched them feeding their young just a few feet above our heads, the nest suspended from a beam with trailing stems hanging down from it, and we could see the tiny chick's head peeping out from a central hole, like the humming-birds on Tobago. Lizard is so named because of the large lizards or goannas that live there; up to two feet long, they come out of holes in the ground and appear to dance together in a most extraordinary way. We became very friendly with one of the members of the staff, a jolly girl, and before we left Esmé told her that she was such a happy person that she would like to take her home. The girl said that it was usually the men who said that, and I could well understand it.

There was something so personal and so private about Lizard that we felt that you could be a bank robber or some other international criminal, and you could do your own thing there without interference.

On the last night on the island Esmé suggested that we should go down to the beach and watch the sunset. It was very peaceful, there was no wind, everything was still and we were quite alone. The beauty came out of the sky that night and the water held it, embraced, the light loitered willingly and the sea was reluctant to relinquish it, they were like two lovers and we watched in silence, there was no need to speak.

We went back to Brisbane for the first test match of the series between Australia and England at the Gabba Ground, called after the district of Woollongabba. Esmé knew her cricket and loved it; when she was growing up in Mumbles she had an Uncle Stanley who used to organise beach cricket and fill them all with enthusiasm, and he gave Esmé and her many cousins the names of famous cricketers of the time, Esmé was Gunn. Uncle Stanley liked a drink or four and Esmé's mother insisted that he was not alcoholic, he was just very sociable but had bad friends, which probably applies to most of us. Unfortunately, Stanley fell into Swansea dock one Saturday night, which brought the beach cricket to a sudden and sad end.

We had good seats at the Gabba just above the sight-screen in the Clem Jones Stand, and just below us was the Wally Grout Bar; at Brisbane they tended to name the bars and stands after famous Queensland wicketkeepers. England lost that game, as so often before and so often since, in three days, but we enjoyed the cricket and being there amongst the friendly and humorous Australian crowd; whether they would have been so friendly and humorous had England won is questionable. At the end of the last day of cricket I was sitting on the balcony of our hotel room watching Brisbane by night and felt at peace, Esmé was inside the room fussing with documents, and suddenly announced that we were leaving for home early the next morning, rather than in two days time, and I had got the dates wrong. This ended my peaceful vigil and the pack-up was fast and furious.

Within three years in 1993 we were back on the Barrier Reef, this time on Heron Island. Our grandson Barney was doing a year's teaching at Geelong Grammar School, and the rest of the family, Bill, Sue, Megan and Rupert wanted to see him, and then with him they wanted to see as much of this great Southland of Captain Cook as they could. We met on Phuket for a few days and then later on Heron Island where we watched them land in the helicopters, new experiences for them all the time. Heron, like most of the Great Barrier Reef and a lot of the mainland, is one great nature reserve; the flora and fauna are so varied, such a plethora of flowers, fish and fowl that it would take much longer than a week to see it all.

No time was wasted and early the first morning we all went to the beach to see the turtles come and lay their eggs, each female comes back to the same beach all her reproductive life to lay her eggs. The staff tagged them with small metal tags and told us that it was not uncommon for a turtle to be seen as far away as the Caribbean, and seen again on Lizard when the time came to lay her eggs. We all watched the laboured wobble up the beach in the early morning light, and the laying of eggs in the holes they dug at the top of the beach; Esmé and I were seeing all this for the first time and were as excited as the rest of the family. There were walks round the island and walks out on the reef conducted by members of the staff. We spent Christmas here, and Esmé and I were daunted by the mountain of food in the dining room, a huge meal in a temperature of 90°F was more than we could manage, so we just had some oysters, mussels and prawns. There were boats going out to the reef at regular intervals, but by now Esmé's brain damage had made it difficult for her to snorkel properly and her vision was very limited, but she tried hard and saw some fish; this was the last time ever that she put on a mask.

We all went on a cruise over the reef in a semi-submersible submarine. There were plenty of fish and we saw many turtles, and you felt that you could really spend the whole of the rest of your life just sitting under the water above these reefs. The coral walls of the reefs here were high and there are very strict rules about stepping on them or even touching them, as the Australians are very determined to preserve all this natural beauty.

At the end of this idyllic week we left with great sadness, and I took a picture of Esmé standing on the jetty wearing her pink Tahitian shirt and white shorts looking brown and happy. We returned to the mainland by boat and then flew to Sydney. We had three nights in the Old Park Royal Hotel on the Rocks just round from Circular Quay, we repeated the Captain Cook Cruise for the family to see the harbour, and this time instead of there being the blue sunbursts of jacaranda, we saw the red clouds of the poincianas. Bill and Sue said they wanted to emigrate to Australia and they meant it. The family went to the Opera House on New Year's Eve for dinner and a concert, and on New Year's Day we all went to the Sydney Cricket Ground to see a day's test cricket with Australia playing South Africa, which they all loved, especially Rupert who is very keen on the game without, unfortunately, having been born with quite the necessary skills.

When Esmé and I left for home next day we were both convinced that we would not see Australia again. As it happened and perhaps unwisely, we did return a year later and spent Christmas in Cairns and New Year in Sydney. Emma came with us and we had a good week on Lizard Island which she very much enjoyed, learning to water-ski and soaking up the sun. Esmé had developed intermittent epilepsy and was at times bewildered, but she knew where she was and seemed happy. We went back to Cairns for two nights aiming to go south to Melbourne and Sydney to see some more cricket and on that first evening in the Reef House Hotel Emma managed to get Esmé into the pool to swim a few strokes, which pleased her greatly. We had a pleasant supper by the pool, Esmé talked animatedly about her early life, and we all went to bed quite happy and contented. At six o'clock the next morning I awoke to find my darling convulsing beside me, her eyes that melted my heart were open and unseeing, in the flash of that sickening second at the break of a day of high southern summer the future had gone, now there was only yesterday. We were twelve thousand miles from home and I was so thankful that Emma was with us, for without her we would never have got home. Esmé was admitted to hospital in Cairns where the epilepsy was controlled, but the drugs that were given to her made it virtually impossible for her to walk or even to stand without support.

After a week we had to make the decision whether to fly straight home from Cairns, or go on down to Sydney as planned, and fly home from there. We discussed this with Michael Suthers, the physician in charge, and he advised us to go down to Sydney in the hope that another six or seven days would give Esmé time to improve a little, and make it easier for us to manage her on the long flight to London. Emma and I had spent Christmas in the Holiday Inn Hotel in Cairns in the company of two hundred Japanese while Esmé spent most of the time in the ward sleeping, and when she was awake it was obvious that her comprehension had been severely damaged. She showed no anxiety and seemed content to let us look after her. In a long life in clinical medicine I had so often found that the loss of the sense of predicament which accompanies serious illness is something to be thankful for; no attempt should ever be made to correct it, and it can be potentiated by giving the right drugs. After a week in the ward in Cairns we were allowed to take her out and get on a plane for Sydney and we spent the last five nights waiting for the Sydney to London plane in the Old Park Royal Hotel, Esmé confined to bed in the room. Emma and I managed to get her into the bath and out again, though thinking back I cannot imagine how we did it; we took her out in a wheelchair to Circular Quay but she was utterly confused in space and time. Emma's video camera had failed but she managed to get it put right and we have a record on video of these ghastly days.

The endless flight home in darkness all the way was indescribable, getting Esmé into and out of the loo was immensely difficult. When we finally got to Heathrow we were met by Michael Hemmings with his minibus, and he made a bed in it so that Esmé could lie flat for the drive back to Cheltenham. She slept all the way, and when we eventually got her into her own bed at home she slept for twelve hours; Emma and I knew that this was the end. Within four months the epilepsy became permanent and within a further four months she was dead. I was so grateful for the love and support of my children when we were in Australia, Emma by her presence and Bill and Cathy by their daily encouraging telephone calls, and it was a tremendous comfort to me to know that they loved her as I did. I so needed their love and strength at this dreadful time. The seemingly endless and timeless river of life and love which Esmé and I paddled together had finally flowed to the sea, taking her with it and leaving me cast away, marooned on dunes of such disseverment and despair that I knew not where to turn nor what to do.

Chapter Fourteen
Jordan and the Holy Land

Neither Esmé nor I were believers. We had long since lost what faith we ever had, and had come to the conclusion that we had no great benevolent power controlling us; we had long ago failed to reconcile human misery with a loving, all-powerful, fatherlike god. Though at different times we both addressed it, this was a mystery too far for us, an unreason a touch too camp. Esmé truly had the humanist's tolerance of the quirks and caprices of others, and felt that it was of paramount importance to help our fellow human beings when we could, if we could, without the comfort and reassurance that by doing so we were making an investment in some heavenly after life. We both very much wanted to see the Holy Land. Our son Bill and our daughter Emma had both worked in kibbutzim in their teens, and we also wanted to go to Jordan in order to see the desert, the Roman ruins at Jerash, and of course the unique rock city of Petra; we found that Bales ran a tour which would give us these opportunities. When we arrived at check-in we asked about an upgrade to business class, but were told that Royal Jordanian Airways did not have business class cabins on their flights, and they had a monopoly of all flights to Jordan. Esmé said that if I really loved her I would have made other arrangements; I have found in our travels that at moments like this it is best to retire to the nearest bar, where a couple of good gin and tonics tended to restore the situation, and this was no exception. As we sat at the back of the plane in steerage we were surrounded by Jordanians returning to Amman, and Esmé got into conversation with them; she told them that she too was a foreigner in England, and was a member of a subject race, being Welsh, but they did not seem to understand what on earth she was talking about. In Amman we stayed at the Philadelphia Hotel and had a room looking out over the city; we had visualised Amman as an ancient Arab city with many mosques and bazaars, but in fact it is modern with the buildings constructed of pale local stone and with virtually no mature trees. The city had mostly been built in the last ten years, and until relatively recently it was just a village.

When we started the tour of the city early on the first morning, the sun was up and very bright, shining on all the white limestone around us; it was almost like standing in floodlight. Hani, our guide, made frequent reference to the Book of Genesis and Esmé observed that at least we were beginning at the beginning. He told us that according to recent archaeological opinion Jordan was occupied as long ago as 7000 BC by settled communities such as Jericho, and he pointed out that armies and migrations of any sort in ancient times had to cross this bridge of land connecting Asia and Africa. He told us to remember Abraham in the Land of Canaan which we dutifully did, and he traced the history from then to the fourteenth century BC when the Israelites left Egypt, thanks to Moses. Esmé told Hani that if Moses had been a committee like our Cabinet at home, the Israelites would never have got out at all; this was appreciated by the other members of the group, but either Hani did not understand or he did not find it funny. He brought us up to date through all the conquerings and invasions, and was given rapt attention by the group. As I had left the guidebook with the best historical description at home, I was especially glad to have this clear and concise account of Jordanian history.

Esmé thought that Hani was probably temperamental; she recorded in our journal that he was very politically motivated and noted that because he was not keeping to the rules of Ramadan he was probably a Palestinian Christian. It came through as he talked to us that he was very pro-Palestinian and anti-American, blaming America along with Israel for most of the current problems of Jordan.

He took us to the Roman Amphitheatre with a forum in front of it, almost complete and with a small museum of local apparel in one of the side entrances to the enormous stage. He then took us up to the Acropolis, past the four royal palaces, and on the top there was a ruined Roman temple and fort which had been occupied by the Caliph of Damascus. We also saw a museum containing many bronze, iron and stone-age implements and weapons.

After a couple of hours looking round Amman, we headed out on the long straight desert road to Azrah, an oasis over one hundred kilometres away, and stopped at two castles on the way. The first was built by Caliphs, a square building on two floors which became a staging post for camel caravans. The desert all around was not of sand but of what looked like hard yellow earth and small stones; this was a very remote place and the airless heat was oven-like; I wondered what would happen if the coach broke down. The second castle was Moorish with domes; it was a palace built for a Caliph for the pleasure of hunting and bathing, and there were frescoes on the walls inside in a poor state of preservation.

We reached Azrah at lunchtime and went to the Government Resthouse feeling hot, dirty and thirsty. We were very ready for lunch which was preceded by "mezes" consisting of several dishes of creamed vegetables; there followed chicken soup, bright yellow in colour, which Esmé diagnosed as saffron, boiled mutton and fruit.

We went to the castle in the centre of Azrah which was occupied successively by Romans, who probably built it, and then Caliphs, and during the First World War by Lawrence of Arabia, whose staff-room we entered. We returned along the desert highway to Amman and looked forward to Jerash, which we were to see tomorrow.

We awoke to lashing rain. Hani told us that there would be two days of this and that we could hire umbrellas when we got to Jerash. We normally took Pakamacs when we went abroad, but we thought that Jordan and Israel would be hot and dry and we had left them at home. It took an hour to get to Jerash from Amman, part of it on the King's Highway; the rain continued to bucket down which made photography at Jerash unrewarding. This is a very big site and still being excavated, but unfortunately they have built a modern town on much of the old city. The initial impression is of hundreds of columns with Ionic and Corinthian capitals lining a long street running south to north. There are two cross streets and a large oval market place, with a theatre to the west, and beside it a small collection of three Byzantine churches in a curious group. The Temple of Artemis is approached by a wide series of steps, and as we climbed we felt that the dramatic appeal of Pompeii was absent here, though it gives the impression of a greater city. There was obviously much unexcavated and we were seeing only a small part of the original city. After three hours we returned to Amman and spent the rest of the day reading in the hotel and watching the rain.

We left Amman for Israel with an early start, and went through mountainous countryside before crossing the River Jordan over what used to be the Allenby Bridge and is now renamed King Hussein's Bridge by the Jordanians. I was expecting great things of the River Jordan, but in fact it was a small cut about half as wide as the River Cam, and the Allenby/King Hussein Bridge was a small metal affair. The two checkpoints, Jordanian and Israeli, are very close together and everything we had with us was thoroughly examined. At the Jordanian checkpoint there was a gun emplacement with machine guns sticking out of it and pointing towards the Israeli side, and the same situation on the Israeli side with guns pointing at Jordan. There were soldiers everywhere, heavily armed, and at the Israeli checkpoint they made me take a photograph of the ceiling to make sure my camera did not contain any Semtex. When we got through the Israeli checkpoint building, there was an hour's delay before we could go off in the coach because of a "military emergency". As well as the gun emplacements there were searchlights on high points, armoured cars and gun carriers. Esmé was quite convinced we were entering a war zone, and suggested that we should take the sights of Jerusalem for granted and beat it back to Jordan. As soon as the coach started for Jericho somebody threw a brick at it and the aim was good.

Jericho is a large oasis town, with many date-palms and cypresses, and as we entered we passed a large sycamore tree on the right side of the road and were told that this was where Zaccheus climbed the tree to get a view of the Lord; we wondered if he was successful. We stopped at the old city of Jericho where the walls came tumbling down, but all that is left of those walls is a round tower which had been recently excavated. The Dead Sea was in the distance with the Jordanian mountains beyond that and the view was arresting.

We lunched in Temptation Restaurant from which we could look up to the mountains where Christ was tempted for forty days and forty nights. Lunch was welcome and consisted of several dishes of delightful cold vegetables and spicy salad, followed by chicken medallions and fried rice.

After lunch the road took us to Qumran where we saw the Essene monasterial remains, and one of the small caves where the Dead Sea Scrolls were found in 1947. In Israel they regard the discovery of the Scrolls by a shepherd in these caves as the most important in the whole world in this century. The Dead Sea was within a few hundred yards of the caves and a few hardy souls among us bathed, but the wind, the rain and the cold made swimming unattractive. Esmé regretted this later because she wanted to feel the sensation of floating weightless in the Dead Sea; it was a missed opportunity which was rare for us, but the weather was appalling and there was nowhere to get dry.

We were on our way to Jerusalem and made a brief stop at the Inn of the Good Samaritan, a yellow concrete building with Bedouin tents all round it and many insistent begging children; we felt we were back in India. There were hundreds of storks circling overhead on their way to Europe; we could see Jerusalem from here, on the hills way in front of us.

Before Jerusalem we halted in Bethany to see the church on the site of the home of Mary and Martha and brother Lazarus. There was a service in process so we peered through a glass door to see the mosaics in the roof. The church was modern but part of the wall outside it dated back to the time of the crusaders. We descended the twenty-four steps into the Tomb of Lazarus a little further up this old Roman road, and entered a mourning chamber leading further down into a burial chamber. The guide said that Jesus raised Lazarus from the dead where we were standing and commanded him to walk out through the door through which we had just entered, having cast aside the shroud which was around him; almost in the same breath he asked us for sweets and pens to distribute to the children outside.

When we got to Jerusalem we were exhausted and cold, and were glad to reach the comfort of the Seven Arches Hotel, where Esmé was touched to be presented with a carnation on arrival. On the way into the city we were amazed at the amount of building in process in the new West Bank Jewish settlements, which had caused so much trouble between the Jews and the Arabs. The Israelis claimed that these houses were needed to accommodate the Soviet Jews who were coming in at the rate of ten thousand per month, but we were sure that in truth they had been built like housing estates over the last ten years to consolidate the acquisition of the West Bank. They looked like little brick boxes tossed onto the top of the hill.

After a good sleep we woke refreshed and the rain had stopped. It was a short coach ride to the Mount of Olives to see, first, the Church of the Ascension, a small domed octagonal church inside a walled courtyard, and round the wall were the remains of eight pillars which were all that remained of the Crusader Church. The central church was a mosque and in the centre of it there was a small rectangular rock polished quite smooth from which, we were informed, Christ ascended into Heaven.

Only a few yards down the hill from here was the Paternoster Church, where Christ was said to have taught the disciples the Lord's Prayer for the second time. This building is a modern Catholic church with a cloister around on which the Lord's Prayer is written in seventy-two languages on a series of plaques, and underneath the church was a cave where the teaching took place. The group was asked to say the Lord's Prayer in unison which they did, with perhaps two exceptions.

A little further down the hill was the Church of Dominus Flevit where Christ wept for Jerusalem, represented by a small black and white catholic church which we could not enter because communion was being taken. Dominus Flevit is half way down the Mount of Olives and from here there is a stunning view of the old city of Jerusalem the Golden. We stopped under a large olive tree and our guide, whose name was Jimmy, gave us an historical survey and, as a member of the group said, he made the jigsaw start to come together. We felt that nowhere else in the world, no other small country such as this has witnessed so much controversy and destruction and still remains of overwhelming significance to so many. Esmé would tell you that she inherited her love of history from her father, who from the time he learned to read to the time that he died aged ninety, read everything of historical interest that he could lay his hands on. She inherited her father's intelligence and she was lucky to have had a highly intelligent mother as well; her alertness, brightness and quickness of mind was such a bonus for me in our marriage, and it is the loss of that mind together with her love which makes my life without her impossible.

Disbelief, anger, sadness, yearning, want, anguish, these are the attendants of loss; they are the components of the deprivation of love, the ingredients of grief and they possess my mind severally or in cruel combination dooming me to despair. When I try to describe the wonderful experiences which we shared I am not consoled. When you love you surrender willingly part of yourself, when you love completely you give all, and when you lose your beloved you lose your reason to be. You are void, nothing, but you cannot die. You must continue to exist as an empty shell, your love fossilised for the rest of time. I am agonised by the constantly recurring memories of every painful detail and development of Esmé's last two years, and I am unable to banish them from my mind or even shroud them in my thoughts; after a year without her they do not dim, they clarify, become sculpted ever more starkly, so that I have no respite from this tyranny, no oasis of peace or contentment in the barren waste my life has become.

From this point on the Mount we had a longish walk between two high walls and came to the Garden of Gethsemane. We entered, shouldering aside dozens of pedlars selling cards, cheap jewellery and mementoes and this caused distress to some members of the group for two reasons; firstly, they had not been exposed to the sort of begging which we had seen in India and Egypt, and secondly the experience of Jerusalem was very important to them in their faith, and they felt that begging and peddling such as this cheapened what they had longed to see.

The Garden of Gethsemane is quite small, and there were eight very old olive trees which had been proved by carbon dating to be two thousand years old, and were therefore probably growing there when Christ was in the garden, which was often for meditation until the evening he was betrayed by Judas Iscariot. We walked round the garden and entered the church, which is modern, and built over a rock in the centre of it on which Christ stood and agonised and suffered for Jerusalem. This was the Church of the Agony and Passion of Gethsemane and of All Nations which had contributed to the construction of the building. They were saying mass around the central rock when we entered and Esmé felt that here in the Garden of Gethsemane there was undeniable beauty and peace. When we came out of the church and looked back across the Valley of Kedron towards Jerusalem, there were hundreds of cemeteries, Jewish, Christian and Muslim. In all these religions it appeared to be important to be buried on the slopes of such a sacred mount to await the coming of the Messiah. Our guide told us that many famous Jews from all over the world paid much money to ensure that they could have burial space here, and they could not rest in peace unless this was so. Writing this in 1996, I wonder if they feel that it was a good investment now that they have the likes of Robert Maxwell lying alongside them.

We left the Mount of Olives and took the coach round the wall of old Jerusalem to the house of Caiaphas, where Christ was taken after arrest. This is built above a dungeon where Christ spent the night before execution, and beside the church there were stone steps leading towards the centre of old Jerusalem down which Christ is said to have walked. The balcony at the back of this church offered wonderful views of Jerusalem and the Mount of Olives, and we saw our hotel on the top of it.

Before lunch we went to David's Tomb, much venerated by the Jews, a small underground tomb with many silver ornaments, lamps, cups and plates above a velvet covered sarcophagus. We came up from here into a large pillared room which was part of a Crusader church, and was held to be the room in which the Last Supper took place. Evidence of this is partly based on the fact that the capital of one of the pillars depicts two pelicans sucking blood from the breast of their mother, the only birds that can do this, and it was an illustration of Christ offering his blood which was given for us. Before entering David's Tomb it was essential that heads should be covered; the women put handkerchiefs over their heads and the men were given cardboard skullcaps if they were not wearing anything else, and my aged panama with the MCC band appeared to be acceptable.

The important visit after lunch was to Bethlehem, now a military and danger area and we were not allowed to enter the market-place because of this. We debussed in Manger Square; Esmé could not believe this, and we proceeded towards the Basilica of the Nativity, jostled and harassed all the way by the pedlars and the stall holders. The cave in which Christ is said to have been born is a few feet from another cave opposite, where the manger is said to have stood. The actual birth spot is marked by a metal cross of David, the ceiling of the main cave is hung with brass oil lamps, and we saw very old mosaic pavements which were found underneath the stone floor of the cathedral above. On the way out we saw the Catholic Basilica of St Catherine who was brutally killed by her father, a pagan king, for failing to renounce Christianity; she was killed over a wheel of fire, and that was why the firework was thus named. I was ashamed that I did not know this, especially as my father and I had both attended St Catharine's College in Cambridge. When we got back to the bus we were thirsty, and I said that there was sure to be a bar near here called Three Wise Men; if there was I could not find it.

The last stop on this very busy and informative day was the Garden Tomb, close to a large rock which looks like a skull and is said to be Golgotha, the actual site of the crucifixion, rather than under the Church of the Holy Sepulchre. In the garden Esmé got into conversation with a Scottish Evangelist who was conducting a tour of folk from a group council of churches; she thought that he was a pleasant Christian fundamentalist, but she took issue with him when he called the Bishop of Durham an unbeliever. There were two chambers in this tomb, one for wailing and one with three places for bodies, and the place furthest in was where they laid Christ after crucifixion. There were literally hundreds of people in the garden, many in large groups holding impromptu services, praying and singing, some praying standing, some sitting and some kneeling; there was an atmosphere of immense devotion and several groups offered us communion. Opposite the tomb there was a large round stone, a replica of the stone which blocked the entrance to the tomb, and we thought that it would have taken several strong men to have moved the original.

At the end of the day, when we were back in the Seven Arches Hotel we concluded that it must have been an extraordinary experience for the majority of the true pilgrims we had seen there; if you want to accept it all, it is there for you to do so; if you do not want to accept it then the commercialism, the rationalisation and the inevitable lack of proof make it easy for you.

We had two more full days in Israel and the first of these began with a visit to the Dung Gate of the old city, so named because they threw rubbish and excrement out through it; we felt that we would be unpopular if we tried that back home in Southam. As we went through the gate the west wall of the old Herodian City was on our right, and is now the Wailing Wall; in front of it were dozens of bearded, black hatted and black coated Orthodox Jews wailing and nodding their heads against the wall.

Further on there was a beautifully laid out area which contained the two large mosques. The first on the right was El Aqusa, a low square building with seven arches in the front of it. Inside there were two lines of white marble pillars, and the floor was completely covered by priceless carpet. Here was where King Abdullah of Jordan, father of Hussein, was shot standing beside the first pillar on the left as we entered; it was very quiet and very peaceful in this mosque. The second mosque is the enormous Dome of the Rock. The actual dome is impressively big, pure gold and with the sun shining on it is the most impressive sight on the Jerusalem skyline. There is a large courtyard, the walls consisting of groups of columns, and the mosque is octagonal and covered with white and blue mosaics, an astounding example of man-made porphyry. The light inside from the stained glass windows coloured a large rock from which Mohammed is said to have been taken up and away to Mecca. Esmé felt that these two mosques had an unpretentiousness and simplicity which made many of the other churches we had seen seem very ornate and trashy, with all their brass and metalwork. Having seen these mosques she was anxious to go to Turkey before she died but this did not happen. We walked from the Dome of the Rock to the south-west corner of the city and into the Convent of the Sisters of Zion, built over the site of the Herodian Antonia Castle, the start of the Via Dolorosa. Underneath the convent we were shown a large water cistern, filled by rainwater, the Struthian pool; and also stone flooring with chiselled patterns on it said to have been made by Roman soldiers who played games on it, and tore up and divided amongst themselves Christ's robes before execution, called the Lithostrata. We walked up the Via Dolorosa, a narrow street paved by stones and flanked all the way on each side by shops selling souvenirs. Part of the way took us through the city market packed with people, local and tourists and as we passed each Station of the Cross, Jimmy the guide explained the meaning to us; we were particularly interested in the Station called Veronica, where a woman was said to have come out and wiped Christ's face with a cloth which then bore the imprint, 'Vera-onica' meaning true outline.

We finished in an Ethiopian church where a priest read to us an account of the conversion of an Ethiopian ruler to Christianity on the road to Gaza by St Philip. This church was part of the Church of the Holy Sepulchre and just above this is a mixture of four different faiths of Christianity, Catholic, Greek Orthodox, Coptic and Armenian. We queued for ages with hordes of pilgrims to enter the second version of Christ's burial place under the centre of the dome of this church. We went in five at a time and a priest invited us to touch the stone floor of the tomb. We then proceeded upstairs to "Calvary" where are the last four Stations of the Cross, and we saw the large stone with a split in the centre of it, created by the Lord when Christ was on the cross. The chapel to the right of the central altar was Catholic and said to be where Christ was nailed to the cross. The other chapel, which was

Greek Orthodox, contained an altar, below which there was a round
hole surrounded by a brass rim, which they told us was the actual site
of the base of the Cross. On the way out we saw another stone, this
time of marble, with oil lamps hung in line above it. This was the
Stone of Unction where they anointed the body of Christ after taking it
down from the Cross. As you listen to all this you get a lasting
impression of a somewhat contrived, artificial and assumed situation,
in a church of unbelievable unattractiveness.

After lunch this day we went to the museum wherein were the
Dead Sea Scrolls; here was the Book of Isaiah and many minuscule
scrolls, written in tiny writing without the aid of a magnifying glass;
they must have been written by people utterly determined that the
evidence of their lives and very existence should survive far beyond
their inevitable destruction.

We had now seen two places claiming to be where Christ was
crucified, and two places claiming to be where he was buried; perhaps
in the future the real place of both may be confirmed.

We bought some gold earrings representing the Menorah, the
seven candles on a candlestick which is typical of Israel, and the next
day we headed back towards Jericho and then up the west side of the
Jordan Valley. We reached Nazareth, which is a sizeable modern
town with Arabs much in the majority and we walked to the Church of
the Annunciation of the Blessed Virgin Mary, a garish modern
building. We were shown a hole leading to the rock where Mary was
visited by the Angel Gabriel and this was an emotional moment for
many of the pilgrims who were weeping copiously. Just round the
corner from here we entered the Church of St Joseph, over the
supposed site of Joseph's carpenters shop, but all we could see was a
metal grill leading down to a deep cave.

We had lunch beside the pretty Sea of Galilee where the water was
only three feet deep, and made enquiries as to the whereabouts of the
kibbutz named Kfar Hanassi, where our son Bill worked many years
before, but we were told it was much further north and we had no
time to go there. We went to Tabtha where the miracle of the loaves
and fishes took place and there was a pretty Byzantine mosaic here
picturing the event. We then proceeded to Capernaum where Jesus
began his ministry and we were not aware that eleven of the disciples
came from this area, the exception being Judas Iscariot. Capernaum
looks like the ruin of a Roman temple, but is in fact the ruin of a

Synagogue, and nearby was the Church of the Beatitudes, with the Beatitudes written round the wall in many many languages.

On the way back to Jerusalem the driver stopped the bus at the gate of the kibbutz where our daughter Emma worked called Gan Hashelosha, an impressive white gateway which opened to a long avenue of tall cypress trees, and we could see some buildings at the end of this avenue. We remembered so well Emma being here and her problems in meeting up with Bill, who had returned to Israel to see Susie, his first love. When Bill was in Kfar Hanassi a couple of years before and was working in the fields of the kibbutz on a tractor, he used to get potted at by Arabs from the Golan Heights. Violence here has not really abated, and on the last night that we were in Jerusalem there was rioting and seven cars were burned.

The next day we returned to Jordan and after crossing the Allenby Bridge we ascended a mountain, Mount Neba, from the top of which there was a fantastic view of Jerusalem to the right, the River Jordan in front and the Dead Sea to the left. There was a small Byzantine church with lovely mosaics, and we were assured that this was the place where Moses died.

We now headed south on the desert highway, two lanes in each direction, the traffic consisting almost entirely of heavy lorries taking loads to and from the Port of Aquaba on the Red Sea. We passed a Crusader fort and Nabothian and Roman temple ruins, and after several hours we came to Wadi Mousa, the village at the entrance to the Siq which leads into Petra.

We were up at 6 a.m. the next morning for the ride on horseback through the Siq into Petra; it narrows to a cleft in the mountain just wide enough to take a Land Rover, and it was a dramatic ride through it with the sides rising up to three hundred metres, almost excluding the sunlight. The famous view through the cleft of the Treasury Building, the first rock-cut temple that you see at the end of the Siq, was extraordinary; it is one of the most complete in the whole city, much of which is ruined, but as you walk along the main street, which is very wide, there are the remains of buildings on both sides. We saw the amphitheatre and were taken into a tomb with graves of varying depth where most of the bodies were buried standing up. All along the right side of the road there are tombs, one of which was said to resemble the Golden Palace of Nero. Much of the rock is streaked with lines of pink, yellow, green and blue formed by the many salts of iron, copper and aluminium which have been imprisoned between layers of rock; this was a feature of the whole of Petra, both inside and outside the buildings. The better preserved buildings are those which, like the Treasury, are protected from the elements.

After lunch we made the big climb of three hundred and fifty steps to the Monastery; this was the biggest building we saw in Petra; it was late afternoon and the soft sunlight on the pink rock and the silence of this place we would remember for a very long time. A little away from the Monastery there was a cave inhabited by Bedouin families and they had a TV aerial; Esmé wondered if they had a Volvo parked round the back. Just before we went to Petra the Government had cleared all the Bedouins out of the old city and rehoused them at Government expense.

We were almost the last to leave Petra, and by the time we got on our horses to ride back through the Siq the sun had dropped quickly behind the high mountains and everything was very quiet. It is a strange place and it had an eerie feel to it. Esmé thought of the hundreds of years until it was rediscovered in the nineteenth century, and said that she had the feel of eternity as she left.

We left the hotel mid-morning and made a brief stop in Wadi Mousa for bread and fruit for a picnic lunch, and another short stop to view the water spring where Moses smote a rock to start it; it was a jagged looking rock and we thought that he must have hurt his hand. We headed across the desert in great heat for Wadi Rum and the scenery was magnificent, with towering cliffs of weathered stone in the distance. The yellow stone, the red sand, and the huge limitless sky took our breath away, there is such emptiness and silence here. Wadi Rum is where several Bedouin tribes live, and is where Lawrence of Arabia, in the First World War, planned to attack the Turks. The main building is a fort with notched parapets and slit windows, currently occupied by the men of the Desert Patrol with splendid colourful uniforms and check head-dresses. You had the feeling that you were truly in an outpost deep in the desert.

The rest of the group went for a drive across the desert in Land Rovers, but Esmé and I thought that we would prefer to walk. We went out of the village and walked across sand, dust and stone, and on either side were small mountains of extraordinary lightened rock. The sun was high, and we were quite alone, and Esmé loved the feel of the place. It was another very different experience for her, we felt so contented, so glad just to be together in these awe-inspiring surroundings, standing on a stage such as this. As we walked back to Wadi Rum we passed several skeletons of animals, mostly goats; the sun went down and as it did so the colour of the rocks changed from yellow through red to purple and the air cooled rapidly.

Wadi Rum is only thirty-five miles from Aquaba and as we rounded a left-hand bend to enter the port we could see, seemingly only a few miles away, the Israeli port of Eilat. We stayed in the Holiday Inn and when we got to the room there was a limiting view of a white stucco wall only a few feet away, and an advertisement in neon lights for a restaurant; Esmé wanted to go back and sleep with me in the desert.

We spent our last day on the beach in front of the hotel; perhaps we should have joined the snorkelling expedition, but we had seen coral fish aplenty and we just wanted to laze and read; I enjoyed watching ships of all sorts plying to and from these two very important Red Sea ports.

As we flew home we both had strong and mixed feelings about what we had seen and about what we had been told; unless your faith and your belief merely needs enhancement, those with doubts may leave with more. Esmé and I had no faith and no belief and therefore we were left with no doubts; we just had each other and we knew that when either of us died, the other would have nothing except the love and concern of our children and friends, and it would be a gap that, however hard they tried, they could never fill.

There were times during our travels when we felt very close to each other, and that afternoon walking together in the desert at Wadi Ruin was one of them; times such as that are very precious to me now, because for the rest of my life wherever I may walk I will walk without her.

Grief cannot be calibrated but it dictates how you arrange your existence. As soon as Esmé went into hospital for the last time I moved to sleep on her side of the bed; in the sitting-room and the kitchen I sit on the chairs she used. Her dressing-table is as she left it: her silver-backed brushes on the left with a box of tissues behind, her spectacles and wristwatch are in front of her Elizabeth Arden face powder and a pot of Opium body cream; in the centre are two small containers, one oblong of glass with a silver lid for her pins and eyebrow tweezers, the other a small gold-painted wooden box the shape of an old fashioned trunk with a rounded top, for her favourite earrings. On the right is a small magnifying hand mirror and behind that two lipsticks and the two perfumes which she used during the last few years, Red Door and Opium, and I have a photograph of her head and shoulders in front of the large mirror at the back. On top of the mirror are perched two small peacocks of brilliant blue which she clipped there. Her pink-edged white-initialled towelling slippers remain under the chair in the corner, her white towelling dressing-gown hangs with mine behind the door, and in the bathroom the plastic cap which she used under the shower remains, together with her talcum powder and renewal creams.

On my desk in the bedroom under the window and opposite the dressing-table, I have seven photographs of her taken between 1971 and 1993 within three feet of me, and I have eleven other photographs of her, and of both of us together, dotted around the house, so that I am never without a view of her in whichever room I may be. Others in their grief may clear the house of everything which reminds them of their lost love, but each time I give away any of her clothing I feel that I am robbing myself of part of her. Students of grief tell me to plan no more than a day ahead, but my problem is so often the next hour; grief demands unreserved acknowledgement of reality, and though some can edit reality I cannot be that selective. During my life I have occasionally been able to cubby-hole worry, and when I could not I could share it with Esmé; now I can do neither, every cove, cavern and canyon of my mind is invaded, possessed totally by this pain, rendering me palsied and paretic in mind and body. I try to free my memories to think of those earlier days and nights of our loving, the breathlessness of her closeness, her touch, the bloom, bouquet and perfume of her body when she loved me, so subtle, so private, so rare, her soft and tender dew-kissed petals open to welcome me, her sweet nectar for me only, but my fugitive mind is too quickly re-captured and returned to the dark dungeon of my deprivation. The pain that you feel in your grief depends totally on how much of yourself you have invested in your love; how you cope with it depends on other factors in your personality. If I can cope with today I simply do not know how I can continue to do it again tomorrow, tomorrow which offered us all those blue horizons and sunlit yonders, but now brings only a bleak tundra of loneliness and hopelessness from which my heart can get neither respite nor relief.

Australia: Picnic on Lizard Island, Barrier Reef.

Jerusalem: The Dome of the Rock, the most splendid building.

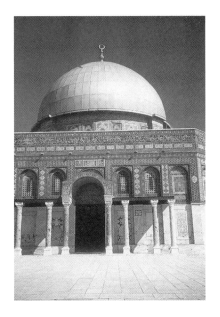

Jordan: The Treasury at Petra.

Jordan: Wadi Rum in the desert.

Papua New Guinea: The village chief at a sing-sing, Central Highlands.

Papua New Guinea: An occupied coffin on stilts, Central Highlands.

Papua New Guinea: Wedding dance, Karawari River.

East Africa: Lions in the Masai Mara, Kenya.

East Africa: A village in the Masai Mara, Kenya.

East Africa: The Ngorongoro Crater, Tanzania.

Morocco: Sahara bound, Tinfou.

Morocco: The Djemaa El Fna, Marrakesh.

China: The Great Wall, Beijing.

China: The Forbidden City, Beijing.

China: Tiananmen Square at peace, Beijing.

China: The start of the Yangtse River Cruise, Chongquing.

Chapter Fifteen
Papua New Guinea

At the end of 1990 we had been to Fiji and were going on to Australia for more cricket and we felt that if we did not manage to fit in Papua New Guinea at this time, we probably never would. Esmé had a social worker colleague, Valerie Best, who had divorced and was about to marry Bob Jones, who was working for Air Niugini in Port Moresby as an advisory engineer; he said that he would be glad to help us in Papua New Guinea and we were grateful for this, because we knew that it was a very strange land, very backward, and we knew that in the centre of the country in the highlands, until the mid-1930s they had never seen a white man.

Papua New Guinea lies just south of the equator and is part of the last of a long chain of islands which extend down from South-East Asia. It forms the eastern half of the huge island of New Guinea, the western half which is Irian Jaya, part of Indonesia.

We flew from the ultra-modern airport at Cairns, just completed, in a Fokker F28 of Air Niugini to Port Moresby in one and a half hours across the Coral Sea. The northern tip of Australia and the southern extremity of Papua New Guinea seemed very close to each other with only the narrow Torres Strait separating them. When we climbed out of Cairns we turned to the north and flew up the north coast of Australia along the outer Barrier Reef, which is a breathtaking sight from twenty thousand feet.

At Port Moresby we were met by a dark fuzzy-haired man holding up a card with our names on it which gratified us, because although we were told that all arrangements had been made we thought that this was probably where things would first start to go wrong; Papua New Guinea was not at all ready for tourism and their infrastructure for it was virtually non-existent. Bob Jones appeared and we felt reassured, and he stayed with us until our onward internal flight to Madang was

due; I noted that the tickets on our baggage were for Wewak, which is
further round the north coast than Madang, and had them changed.

When we were about to board the Madang flight we were held
back and switched to a flight forty minutes later, which itself left
thirty minutes late; the airport appeared to be in total chaos. We took
our leave of Bob Jones and arranged to meet him for a drink in the
Islander Hotel when we came back through Port Moresby to return to
Australia.

The dreaded disaster happened at Madang: for the first time in
over twelve years of long-haul travel our baggage did not appear. We
were met by a pleasant young man from the Madang Resort Hotel
who discovered that they had failed to take the bags off the plane, and
in spite of the change of labels they had still gone on to Wewak; this
young man's name was Burex. Esmé kept calling him Durex, so we
had a discussion and agreed to compromise and call him Freddie.
Thereafter whenever we called him Freddie he was absolutely
delighted and fell about laughing, but I am not at all sure that he
understood our reasoning; he kept saying, "I am the Freddie". At all
airports in Papua New Guinea, other than Port Moresby, the locals
crowd the airport to see the planes, invading even the runway, and
nobody seems to mind. There was a large crowd of men, women and
children in this little airport at Madang, and we had to extricate
ourselves and go with Burex/Durex/Freddie to the hotel, and hope that
our bags would arrive in due course; all we had were the shirts and
shorts that we stood up in and our sponge bags. It was very hot and
very humid, and it took rather more than the tropical Papuan drink
which they offered us in the bar to reassure us. We went to bed and
our bags had still not arrived after breakfast next morning.

We decided on a harbour cruise in the motor launch owned by the
hotel and driven by a nice young man named Paul, who had trained in
Brisbane to be an aeronautical engineer but was having difficulty in
getting a job. He took us round an unexpectedly large harbour; our
snorkels were in our bags in Wewak and we could not explore
underwater which was a great pity, because we knew that there were
many World War II wrecks just below the surface that we could have
viewed with a snorkel and mask. Paul took us to a pretty island called
Krangket, where there was a lodge with laid out gardens and we
walked across to the ocean side where Pacific rollers were crashing
onto rocks, and palm trees and colourful shrubs were everywhere; on

the boat in the lagoon the water was so peaceful and calm, a strange contrast to the huge seas crashing on the beach only a few hundred yards away, and there were many islands, cays built up on the coral. When we turned back towards the hotel Paul pointed out a mountain to us, and told us that a famous lookout was on the top of this, from which local Papuans watched Japanese troop movements well behind their lines, and sent information back to the American and Australian headquarters further inland; many died dreadful deaths at the hands of the Japanese when they were caught.

Back at the hotel there was still no sign of our bags; by now our shirts and shorts needed urgent laundering and we sat on our balcony reading, wrapped in towels, while this was done. I made repeated enquiries about the bags but was always met with a pleasant smile; there is a timelessness about Papuans which, at this point, made me want to shoot the lot, but I could not get my hands on a kalashnikov.

Locally carved and painted wooden masks are important in Papua New Guinea, and were more often intended as a house decoration than as something to be worn. We found a Chambri mask to decorate the chimney-breast at home and bought it; it was about two and a half feet long, ten inches broad and consisted of a lovely face with a baby crocodile above it. The face was painted with red, black and grey stripes, the background to the mask was grey, the eyes were cowrie shells, the lips were black with white spots, the inside of the mouth showed red, and there was a long red tongue hanging out of it, which is the sign of welcome in Papua New Guinea.

The next morning we prepared to depart for Mount Hagen, which is the central point from which planes depart for the highlands and to the Sepik River and its tributaries. Some ten minutes before we left the hotel, and as we were standing outside, Burex/Durex/Freddie arrived in a minibus with our bags in the back, with the inevitable wide-mouthed grin; Esmé said that she was sure he would grin on the gallows.

The internal airline in Papua New Guinea is Talair, and their planes are the Model T Fords of the air. When we were about to board this plane I saw the Australian pilot kicking one of the tyres, and he said that with Talair, ground maintenance simply did not happen. I told him that that did not give me too much confidence, and he said that he was up there too, "mate". I reported this to Esmé when I got into the plane, because I felt that with a love like ours not only joys but anxieties should be shared; she said that if I really loved her I would not have brought her to this godawful country in the first place.

We flew to Mount Hagen over forbidding jungle-covered mountains. At Mount Hagen airport we had a two hour wait for motor transport which was to take us to Ambua Lodge, twenty-four kilometres up in the mountains. The terminal building was a large hut where arrivals and departures mingled with the local populace, who came to spend the day. There was a woman squatting on the floor with an infant sucking and tugging at wizened breasts, long since visited by milk. The smell of stale bodies was curiously overpowering, and Esmé thought that the children were covered with weeping jungle sores or impetigo, or both. Everybody seemed very happy, they were very interested in us, we were a peculiarity to them, they came up very close and looked us up and down, front back and side; I told Esmé that any minute she would get an exploratory prod with a finger to see if she was real.

Eventually a Toyota Landcruiser drove up, a man got out, shook us warmly by the hand and said that his name was John, he was a Huli tribesman, he had been to school and spoke English. The Landcruiser had a windscreen that was totally opaque, and he told us that as he drove into the airport somebody had thrown a rock at it. We got into the back and awaited developments.

I cannot possibly convey the humour of the next half hour; John, such an earnest man, was nonplussed and already there were ten or a dozen Papuans standing around and giving him advice. There was much talking and touching of the windscreen, I suggested to John that he should simply punch the windscreen and navigate through the hole that would create, he took his cap off and said that he wanted to think. We got out and he and his advisers poked at the windscreen and then jumped back as if they had just tickled a hand grenade. John got back into the vehicle, picked up the jack and I had great hopes that a decision had been made, but he thought better of this and picked up a screwdriver and started to lever out small pieces of the windscreen, cheered on by the crowd, now more than fifty strong. It took thirty minutes for John and his friends to pick out enough of the windscreen very slowly, one piece at a time, for him to have a view of the road, through a hole no more than a foot in diameter.

We got going. The road was very bumpy and what was left of the windscreen began to fall into the vehicle; John stopped, and again a crowd collected in no time. We had reached the foothills of the mountains and the people were strangely clad, the men had paint on their faces and Esmé was quite convinced that she would end up in a stew, like her grandfather in Sumatra, and she said that we were really too old to die that way, and we would be very tough to eat anyway. I still had faith in earnest John and he took up the jack again, now with a very determined expression, and bashed it all round what was left of the windscreen; we were able to continue with a tropical wind and thick dust in our faces and John was triumphant.

We passed a market in a village where there was a commotion, with people standing around a man lying beside the road, very blood stained and apparently unconscious. John stopped and went to investigate; he came back smiling broadly and said that this man had stolen some money and had been beaten up by the police, who had gone to fetch a car to take him to jail.

We had now reached seven thousand feet and we had wonderful views across the enormous Tari Basin. At Ambua Lodge we occupied a straw hut, and after a late lunch John took us on a walk through a rain forest, over rope bridges hundreds of feet above rushing torrents, and stopped at the top of a cascading waterfall of the purest clear water. He then took us in the Landcruiser up to nine thousand feet where we were equidistant from the summits of two mountains, Mount Kewala and Mount Ambua; the air was cool and fresh and in total contrast to the humidity in Madang and Port Moresby. On the way back to the lodge John wanted so much to show us Birds of Paradise, and asked us to stand very still in the road and wait; we heard clattering calls but did not see the birds, and he promised to take us out the next morning if we would get up early enough, and he would guarantee sightings. Dinner in the lodge was round a lovely open log fire which we appreciated, because at this height the night was cold.

We were up at 5 a.m. and the dawn of this new day was a wonderful sight, with the Tari Basin filled with white mist like cotton wool and only the tops of the mountains visible. We returned to the woods and waited in silence; nothing happened for what seemed an age, and then in the distance and getting louder, was the clatter we had heard the day before. John motioned to us to keep still and quiet, and then a Duke of Saxony Bird of Paradise flew into the top of a tree less than twenty yards from us; it had long feathers like sticks coming out of its head, which it waved and twisted, and John told us that this was a mating show for the female. We saw plenty of Tiger Parrots, which are very pretty green and red birds, and then further down the road after more waiting we saw a Ribbon-Tailed Bird of Paradise; we had a long sighting of this through our binoculars; it was absolutely beautiful, bright blue, with a purple head and two long white feathers for a tail. When we returned to the lodge for breakfast, on a tree just outside the gate we saw another Ribbon-Tailed Bird of Paradise and we felt that we had achieved something, and that we had earned our breakfast, for quite often there were no sightings.

After breakfast there was a long all day trip in the Landcruiser back past the airport to see a Sing-Sing, and on the way we encountered a large crowd of people walking down the road in what appeared to be their best Sunday clothes. Our guide today was Andrew, and he told us that they were going to church, the choice was between Seventh Day Adventist and Roman Catholic. Andrew said that there was a certain amount of Christianity in Papua New Guinea, and that cannibalism had really been stopped by Christian missionaries.

At the Sing-Sing there was an open area surrounded by trees, and all along one side were seated the villagers; on the open ground there were eight or nine young men painted in brilliant yellow on the face, lips painted red and bodies and legs covered with a red ochre. They had startling head-dresses, made of the feathers of the emu, Bird of Paradise and the cassowary. The men wore a small apron over their genitals, and the women grass skirts; some of the men had brown wigs, but there was one elderly man who seemed more painted than anybody else, who strolled around posing for photographs and who was the village Chief. The dancing was rudimentary, repetitive and accompanied by beating on drums; every now and then they all gave out wild cries and Esmé said that this was one of the most weird and primitive scenes that she had ever witnessed.

We went to another village where we saw how native burials were carried out, and we were met by the Chief with an enormous head-dress who made a speech, which was interpreted by Andrew as a welcome. He picked various leaves from trees around him and when immersed in water they made a drink which gave him protection from his enemies, and then he showed us his house, which was a hut with only one room, and appeared to be the residence of himself only. Next door there was a smaller hut where his wife slept with a family of pigs; men and women do not cohabit in this part of the country, they live in separate huts, and when Esmé asked the obvious question the answer was "in the bushes". I could see that she rather liked the idea of this, I hoped that it brought back happy memories.

The Chief showed us with pride the family tomb where there were seven skulls, painted in red, yellow and green. The rock in the back of this shallow cave had two carved prominencies resembling breasts, a hole below them like a navel and below this there was a vertical aperture chiselled out to represent a vulva; the skulls were arranged in line with the breasts, because babies suckle with their heads close to their mother's breast. We thought about the cliff graves we had seen in Torajaland, and how important was death and the management of it to these primitive peoples.

After lunch we went to a wig-growing school, where young men paid for their education while they grew their hair. Over an eighteen-month period they grew enormous wigs, the long brown hair gathered into a circle so that they looked as if they were wearing large circular hairy helmets. They were in their middle twenties, and while they grew their hair they remained rigidly celibate; if the schoolmaster caught them with a girl they were expelled. After they completed the course they returned to their families, and either they kept their hair or they cut it off and sold it as a fully-fledged wig.

After this eye opening experience we made a brief stop at a burial ground, where there was a coffin on stilts six feet above the ground which contained the body of a woman who had recently died. Decomposition was rapid in the heat and humidity, and the normal custom was for the relatives to sit underneath the coffin and as the body decomposed the fluids or "humours" dripped down upon them. The stench was awful, they smelled to high heaven, but as they moved among the people they were thus honoured in their bereavement.

The variety of apparel which you see in Papua New Guinea is limitless: there is western dress, men with shirts and coats, even blazers on top and only a genital apron below or gourds, often bright yellow in colour; and there are almost naked men with straw skirts and head-dresses. They wear anything they can lay their hands on, and we were told of the head waiter in a hotel who wore a shirt with a stiff collar, a tail coat and a penile gourd underneath. The women hanker after western style dress but they always wear a billibong on top. The children are all barefoot and filthy, and many have widespread skin eruptions, especially on the legs. Esmé noted the almost complete absence of gross congenital deformities, in contrast to India.

On the way back to the lodge Andrew told us that the burial ground and the wig school had been open to tourists for only the past two years, and the Huli country was the last to be reached by the white man; we found it easy to accept that cannibalism was only stopped relatively recently.

The next day we left for the Karawari River, which meant going back to Mount Hagen and flying to a landing-strip on grass beside the river, and a flat-bottomed motorboat took us up river to Karawari Lodge. The river is a tributary of the main river, the Sepik, and was in flood with fast-flowing yellow water. The Lodge is built of bush materials and on the lines of a Haus Tambaran spirithouse of which there is one in every riverside village. The main reception area and lounge were very attractive, the walls literally covered with painted wooden masks and figures of every conceivable pattern, all made by local people; most were for sale, with the exception of those which had been made prior to 1963, which were regarded as antiques and not to be exported.

After lunch we were introduced to Felix, who was to take us further up-river to a sago palm plantation and instruct us in the way the people used sago, which was very important to them mainly for food, but no part of the sago palm went unused. As we cruised up-river both banks were lined with feathery wild sago, bamboo, wild sugar cane or pitpit, and broad-leaved lush breadfruit trees. We moored at a village where we had a demonstration of how they pound the sago pulp in a hollowed out palm trunk; they soak it in reed baskets, squeeze it out and put it in their long canoes and it makes a creamy substance which they make into sago cakes in a bowl, using a large crude wooden spoon. The heat and humidity on this steamy equatorial river and the primitive life on its banks made the Amazon seem civilised.

By the time we got back to the lodge it was early evening, and insects of many varieties, including mosquitoes, were busy; we had mosquito nets over the beds and we lit mosquito coils in the room and on the balcony, and liberally used our Timor spray, but these mosquitoes were well trained Kamikazes. Before supper we bought an "ancestor". He is eighteen inches high, made of dark wood, he has a long face with cowrie shells for eyes, a long nose pierced at the tip, and through the hole is a small piece of string tied in a bow; each ear is also pierced and there are three pieces of string hanging from the ears on each side. His head-dress is represented by seven vertical cassowary feathers, his body is long and there are decorations carved on it, his legs are short and he has a short skirt made of string, and string armlets and anklets; he now stands beside the fisherman's god from the Cook Islands and we often wondered what they talk about, on the dining-room window-sill.

After we had bought our ancestor, Esmé, with the greatest delicacy, lifted the string skirt, announced that the member was unshorn and accepted that this must be the norm in Papua New Guinea. I was glad that she did not ask me to do a population survey, because I knew that most of these sportsmen packed bows and arrows, and I had no wish to end up like King Harold. Esmé was intrigued by their "payback" arrangements; if somebody from one village steals a pig or molests a girl from another village, the resulting punch-up takes the form of shooting at each other with bows and arrows until honour is satisfied, and this may well end in death.

Esmé heard the pattering of feet on the balcony in the middle of the night and suggested that I should go out to investigate; I made the lame excuse that I did not want to disturb the mosquito net and told her to put her head under the pillow and the feet would go away.

They woke us with tea, cinnamon buns and dough cakes. We had an early breakfast on our balcony in the dank and misty dawn and were briefed about the adventures ahead of us; Esmé and I were ever ready voyagers to as yet unseen delights, and in our travels we were rarely disappointed. We were going up-river to the lakes, we were issued with a picnic lunch, and took bottles of lager which we trailed in the water in an effort to keep it cool.

We turned into a tributary of the Karawari, quite narrow, the foliage on each bank arching above us almost obliterating the sun, and there were many river birds, heron, cormorant, egret and eagles. We stopped at a village which had a little church with a simple wooden cross over the door, another over an altar which was a large tree-trunk, and the pews were simple logs. We were shown the "Department of

Education" which had a straw roof and wooden walls, and there were rough wooden desks for about seventy children. In front of this building there were six large boulders which were Blood Stones, where they used to pour the blood of the men they killed in battle in a ceremony to initiate their young warriors.

When we left here the river widened into a lake, and we had our picnic in the middle of the lake because the insects made it too uncomfortable to have it on the bank, according to our guide. There were five of us in the boat; one of the women required a 'comfort stop', and when we got to the bank Esmé felt that she ought to get out with them to be on the safe side; she got stung and wished she had stayed in the boat.

On the way back downstream we stopped at a village where the people were considered backward because they could not fish or build canoes out of sago palm trunks; they got their fish by making a poisonous fluid out of vines, putting it in an enclosed part of the river, and collecting the dead fish from the surface. Their immediate ancestors had lived in the swamps and had been moved to the riverbank by the Australians when they took over Papua New Guinea after the Second World War. They showed us an old Haus Tambaran spirithouse, which had survived the missionaries who burned as many as they could. It was large and on the walls there were bark paintings, and we were treated to a flute recital given by two men; the flutes were lengths of bamboo five feet long with a side hole at one end; before they got going there was much experimental blowing, and they pulled vines through the flutes to get them ready. They tried several and discarded them, but eventually they began to play, the noise was cacophonic; it was like listening to the London Philharmonic wind section tuning up on a very bad day.

Immediately opposite this village on the other bank we were allowed to watch a marriage ceremony. The men were much decorated and the women painted also, and they all jumped up and down chanting, the women half naked, and so well endowed that we kept ready to duck. At a signal they formed a column and danced toward a wooden hut in which sat the bride and her best friend: when they got to the hut the best friend was ceremoniously replaced by the bridegroom, the door was locked on the outside with much leaping about and the making of lascivious and libidinous gestures. They then danced off into the trees and it was all as simple as that; Esmé said that she hoped they would not leave it too long before coming back to open the door, because in stifling heat like that you could have too much of a good thing.

We had a long peaceful cruise back to the lodge. There was a storm brewing, everything in our room was soaked through and I was worried about my camera and films. A seven man bamboo band entertained us at supper and soon after we got to bed the storm broke; we went out onto the balcony and felt quite overwhelmed by the intensity of the sound, the vivid light and the force of the water which was cascading down with the noise of a thousand kettle drums on the roof just above our heads; thoughts of further sleep were superfluous. This storm was one of the excesses of nature which we experienced in the tropics along with the impossible heat of the sun, and we loved it. The next morning we were offered a visit to a village nearby where there was a skin cutting ceremony about to take place. This involved the making of curved cuts through the skin to the muscle on the upper body and upper arms of young men and was an initiation ceremony denoting the reaching of manhood. After they made the cuts they rubbed in clay and ashes to ensure healing by raised keloid scars. We discussed this and decided that ritual mutilation in any form did not attract us and we gave it a miss. At noon we flew back to Port Moresby and Bob Jones came to the Islander Hotel, and suggested that we should go to his bungalow and have a couple of beers there; we saw on his television that Margaret Thatcher had been deposed. Bob was a delightful companion, he always seemed so cheerful; I suppose he had to feel that way because with the job of trying to keep the planes of Air Niugini airborne and with the local staff at his disposal, if the problems had really got to him, he would have been in acute depression; Esmé was quite delighted that he and Valerie were to be married. We had a late supper back at the hotel and went to bed.

Early in the morning I awoke feeling that something was wrong, and I realised that I had left my black handbag in the dining-room, containing everything of importance, credit cards, money, airline tickets and passports, and Bob Jones had warned us that thieving was worse in Port Moresby than up-country. I asked at the reception desk whether a bag had been found, they explored the safe, and said that no bag had been handed in; after another two hours with my constant enquiring they produced the bag with nothing removed. It appeared that a member of the dining-room staff had seen it when he was clearing up to go home, and because he could not get hold of the key to the safe, he put it in the back of a large fridge and failed to tell anybody. We celebrated the recovery of the bag in the hotel shop, where we bought two crocodile teeth for Esmé's tropical necklace.

We flew out at midday for Brisbane; it was very hot and so humid that you felt that you could grab handfuls of the air and drink it. We staggered across the tarmac soaking with sweat, and mounted the steps into the Qantas jumbo; at the top of the steps a steward asked us if we would like our cold champagne where we stood, or would we prefer to wait and have it when we got to our seats. Esmé made a quick decision, so we had one there and two more as soon as we got to our seats; the cool air in this plane was bliss after the steam heat of Port Moresby.

For us both, seeing the world was always our ambition, and it has been said that when the ambition of a lifetime is fulfilled something has gone from life itself; but we found that as far as our travelling was concerned, when an experience had been lived through and relived again and again with the help of photographs and chronicles, the irritations and discomforts were easily forgotten, and we were left solely with the satisfactions, the pleasures and the joys and were filled with thankfulness for our luck in life.

It is six years since we went to Papua New Guinea, and no doubt the facilities for tourism have been developed and improved; I am just glad that we saw that extraordinary country before too much had changed, side-tracked as it had been for so long on the highway to civilisation.

We felt when we left that this country had such opportunities to thrive in world-wide commodities, especially coffee, cocoa, and palm oil which had largely replaced copra, and there is also an immense timber resource, as yet virtually untapped. The people are an anthropologist's dream and fascinated us. I was sorry to miss the World War II relics and especially wanted to see the Kokoda Trail where the Japanese were finally stopped by the Australians and the Americans, but it was not possible to fit this in. Esmé had been diligent in writing up the journal each evening, sometimes in uncomfortable circumstances, and we flew out with this and the trophies of crocodile teeth, the Chambri mask and our ancestor, and of course our wonderful memories.

Reading the journal again now, Esmé has made a point of describing the boats on the Karawari: some were simple dugout canoes, some motorised, some of them were more ornate with carved crocodile head prows which they called puk-puk. Wherever we went in the world each country had its own distinctive type of boat, the clattering long-tail boats and rice barges of Thailand, the fussy sampans and junks of Hong Kong, the houseboats and gentle shikaras on the lakes of Kashmir, the long riverboats on the Amazon, the tranquil feluccas on the Nile at Aswan and the larger riverboats on both the Nile and the Yangtze, and also on the Yangtze the domed roofed barges and the flat fishing boats with their huge funnelled nets. We always felt that the boats were as much part of each scene, and as typical of it, as the buildings.

Chapter Sixteen
East Africa

Toward the end of 1991 our son Bill and family decided that they would be able to join us in the Seychelles at the end of our proposed safari in Kenya and Tanzania; they had never been to the tropics and their appetites were whetted by hearing our descriptions.

For Kenya and Tanzania we had to kit ourselves out with safari shirts and shorts and I had to change my camera for something better, especially with a more powerful zoom lens, in order to capture on film the game we were going to see. This holiday was really Esmé's idea. I wanted to see big game but did not give it top priority, but in the event it was certainly one of the most arresting and interesting holidays we had.

Esmé and I had the good fortune to be able to get to like what the other liked, and enjoy what the other enjoyed, and this was the gilt edge to our love affair. To share and really want to share, to care and really want to care, to please and need to participate in the pleasure, those are the feelings of love. Now that she has gone I cannot even tell her that I love her, condemned as I am to this cruel continuum of emotional continence. There is nothing positive about grief, it enhances nothing, enriches nobody, brings only impoverishment and pain, and for some it brings guilt as well. There is no stereotype for the pain, it is individual, particular, private and personal, and with every lancinating shaft of it, each torturous twist a little of you dies, but never enough.

When you lose the person you love with great suddenness, the first reaction must be one of freezing numbness and shock; you are paralysed mentally and physically though you will probably function for a while until reality will no longer tolerate your refusal to accept it, and then you begin to grieve. If your loss comes after a long progressive illness, you may be half ready to face life without your love because you began to grieve when you knew that there could be only one outcome, and that moment reached weeks or months before the end. Counsellors will suggest this, but you are so busy coping practically and emotionally, that you have no time to contemplate the selfishness of your own grief; when this finally comes and you no longer have her there to care for, try to reassure and keep happy, pretend to about a future which you both know is not there, you are not shocked, you are filled with the powerful desire and even determination to avoid living on without her. You have both been forced to play a cruel game and lost, and because you know that you never had a chance of winning you are consumed with resentment, with jealousy of those who have not yet had to play that game. When she went more than half of me went with her and I exist as a hopeless remnant. I know that I can never be hurt again as I have been and this makes me feel curiously invulnerable, with a strange sense of freedom. Nothing matters anymore except the love of my family and the need to avoid hurting them; these are my only reasons to continue to try to live.

Before going to East Africa we had read *White Mischief* by James Fox, had seen the film of that book and also *Out of Africa*. We spent the first night at the famous Norfolk Hotel in Nairobi, and Esmé asked if the snooker table was still there, the snooker table on which games other than snooker were played, in which cues were not needed, but rests almost certainly were.

It was planned for us to go for a drive around the national game park on the outskirts of Nairobi on the first afternoon, but they had forgotten about us. Eventually we had a foreshortened circle of the park, which was really intended to be a haven for sick and wounded animals, but according to Kennedy, who was our guide, at least half of them had to be destroyed. We saw a few somnolent lions, a leopard, a cheetah, some very tame zebra and spotted hyenas, which are highly unattractive. In the main park, which is less than ten miles from the centre of Nairobi, there is quite a profusion of animals; we saw giraffe, water hog, impala, hartebeest, African buffalo and waterbuck. Esmé was particularly delighted with the birds, red-eyed partridges, little shrikes, and secretary birds with crested heads like a fan, and long tails; Kennedy told us that they were of the vulture family, but they were very much more attractive than vultures, and Esmé wanted to take one home.

Back at the Norfolk we took things easily in the bar after getting ready for dinner, as we knew that during the next week we were going to be very much on the move, with early morning starts to each day. Esmé loved the Norfolk and she wrote in the journal of the comfortable ex-colonial atmosphere, with everybody welcoming and friendly, and there was absolutely no subservience, which especially pleased her.

We had to reorganise the packing because we were limited to a small case each, and we restricted ourselves to two grips. Esmé said that if I really loved her I would have found out about this back in England, and she would then have avoided having to pack and unpack two suitcases and a grip twice in two days; this necessitated us going down to the bar a little earlier than usual! We had dinner on the Lord Delamere terrace and had an early night. The Norfolk is very much the hub from which people radiate out into the various game parks of Kenya and Tanzania, and next morning there were many people waiting around for their minibuses, dressed for the occasion as were we in our new safari apparel.

The drive to the Ark Game Lodge first took us through lush green country with coffee plantations and cattle grazing before opening out into broad grassland. Eventually we left the main road and bumped our way up to Aberdare Country Club where we had a curry lunch without risking the salads; Esmé said that she had no intention of spending the next two weeks at close quarters with me in game lodges and camps, not to mention Range Rovers, in a state of acute diarrhoea. She said that she had read about somebody on safari who had to get out of a vehicle for urgent relief and got mauled by a lioness; I wondered if my wife's vivid Welsh imagination was at work, but I kept off the salads throughout the whole trip just in case.

The Ark is less famous than Treetops, but is beautifully positioned, standing up on higher ground with a water hole and salt lick in front of it. As we drove to it we saw many colobus monkeys in the trees and plenty of elephants. We arrived in the late afternoon and went out to the viewing terrace to await the visitors to the water hole, with binoculars and camera primed; in the two hours before dinner we saw bush buck, buffalo, warthog, elephants and a lioness charging across the open ground chasing a warthog.

After dinner we took up position indoors in front of an enormous window; we saw hyena, and two rhino squaring up to each other with much bowing of the heads, until the smaller one backed off and loped away. We were taken to the bird table where there were dozens of brilliant tropical birds, with a bushy-tailed mongoose underneath feeding on the scraps. Esmé recorded bird sightings of yellow-billed oxpecker, Egyptian geese, Augur buzzard, swifts, hammerkap, speckled mouse bird, sandpipers, crowned hornbill and many weaver birds, and she was utterly fascinated. Many elephants came to dig up salt with their trunks and they had a great air of peace about them. There was a suckling baby elephant and we nearly saw a mating, but they thought better of it and Esmé wondered if the floodlights put them off; she said that she never had and never would perform under floodlights herself, and I can vouch for that, for her the lighting always had to be tastefully subdued. After this first night at the Ark Game Lodge we moved on to Mount Kenya Safari Club, picking up the case we had left at Aberdare Country Club on the way. When we were planning this trip with Julian Taylor back in Cheltenham, who made all the tour arrangements for us, he said that we should have two days of luxury at Mount Kenya Safari Club, where dressing for dinner was obligatory with jackets and ties for the men. Our room gave the promised view of Mount Kenya, the whole place seemed almost empty and we wondered if this was because of the state of political unrest, but we were assured that people would really start to come here in mid-December. Walking across to dinner there were wide lawns on which we mingled with prancing peacocks, Egyptian geese and marabou storks, as well as a sacred ibis. We browsed in the gift shop, where we marked down a soapstone head for ourselves, some earrings for our granddaughters and bought some postcards to send home. It was so cold that they lit a huge fire for us in the corner of our room, and we found it difficult to believe that we were sitting in front of a log fire on the equator, albeit seven thousand feet up. As we went to sleep with the fire burning, Esmé said that it reminded her of her childhood, when her parents would light a coal fire in her bedroom when she was ill.

I wanted to take a photograph of Mount Kenya in the rising sun, but it was shining directly into the camera and I had to wait. Mount Kenya is cloud-free until mid-morning and then quickly becomes covered and invisible; as the morning was warm and sunny we tried to get in some tennis, but Esmé pulled a thigh muscle and we repaired to the poolside and had a swim instead.

In the club lounge at 4 p.m. all the tables were laid up for English afternoon tea, with plates of thin delicate sandwiches and a central cake stand on each table; we could almost see our mothers sitting there.

We had a drink on our balcony where we made friends with a Tacazze sunbird, a lovely little bird and almost tame. We had an early dinner and bed, because after two days of doing absolutely nothing in this plush club, which seemed to be in a time warp, the real safari would begin when we got to Little Governors Camp in the Masai Mara Game Reserve.

We flew in a small plane which took off from a bumpy grass field, passed over the northern end of the Aberdare mountains and then over the Rift Valley, with mountain ranges hundreds of miles apart on each side. The land below was cultivated with many small farms clearly marked out, and there were small houses dotted all over this huge area; as we neared Little Governors Camp we saw herds of game.

We landed on another grass field even more uneven, and a jeep took us to the edge of the camp, where we were put down on a river bank and hauled across the river in a punt by a Kenyan hauling on a rope. From there it was a short walk into the camp, which consisted of sixteen large tents, with full shower, WC and bidet facilities at the back. Lighting was by a calor gas lamp at the front and a paraffin lamp in the bathroom at the back, which reminded us of those years camping with our children all over Europe and filled Esmé with nostalgia. There was a central tent with bar and dining area but we took meals under the trees outside; the ground sloped down to a wall, there was a deep trench on the far side of it, then open grassland with a water hole, and about three hundred yards away the bushes and trees. It was like sitting in the stalls of a circus waiting for the show to start.

As we had arrived at lunchtime, we had a quick lunch and went off for an afternoon game drive finding ourselves in a four-wheel drive Range Rover with a pleasant young German couple. Our driver was David, and for the next two and a half hours we were driven all over the flat savannah country and shown game; there were some wildebeest left behind after the migration to Serengeti, attractive little Thompson's gazelles, waterbucks, baboons and two prides of lion. It was a windy day and the dust was thick.

We had a welcome shower and some drinks before supper by a camp fire of dead tree branches, we were told that there were no mosquitoes, but we lit a couple of coils and sprayed the tent liberally to be on the safe side. There were frightening animal noises most of the night, and I was sure that one of these was a laughing hyena, but Esmé said that it was the ghastly Yorkshireman we had met at dinner, who told dreadful jokes and then brayed with laughter at them.

The whole of the next day was spent driving about the game reserve, and we got very close to a lot of lions, both prides and in couples, and a few trotting about alone. David stopped the Range Rover within a few feet of a couple of lions who were obviously mating, though during the time we were there watching, the lioness kept her bottom firmly on the ground. David told us that they mate on average eighty-four times in twenty-four hours when in season, and this made the young German neurologist say something to his wife in German, which Esmé, who knows some German, could not understand. His wife told him in English not to be disgusting and to behave himself in front of these elderly English people. We got to know this young couple very well; part of his neurological training had been done at the National Hospital for Nervous Diseases in Queen's Square, London and his wife looked just like Julie Christie.

This day we saw a cheetah in a gully with four cubs like large kittens, about two weeks old. We saw crocodile and hippopotami on the bend of a river, and birds that we had not seen before, black billed bustards, black headed heron and several different plovers, wattle, senegal and crowned plovers, and on the way home there was a martial eagle. Just before we reached the camp, we found a leopard lying on her side in a hollow, stretching and yawning, turning over and ignoring all the attention. When we got back to the river bank David showed us his rifle which he kept under the dashboard, and he told us that there were two men with shotguns parading the camp all night.

It was a very early start next morning and we drove out with the glorious early morning African sun coming up to the left of us; there was a slight breeze and we saw more game on this early run than later in the day. We returned for breakfast after two hours, and filled ourselves with fried eggs, bacon, sausages and tomato, followed by a plate of tropical fruit, for which we were more than ready.

David took us to a Masai village, where the dwellings were so primitive that Esmé compared them with the straw hovels we had seen in Papua New Guinea. The whole village was surrounded by a flimsy fence which certainly would not have kept out a lion, but David told us that lions do not attack the Masai; until recently, they had a tribal custom that each boy on coming of age should kill a lion, and according to David this had resulted in a healthy respect for the Masai by the lions. We went into some of the houses which were built of mud, and in the roof there was a small slit-like aperture which was for emitting smoke and letting in light, but not fulfilling its function for either. There were cowhide strips on the floor of what was called the sleeping quarter. It was not possible to stand upright in these houses and the people must have had a very uncomfortable life, which they shared with goats. David told us with some sadness that soon all these people would be housed in brick houses and thereby lose their traditions and their heritage; he himself was a Masai, at the age of seventeen his father sent him to a missionary boarding school, and whenever he went to and from the school he had to walk fifteen kilometres through country in which animals of prey roamed freely.

This last game drive ended at lunchtime, and after lunch we left Little Governors and flew back to Nairobi, where we were met on the grass landing-strip by the Norfolk Hotel courtesy bus driven by a delightful Kenyan named Flamingo. Esmé felt as if she was coming home when she entered the hotel, she really loved it there. We received instructions before dinner about the Tanzanian leg of the safari from Kennedy, who told us that Flamingo would drive us to the border.

We headed for Tanzania after an early breakfast, picking up three Chinese girls on the way. Nairobi is a large modern city and it seemed to take a long time to get through the suburbs into open country. As we neared the border the land became more arid and the earth red, and at the border Flamingo handed us over to Albert, a serious, studious young man, who was to be our driver and guide all through Tanzania.

We now had a Range Rover to ourselves, but we missed the young Germans because they had a good sense of humour and were good company. After a one-and-a-half-hour drive we reached the town of Arusha and went to the Meru Hotel for lunch. Paying for lunch was complicated, because first we had to change traveller's cheques into

Tanzanian shillings as they wanted hard currency and the credit card was a thing of the future. Esmé maintained that we should always go abroad equipped with the mighty dollar, and a sheaf of one dollar notes for tipping.

On the way to Arusha from the border it was made painfully obvious to us that the roads were much worse than in Kenya; they were strewn with large stones we felt as if we were on the back of a circus motorcycle. Before we left Arusha, Albert took us to the back streets where we picked up an icebox with beer and orange juice for the morrow from the "Florida Bar".

We saw few other vehicles on the road to Lake Manyara, where we were to stay at Gibb's Farm. The 'good' road ended after seventy-five kilometres, and we made a right turn on to an appalling track with a sign pointing to Lake Manyara. We hoped that the lake was fairly close, but it was two hours along one of the roughest and dustiest roads we had ever known, before we got there. The lake was big and beautiful, and we climbed up along the west side of it, Gibb's Farm is high up and we had a cottage from where we could look down to the lake across acres of coffee bushes.

We acquainted ourselves with Tanzanian beer at Gibb's Farm called Safari, strong and with a very pleasant taste, very like Singha beer in Thailand. Our first impressions of Tanzania were of immense space with very few people, a poor country and virtually no tourists; we liked Gibb's Farm which was run like a private farmhouse, and you felt part of the family.

I was woken in the middle of the night by heavy thumping on the roof of the cottage and, as I have written previously, with a love like ours it was very important to share the fears as well as the happiness. It was not that I wanted to worry my wife, but I did not want her to miss any experience; as when I was dying in La Paz, I kissed her to wake her and I told her that there were many heavy wild animals jumping up and down on the roof. She listened for a moment and then said that they were bush-babies or small monkeys, and that if I really loved her I would have read that up in the guidebook and not woken her unnecessarily. There was then a very heavy thump indeed, and I said that if that was a bush-baby it was very post-mature, but she had already gone back to sleep, and I was cut off from further reassuring conversation. I lay thinking how glad I was that there were heavy metal grilles on all the windows.

The next day held for us the promise of the Ngorongoro Crater, that gigantic volcanic ulcer in the Rift Valley, the timeless cleft in the surface of this vast continent. The crater is twelve miles in diameter and in the bottom of it there is dried grass, salt and freshwater lakes, trees are sparse but there is plenty of bush vegetation. Esmé stood and looked all around her and said that it was not so much the animals that we were to see, for we had seen those same animals in the savannah, the uniqueness of this situation was that never before had we stood together on the floor of one of the world's most massive volcanoes. We had not seen flamingos and there were million upon million of these ungainly pink birds on the shore of the salt lake, with hyena and jackal watching and waiting to grab the unwary, and when the flamingos took off en masse the whole sky went pink. We saw lion and black rhino, but by this time we were no longer amazed by game.

During our travels, so often did we see breathtaking examples of the lavish artistry of nature, like the Ngorongoro Crater, but when they were wedded in perfect harmony to the inspired creations of man, as the Andean peaks to secret Macchu Picchu, the peaceful Jumna riverscape to eternal Taj Mahal, the incandescent pink cliffs of the Saharan edge to the Temple of Ramses at Abu Simbel, the huge Pacific sky and the vast and lonely ocean to the vigilant, pensive moai on tiny Easter Island, we were transported to the very highest realms of wonderment.

After a long drive back to Gibb's Farm, covered in red dust and caked with sweat, we fell into the shower. We were so dirty and such was the urgent need for us both to feel clean again, that we showered together. Esmé asked me when we last did this, and I was ashamed to say that I could not exactly remember; if she had then said, "If you really loved me..." I would have killed her; she probably knew, and that was why she did not say it.

We faced next day a two hundred kilometre drive to the Serengeti. Initially mountainous and green we later drove through very dry, barren country and before reaching the Serengeti National Park, we stopped at Olduvai Gorge, where there were extensive excavations. Much had been learned about man's early ancestors here, and this was where Dr and Mrs Leakey discovered very important skulls and skeletons, digging down through four layers. The fourth layer was black in colour, the third was red and together they represented five hundred thousand years of time; we could not easily wrap our minds around a time-span of this nature.

We went into the museum where there were informative charts about Hominis Habilis and Hominis Erectus. I asked Esmé which one she thought I was; she just kissed me and said she loved me, and that I should work out the answer to that one by myself.

After the Gorge, in two hours we came to an arch on which was written Serengeti National Park. We were in a seemingly limitless plain with hardly an acacia tree in sight; dotted over it there were mounds of granite boulders up to one hundred feet high, known a kopjes; the magnitude of the sky reminded us of the Pacific.

We reached Seranera Lodge where we were to spend two nights. Almost at the entrance to the Lodge there were some tall trees. Albert became excited and told us to keep quiet; he reversed very slowly and stopped under a large acacia tree. He pointed upwards and we could see three leopards lying on branches toward the top of the tree, with the remains of a young zebra hanging from another branch, which was obviously their larder.

Seranera Lodge is built on a kopje, and on arrival we were told that the water supply had failed entirely, both hot and cold; they hoped that they could do something about it but we had no confidence; they warned us to keep bedroom doors and balcony windows shut to keep out baboons. During the next two days we traversed the Serengeti; a land without ends or borders, a place without boundary or restriction of any kind. You felt you could walk in any direction, time stood still and the game seemed to have so much more space even than in the Masai Mara.

In the Serengeti we saw a wider variety of birds and Esmé chronicled more than fifty. The Emerald (Hoopoe) Cuckoo was arguably the most beautiful bird we had seen, including the Paradise Birds of Papua New Guinea; with the Emerald Cuckoo you get a flash of brilliant green, it turns the red sunlight itself into green. Another particularly attractive bird was the Blue-headed Bee-Eater and it perched on a branch just beside us with a large succulent bee in its beak.

During this game drive Esmé talked to Albert about his family and his background and his aspirations. He told her that his wife wished to do a PhD in a foreign country next year; he seemed to think that he had married above himself; his English was not good but he had ambitions for his two little girls. With her never ending concern for the underprivileged Esmé was upset by her conversation with Albert, because whatever were his aspirations, his horizons were so limited by his birth.

We were having a rest on the bed before supper at the Lodge, I had opened the balcony window a little because we needed some air, we both dropped off to sleep and I awoke feeling uneasy. When I opened my eyes and lifted my head from the pillow, I was face to face with a large and malignant looking baboon sitting on my feet. This was another of those occasions when I felt that with a love like ours both the unattractive as well as the attractive should be shared, but as if by telepathy Esmé woke, quickly realised the situation, and to her everlasting discredit rushed into the bathroom and locked the door, leaving me alone and deserted to face my evolutionary predecessor. He leapt from the end of the bed onto the desk below the mirror, whereon was the black bag containing everything of importance lying open. He picked up a pen, ignored the black bag, turned round to look in the mirror and his back was towards me. He was the size of a three-year-old child and I had a view of his red bottom, and blue scrotum hanging down like an overripe aubergine. Esmé was shouting advice to me through the locked bathroom door, and as I watched this half human beast he jumped back on the bed, then through the open balcony window clutching the pen, and I shut the window after him. My wife emerged from the bathroom and said she was proud of me; it was one of those moments in a marriage when you have to remember how well you understand each other.

We had one more day left and we would leave the Serengeti, and soon East Africa. For the dawn game run we started in the half-light, and during the two hour drive we saw at close hand a leopard with cubs playing in the grass, with a zebra hanging up in the tree which was their home. There were hyenas in a pack and one of the adults was playing around with the head of a wildebeest. Looking across the endless plain we saw a huge herd of wildebeest, and imagined what it was like when they assembled for the big migration north to the Masai Mara.

From the Serengeti our journey took us back past the Ngorongoro Crater, and after lunch we sat looking across the crater which is big enough to have several weather patterns; it has hot sun, dark cloud, heavy rain and mist in different areas. We bumped our way back along the red dust road past Gibb's Farm to Lake Manyara.

We spent a night in transit and next morning had a game drive round the Lake Manyara National Park which has a large lake with many hippopotami lurking under the surface to avoid sunburn; the scars that you see on hippopotami are caused partly by fighting but are mainly the scars of sunburn. There were many bubbles and Esmé thought that it was a strange way to spend the day, standing underwater belching and farting. There were buffalo with their oxpecker jockeys picking the ticks out of them, and as we walked back through a wood we saw several Trumpeter Hornbills; but the main feature in this wood was a large pack of baboons of all ages, copulating as if there would be no tomorrow. Esmé was surprised that the females did not seem to look round to see who it was; she said that she herself would always want to know who it was; I could only say that indeed I hoped she would.

We had a longish drive along very dusty roads to Mount Kilimanjaro International Airport where we boarded a four-seater Cessna 2 aircraft which we had chartered, to take us back to Nairobi. Never in our lives had we been so filthy; we were covered in red dust and we longed to get back to the Norfolk Hotel and clean up. Flamingo met us at the airport in Nairobi and took us to the Norfolk where we fell into the shower.

We had come full circle and on the morrow we would wing our way across the Indian Ocean to the Seychelles, where the family would join us.

Chapter Seventeen

Morocco

In April of 1992 we decided that we would go to Morocco. Esmé wanted to start at Fez, the most ancient of all imperial capitals and, as far as the medieval flavour is concerned, the most complete city of the Arab world; we felt that we would give Casablanca a miss, though our plane landed us there and we had to wait three hours before getting another to Fez.

A grinning Arab in a djellaba named Rashid met us, took us to the Palais Jamai Hotel in a large air-conditioned Mercedes with a uniformed driver and Esmé loved the style. This was a nineteenth century Vizier's palace with wonderful views of the city below; we knew that it would be expensive but we felt that we would rather spend our money here than later on in the Hotel Marmounia, made famous by Winston Churchill, in Marrakesh and we had a room with a balcony overlooking the medina. Certain things gave Esmé unusual pleasure, and she had much looked forward to Morocco because she knew that it was quite different from anything that we had seen before. Here on the evening of our arrival she was full of anticipation of what was ahead; we had very special things in our lives together and special places and I felt that this was to be one of them.

We explored a little before dinner, we walked through the gardens in front of the royal suite, we found the tennis court, we did a few lengths in the pool, and had dinner in Al Fassia Restaurant in the hotel. We went to bed early because we had been up most of the previous night listening to the results of the general election.

We awoke on the second morning and met Rashid in the front hall, an impressive room with much wood carving and mosaic tiles. Our plans to have a long, undisturbed night had been destroyed by a screaming muezzin in his tower at 4 a.m. calling us to prayer. As we lay there listening to this hideous noise, I remarked to Esmé that he lacked the tonal purity of the castrati of seventeenth century Italy. She felt that they must be cutting off his hand and being economical with the anaesthetic. We had heard muezzin from Kashmir to Sumatra but never anything quite like this; he woke the birds in the date palms just outside our window, and with them, the muezzin, cocks crowing and peacocks shrieking, we had to concede the night.

Rashid walked us from the hotel into the medina, and we spent the next two hours strolling through very narrow alleyways packed with people, donkeys hopelessly overloaded, and mules which butted and jostled us. Some of these alleys were open to the sky, others were covered by wooden lattice to keep out the sun. We were not allowed inside the mosques because it was Ramadan but we could peer through doorways. Rashid showed us the Attarin Medersa, a medieval college with a courtyard surrounded by fantastic wood and stucco patterns and lovely Islamic arches everywhere. We crossed the Place Sapphirine with a huge fig-tree in the middle; there were metalworkers hammering away at copper and bronze bowls and trays, and we went on to a stinking building which was open in the centre and which was the tannery, with men wading about in stone tanks containing filthy water and animal skins. On the top of this building we had a good view of Fez from a different direction, and looking down into a neighbouring building we saw a dyer's souk with many stone tanks containing dyes of different colours, yellow, red, blue, green and black; there was a date market nearby and also a woodworkers' area where there was a delightful smell of fresh cedarwood. After a late lunch we spent the afternoon swimming and at sundown we went to the tennis court and had our usual knock-up, with Idriss the coach acting as ball-boy. Esmé felt that she could get used to having ball-boys to serve her with balls and expected me to arrange this when we got home. Idriss obviously felt that Esmé's backhand required attention and he insisted that she had fifteen minutes with him which pleased her greatly. Dinner at the Al Fassia Restaurant consisted of shoulder of lamb with a quite delicious sauce which we could not diagnose.

We had two more days to spend in and around Fez and we decided to go to Meknes, an hour and a half away by road and the Imperial City of Sultan Moulay Ismail and his mausoleum; we had also been advised not to miss the Great Gateway of Bab Mansour. For the day in Meknes, Rashid handed us over to Brahmin, and we felt that Rashid was obviously an entrepreneur, and that he had at his beck and call transport of all kinds, from donkey carts to gleaming Mercedes; he said that we were to pay him for everything at the end of our stay, and that he would see to it that the others had their share; we wondered what share that would be.

On the way to Meknes the countryside was hilly and the crops sparse; the drought had hit everywhere very hard, and the corn was only a few inches high instead of two feet. We passed through olive groves and lines of fig-trees; all along the road the trees had their trunks painted white and the traffic was very thin. There were people in the fields planting onions and other vegetable crops, and we could imagine that in normal climatic conditions at this time of year the slopes of these hills would be verdant.

Our first stop was a large Roman city site known as Volubilis, and we walked up a steep stone path to the city where there were foundations of many houses, paved roads, some columns and in the distance what looked like a triumphal arch. This was a big site and probably largely unexcavated, but we felt that it was not of the same importance as Pompeii or Jerash. Just before Meknes we looked across a valley and saw the old town of Moulay Idriss; there were piles of white houses on the hill opposite, and this was the burial place of Moulay Idriss, Morocco's most venerated saint and creator of its first Arab dynasty. He was the great-grandson of the prophet Mohammed, and he fled to Morocco from Damascus following the great civil war in seven hundred and eighty-seven AD.

As we drove round the walls of Meknes we tried to imagine the cruelties of the fifty-five year reign of Sultan Moulay Ismail from 1672 until 1727; at a time when everywhere else in Europe enemies were routinely tortured on the rack and burned, Ismail was cruel beyond belief; he made Genghis Khan, Vlad the Impaler, and Attila the Hun look like amateurs when it came to ruthlessness. He would slash off the head of the eunuch who was holding the stirrup as he mounted his horse if he felt like it, and he would batter skulls in when he viewed the work on his buildings in order to show his subjects who was in charge; he is reported to have said that his subjects were like rats in a basket, and the basket must be shaken regularly or they might gnaw their way through. His construction programme was obsessive, and he designed and even worked on many of the buildings himself.

Esmé hated hearing about cruelty, it was complete anathema to her and she claimed that it was because of the subjugation of the Welsh by the English; I never argued about this, but I did feel that whenever I went to Cardiff Arms Park it seemed to be the other way round.

Meknes is really two cities, a medieval city surrounded by a high turreted wall with its many gates, and the modern city alongside. The mausoleum of the Sultan is in the Berber Mosque, the only mosque open to people of other religions, beautifully decorated with mosaics on the walls and the floors of three courts, and with the mausoleum in the centre.

We went through the medina which was much like Fez, and walked through the immense gateway of Bab Mansour along the main street at the edge of medina called Rue Dar Semen; Esmé thought that this was curiously named, with which you had to agree,.

Sitting here and writing this book in Kuching in Sarawak, in a tropical garden and looking out to the South China Sea, I cannot but think how much she loved places like this, they were part of her very soul. Having to be here without her twists the permanent ache inside me; she would understand that I cannot be happy, but she would want me to try and I do not know how to begin. Bereavement places you in a situation of isolation and quarantine, for your acquaintances, not so say your friends, find themselves in a bivious untenable position; they are discomforted by your pain but they cannot share it with you. They have two courses open to them, either they will stand aside and await your recovery in time or they will seek to immerse you in social activities to help you realise that normal life still goes on, and in this way your pain may be eased, for themselves if not for you. In your grief you will find friends who may surprise you with their need to be closely involved with your loss and longing; you are grateful and you love them for it because they understand that all you want to do is talk about your love, her suffering and your own until the sheer repetition of it dulls your grief. It hurts you to think that any facet of your joint suffering must be denied, erased from the agenda of others. You feel a failure because you should be doing better and this merely exacerbates your feeling of utter desolation.

You see people whom you know suddenly finding an absorbing interest in a shop window as you walk along the street, and although you may find this upsetting, if you are honest you have to admit that in their position you might do just the same. There is a reassuring, rewarding and comfortable rhythm to life when you live with someone you love. Daily routines and events, however simple, and the quietnesses of love's understanding have meaning and purpose because they are shared. When you are alone there is only the repetition each hour of each day of the unchanging rhythm of loneliness and longing, an insistent riff from which there is no escape.

On the way back from Meknes to Fez we took a different road, but the scenery was very much the same. At one point on this road there was loud hooting and wailing of sirens, and we were motioned by police on motorcycles to stop at the edge of the road. There came a posse of fast cars proceeding rapidly in the direction of Fez, with motorcycle outriders, all armed, and with military vehicles in front, alongside and behind. Brahmin said that they were transporting Arafat who was paying a visit to Morocco.

Back in her beloved Palais Jamai, Esmé acquired the Sunday Telegraph, which we divided and read on the terrace by the pool with our sundowners. We again dined at Al Fassia and had delectable pigeon and chicken dishes to the accompaniment of a four-man band, consisting of strings and a pipe; Esmé wrote in the journal that she found this music non-seductive.

The next day, our last in Fez, we met our guide for the day, Charlie Brown, a somewhat un-Arab name, and he took us through the souk to the far side, to the Bab Bongeloud Gate with blue tiling on the outside and the colour of the city of Fez, green, on the inside because green was the colour of Mohammed. The main purpose of this morning dawned upon us: Charlie Brown's remit was to take us into Fez and get us to buy things, which we resisted; it was not that we were reluctant virgins, it was just that we felt that we did not need anything, and the window-sill in the dining-room was becoming rather crowded. When he realised that he was on a loser, Charlie Brown took us back to the Palais Jamai.

We had the afternoon free and in the evening we did a tour of the ramparts of Fez; we discussed the mosaics that we had seen in Fez and compared them with elsewhere, especially India; Esmé found them all enchanting, she described them as a harmony of colour and told me that Babur, the first Mogul emperor, introduced them.

We had an early start the next morning, because we were to drive over the Atlas mountains on a long road which eventually, after two days, would bring us to Ouarzazate, with an overnight stop at Er Rachida.

Our driver for the rest of our time in Morocco was Abdullah, and when he met us he told us that we were going in a Peugeot 504, and that we were fortunate because the Peugeot 204 was unavailable. Looking back on this very long journey, which took a full two days with stops, being confined in a Peugeot 204 would have been uncomfortable.

Abdullah said that we should have been his responsibility from the moment that we arrived in Fez, but he became involved with other clients and was unable to meet us, hence Rashid with his collateral arrangements. Abdullah was young, knowledgeable and a good guide, and obviously had ambitions. We drove out of Fez, across a wide plain, barren in the drought, before coming to the foothills of the Middle Atlas, when we began to climb. Hereabouts Esmé announced that she had acute earache and asked me to do something about it; she also said that we were going to climb higher and higher over these bloody mountains and she could end up permanently deaf, if that was what I wanted.

Here was another of those occasions in married life when, however much you know you love your wife, you dare to wish that perhaps you were travelling with somebody else; I banished this treacherous thought immediately from my mind and reached in my shoulder-bag for painkillers; unlike on Easter Island I had them with me here. I gave her two aspirins and two codeines and reassured her, and told her that I loved her, and that when we stopped for lunch I would add to the therapy a strong gin and orange or three.

As we climbed the mountains the scenery reminded us of the Alps, with pines and olive-trees in profusion. We passed through Ifrane, high up and the summer retreat of wealthy people from Casablanca and Tangier; above the town there were ski slopes, further on the trees became scarce and we passed through snow piled up on either side of the road. Abdullah said that we were now at six thousand feet. From here we dropped down to a stony plain and stopped at Midelt for lunch, and so also did eight coaches of tourists. I was able to dispense further therapy for Esmé from the duty-free and she seemed to be a little better after lunch.

From here to Er Rashidia we crossed a desert and the only people we saw were shepherds and goatherds. We passed through the Gorges der Ziz, an extraordinary green cleavage in an otherwise barren yellow and red country; there was nobody here at all, and as we stood looking down at the Gorge there was literally not a sound, the silence and the stillness of this place buffeted the mind, and Esmé wrote in the journal that she could well understand the obsession that people had with the desert.

We saw villages with flat mud walls and holes for windows, we saw Bedouins with their black tents and their animals, and what grass there was, was in brown tufts and only good for goats; we noted that the Bedouin people carry their water with them wherever they go.

Eventually we came to Hotel Rissani at Er Rashidia which was packed with people, and although we had a reservation they told us that there was no room for us. We waited an hour while Abdullah prayed to Allah to get us in, and his prayers must have been heard because eventually we did get a room in this oasis on the tourist route.

Abdullah warned us that the next day would be our longest day on the road and we would traverse the Valley of a Thousand Kasbahs. We were off at 8 a.m. and he headed across the South Moroccan Desert towards Erfoud, because he wanted us to see the sand-dunes of the Sahara. We passed through villages where every house looked the same, square with pinnacles at intervals round the walls and turrets at each corner; each one was a little kasbah. Abdullah was worried when we got to Erfoud that there would be no Land Rover available to take us to the dunes at Merzouza, but eventually he found a friend who provided a very ancient vehicle, and we drove in a cloud of dust across dead flat stony desert for an hour with high mountains in the far distance. We followed a line of telegraph poles carrying the line to the last village in Morocco before the Algerian border thirty kilometres away. We passed a remote auberge, and eventually saw the sand-dunes far ahead of us, Erg Chebbi, the biggest dunes in Morocco, one hundred and fifty metres high and fifteen kilometres long. We bumped across the desert 'piste', sometimes along the tracks of previous vehicles and sometimes across virgin desert, there were striped posts stuck in the ground at intervals, presumably to guide the drivers, but our driver took no notice of them. When we reached the dunes we turned to the right and stopped at a small building at the foot of the dunes, where we were served with atrocious mint tea. We staggered a little way up the dunes, so that we could say that we had done so, it was like walking up the front of a huge granular tidal wave.

We got back in our Peugeot after a quick cold beer, and two hours later we arrived in Tineghir for a late lunch; we had driven across hot desert all the way with snow-capped High Atlas mountains far away to the north and with Moroccan villages at intervals along the road.

At Tineghir we went into Todra Gorge, very narrow and as you stand at the bottom of it by a stream you look up dominating walls of rock three hundred metres high on both sides. As we stood and beheld this, Esmé told me that she was sure that I would like to know that the pain in her ear was better, but that she now had a total blockage of the sinuses. I reassured her that it was probably just the desert dust, and that when we got to Ouarzazate all would be well; on these occasions you have to think of something to say.

We had lunch in the centre of the Gorge and then pressed on towards Ouarzazate, having time on the way to look at the Dades Valley and Gorge from a distance. We got to Ouarzazate in the early evening as the sun left the desert; we were too tired to eat dinner and Esmé told me that she felt that she had shown commendable fortitude in surviving this long, long journey in such severe upper respiratory discomfort. The hotel had a well-stocked bar and a pleasant restaurant, and I had great hopes that she would be granted alleviation, if not cure tomorrow; meanwhile it was a question of antibiotics, analgesics and sleep.

We insisted that the next day would be completely at rest and Abdullah agreed to this, he joined us for a drink at lunchtime of orange juice and soda and Esmé, as I knew she would, delved into his upbringing and his family life generally. He said that he had gone to primary school and then to boarding school in Agadir and his brother was in his last year at university, training to become a teacher of English. He said that Berbers have great respect for their women and that his sister never went to school and could not read or write; she married at the age of eighteen and Berber women were kept at home in order to protect them; his mother never went out of the house except to go to the souk occasionally, heavily veiled.

The next morning we drove almost due east to Zagora and we had great expectations of the Draa Valley. We went into the mountains, passed over a high point and saw the valley below, narrow at first, but it soon became very wide and looked like an enormous ribbon of green between the two bare mountain ranges. The mountains on the north-east side were high and sheer, and level at the top, which reminded us of The Grand Canyon; those on the opposite side and further away from the river were irregular, like huge serrated teeth. There were villages all along the river, some with kasbahs and some without, many of the houses seemed to be ruined and when they fall down they simply build another one on the top, they are built mostly of mud from the riverbed, have a short half-life, and have an attractive pinkish light brown colour. The people are dressed in traditional black for the women and bright coloured djellabas for the men, but the younger people wore modern western style clothes; Esmé here felt the need to change from skirt into trousers, which she did in the confines of the Peugeot with skill and decorum without attracting a crowd.

At the exit from Zagora we saw a sign which stated 'fifty-two camel days to Timbuctou' and headed back into the Sahara for a short trip to Tinfou, where we had another sand-dune scamper and watched a camel being treated for stomatitis. Its mouth had been filled with methylene blue and the 'vet' was emptying syringe after syringe of fluid into the scruff of its neck, which it did not seem to like very much, judging by the bellowing, not surprising since the syringe was like the barrel of a four ten shotgun.

On our way back to lunch we stopped briefly at a mental hospital where mad people could come off the street, and be allotted a place on the floor of the cloisters which surround the courtyard of what was the tomb of a holy man many centuries ago, a Zaouia. We were shown round this and also into a library which contained thousands of old books written in Arabic; there were Moorish books on astronomy, algebra, geometry, law and medicine, most of them written in the seventeenth century. The Imam in a blue djellaba who showed us round, asked us for the entrance fee of ten dirhams and Esmé discovered that there were pockets in djellabas and that was where our money went, rather than on the tray by the door.

After lunch of chicken salad, bread and rosé wine among brightly coloured shrubs we retraced our steps back along the Draa Valley, to Ouarzazate and we imagined the camel caravans coming in from East Africa with spices and other merchandise, including slaves, along these age-old southern routes in Morocco; we were fascinated by the desert scene.

Next day we took the road to Taroudant and the famed Hôtel La Gazelle d'Or; we stopped on the way at Kasbah Tifoultoutte, an old kasbah which had been rebuilt and was now a hotel, once a large rectangular fort, situated high up on a hill. We clambered up the steps to the roof where there were storks nesting in two of the corner turrets; this was the hotel where the cast of *Lawrence of Arabia* stayed while filming. A mile further on was Ait Benhaddon, a huge kasbah on the opposite side of the river, quite derelict in its upper part but the lower part had been rebuilt with various buildings added at the instigation of Omar Sharif for the filming of *Lawrence of Arabia*. We were still in high mountains and negotiated many hairpin bends for what seemed an age, eventually crossing the Tiz-n-Tififft Pass, one thousand six hundred and sixty metres high and showing rocks with striking layered strata, all very bare and bleak.

We came down off the mountains, entered the plain and the road was dead straight for mile upon mile. There were endless plantations of argan trees, which bear a yellow-green fruit rather like an olive, and we saw the goats climbing up the trees to get at the fruit; the kernels pass through the goats and are retrieved from the dung and processed to provide argan oil, a very expensive substitute for olive oil. We stopped at a small café where there was a well from which Abdullah drank water out of a tin, which we declined to do; an old man was measuring and weighing out saffron, this was the only area in all Morocco where saffron was grown, and we sampled saffron tea, pleasant to the taste, sweet and hot, and Esmé bought two grains of saffron for thirty dirhams.

We had lunch at the Hotel Salaam, an old palace, on the outskirts of Taroudant, and in the heat of the midday sun we lunched under palm and banana trees.

In mid-afternoon we arrived at La Gazelle d'Or and were relieved that the Duchess of York had finished taking her pleasures there and returned home along with an army of photographers. The hotel consists of separate and discrete cottages with a very tasteful central congress area and a large pool; having been on the dusty desert road for days we felt that we owed ourselves a little luxury in peace, and here was the very place for it.

An Irishman named Adam played a grand piano in the drawing room bar before dinner. We ate dinner outside under bougainvillaea and frangipani, the men wore ties and jackets, the women designer outfits. Esmé said that she got the impression that this place was a trap for the upper classes wanting to have affairs, and judging by their behaviour in and around the pool they were obviously having them; she felt that the three linked drawing rooms, with the piano tinkling away, the gold braided velvet drapes and pelmets, and the furniture, together with the conversation of the people, reminded her of the curtain going up on a Noël Coward set in the thirties.

We roused ourselves to hit a tennis ball at each other for a while the next morning, and lunched by the pool, listening to the inane conversation, not of film stars, politicians and royalty, but of mature London yuppies, divorcées and their lovers. That night we found a semi-private extension to the outside dining area and we had dinner under bamboo trees. Above us the Moroccan night sky was a limitless cupola of the deepest purple studded with scintillant stars of unusual brilliance, and the moon's floodlight would have made ancient Pharos' lighthouse seem like a guttering candle. When I remember nights like that I feel that those same stars, that moon and the sunlight by day, which all so became her, now taunt and mock me and try to persuade me that I might live less painfully in total darkness.

Esmé gained much from her discussions with Abdullah, a highly intelligent man, and as always during our travels, she needed to find out and relate to the predicament of the people; she always said that anybody who considered that they were born better and had rights of birth above others, or believed in a god in whose kingdom that prevailed, filled her with disgust. In the souk at Taroudant I bought a small Berber figure carved in stone, with a nice face and wooden earrings, and Esmé named him Abdullah.

We had three more days in Morocco and headed for Marrakesh, over the mountains again and with lovely alpine flowers, especially lavender, in profusion and the mountain air was so cool and clean. We stopped at the summit of the mountain which was called Tizi-n-Test where there was a small café and a shop selling fossils; the shop was an old delivery van cemented into the rock to prevent it being blown away. Here Abdullah told us of the medical history of his family and he was particularly concerned about the death of his father from a cerebral tumour; after the onset of a headache his father had first consulted the Marabout, because they were good Muslims, and this delayed the diagnosis long enough to ensure inoperability and death.

We reached Hotel Es Saadi in the early afternoon, and after much bargaining we obtained a room overlooking the pool which the Ashbys, our friends in travel, had strongly advised us to do; the first room which was allotted to us looked out at the back over a large chicken-run, and we had no intention of spending the last part of our holiday in Morocco watching chickens treading on each other. We found English papers and caught up on the news, and in the evening dined in the souk at the Yacoute Restaurant, starting with an aperitif on the roof while a local musician played the lotar, or Berber lute. We sat on stools in candlelight and Esmé said that it was a long time since she had looked at me across a barrel in candlelight; she told me how happy she was and how much she loved me, and I made a mental note to find somewhere back in the Cotswolds where there were barrels and candles.

The last day of our holiday was spent sightseeing in Marrakesh. We saw the Saadian Tombs, where many important people are buried in graves both inside and outside the building, each covered in tiled mosaics; we saw the El Badi Palace, which is in ruins and must have been very beautiful before it was destroyed by Moulay Ismail, and nearby was modern Palais El Bahai, built in 1984, which Abdullah considered very vulgar. The Djemaa El Fna, a large open area in the middle of the old city, was the central market place with many stalls and much coming and going, but our guide for Marrakesh, whose name was Ibrahim, began to lose interest in us when we refused to go into a carpet shop.

On our last night we took a taxi to the Fantasia, a Moroccan show. Here we joined thousands of tourists in large tents around a central area like a parade ground, and had dinner in a tent sitting on cushions on the floor. During dinner we were visited by a group of singing and dancing Moroccan women who gave us an exhibition of Moroccan belly-dancing; we agreed that this did not compare in any way with the South Pacific, and when the women sang Esmé said that it sounded as if they had caught their feet in a trap. We were due for an early start for home next morning and we left before the Final Grand Spectacle; we both felt that we could do without this and went back to the hotel and to bed.

On the way home to London we told ourselves that we had seen East Africa and North Africa and that we must now go to South Africa as soon as the political situation became stable. This very soon happened with Mandela, but Esmé did not live long enough for us to go. So much would she have loved to see that beautiful country, and perhaps watch cricket there, but apartheid appalled her; I was so very glad that she lived long enough, and retained her comprehension sufficiently, to appreciate Mandela's victory in the elections.

In Morocco we intentionally avoided the cosmopolitan cities of the north, Casablanca, Rabat and the large coastal resort of Agadir further south, because we wanted to see the genuine Islamic and traditional aspects of the country. Although Morocco can be reached by an hour's ferry ride from Spain, the culture and traditions of the country are unfamiliar and so very different from those of Europe; Fez particularly makes you feel that you are firmly back in medieval times, with its delightful Islamic architecture, times when the Moroccan empire extended from northern Spain to Senegal. On our journey we saw very contrasting scenery, from the high forbidding Atlas mountains to the scrub of the sub-Sahara and the sand, stones and emptiness of the desert itself; and around the oases near Tineghir, Zagora and Erfoud the mile upon mile of date palm plantations; on none of the many journeys we made were we so quickly in such a different culture and civilisation from home, as when we went to Morocco.

Chapter Eighteen

China

By 1993 many companies offered comprehensive tours throughout China. We decided upon a tour with Jules Verne which they called "China the Beautiful", but as we were later to find out, much of China is not so beautiful, though everything we saw during a three week non-stop trip involving eight planes, five trains and five boats, was never less than interesting.

We were due to fly to Hong Kong with British Airways in the middle of April and in January Esmé developed an irregularity of the heart which, though intermittent, was of a potentially serious nature, and two and a half years later brought about her death. We agonised as to whether we should go to China but she was insistent; she was given tablets to control the heart rate and we flew to Hong Kong hoping for the best.

Esmé's courage throughout the whole of her two years of progressive neurological insults, each leading to further deficit, was monumental; she well knew during the whole of this time until she entered her final coma eight weeks before she died, that her brain was being removed piecemeal, and her sole concern was to make things as easy as possible for the rest of us who loved her. It is impossible to convey the degree of frustration caused by the permanent loss of perception, especially when coupled with the loss of vision to one side. You can see the objects you need for everyday living if you keep them in your left visual field, but you cannot recognise them. You cannot wash or shower until you are piloted to the bathroom; you can see toothbrush, toothpaste, soap and shower cap but you cannot use them because you do not know what they are for. If you can find the loo you can wipe yourself only if the paper is handed to you; if your clothes are laid out for you on the bed you cannot put them on because you cannot tell which garment is which. Esmé was never able to hook or unhook her bra from the moment she had her second stroke. She tried so hard to be independent and when she emerged from the bedroom one morning grabbing the handrails I had put up for her, delighted because she had found her shoes and put them on without help, my heart broke because they were on the wrong foot. It amused her greatly that having spent the earlier part of our relationship undressing her whenever I possibly could, here I was toward the end of it still doing so, but now I had to dress her up again as well. We had always been very close, but in the hell of her affliction we became as one. It helped me to know that she was so happy for me to do everything for her, the most intimate things, and I knew that if our positions were reversed it would have been just the same. Our examination was unrelenting and merciless, and failure was not an option until convulsions and coma carried her away from me and tore us apart for all time. Now I touch her clothes in her cupboards and drawers repeatedly and I look in every pocket, hoping to find some forgotten handkerchief which might still smell of her; a few strands of hair in her hairbrush are all that I have left of her. My fear, sometimes approaching panic, is that before I can manage to die she will be traceless and that in my increasing decrepitude of mind and body I will continue to mourn the loss of a love that was just a fantasy.

We were glad to be back in Hong Kong which had excited us so much when we first saw it sixteen years before, but it was now all very different. Instead of the Typhoon Shelter being full of junks and sampans it was virtually empty, and the harbour was contracting due to the continual reclaiming of land from the sea. We felt that if this continued at the current rate Hong Kong Island and Kowloon would soon be contiguous, and our beloved Star Ferry would be no more.

As I write this chapter I have moved along from Sarawak to Sabah and if I were a giant with sufficient strength, I could throw a stone due north from here on the beach at Kota Kinabalu, and it would land in Guanghzou where we ended our tour of China, having crossed the whole width of the South China Sea. Before I finish this chapter and this book I shall have moved round the top of this enormous island of Borneo to the ancient port of Sandakan, where I shall sit and think of those early century ships of sail and steam coming and going on the old shipping routes between the Americas and Singapore.

In Hong Kong we gathered ourselves together for what was to be a very arduous journey, physically and mentally. We took a junk cruise that first evening to Lamma Island for a Chinese banquet; the cruise took one and a half hours through the harbour past the fantastic Hong Kong night skyline on our left, and Lamma Island which twelve years ago had been the centre of much bustle with a very busy market, now appeared to have been turned into one enormous chain of waterfront restaurants, with seafood in every conceivable form in great abundance waiting to be selected in huge seawater tanks. Our banquet consisted of nine courses, and we got into conversation with a couple who had just finished the previous tour and were enjoying their last night before flying home. They warned us of the hard work that lay ahead of us and appeared to be quite exhausted, but they told us that there were two sorts of drinkable white wine in China called 'Dynasty' and 'Great Wall'. After talking to these people we felt that we were about to embark on a second Long March, and without Mao Zedong.

The next day was at leisure in Hong Kong. We crossed on the Star Ferry to Kowloon, bought postcards and had a beer in the Ocean Terminal and lunched in the Hong Kong Hotel of happy memory.

We left Hong Kong for Guilin. The scrum to get through Kai Tak Airport was awful, and we felt that the sooner they built the new airport the better. Guilin was an important city, a Ming provincial capital and during the 1930s and the Second World War it was a communist stronghold; its population increased immensely and was now 300,000. The main reason for coming here was to see the limestone peaks and to go on a cruise down the Li River. A coach took us to the river, and on the way we saw a motorcoach with the roof completely covered with hundreds of ducklings under a net; our guide told us that every space on every vehicle in China was valuable, the record number of pigs that could be transported on a bicycle was six, and he knew a man who had moved house entirely using one bicycle. The Li River boats are large three-decker cruisers, there were about forty of them all going down river and ours was pulled by a tug, which gave us a less noisy cruise because the tug was at least fifty yards in front. On each side of this wide, rapidly flowing river there were tall slender limestone peaks sticking up directly from the flat plain, hundreds and hundreds of them and many of them hundreds of feet high, all covered with vegetation. There were many bends on our journey down the river, some of them with minor rapids, and every mile or so along the bank there were small fishing villages with their boats moored; but for once during this tour there were few people.

We eventually came to Yaoshong, a small town packed with tourists from the boats, with stalls everywhere selling mainly rubbish; a few old fishermen fascinated Esmé with their tethered cormorants, and for ten yuan they let you photograph them. The Chinese must be the most practical people on the face of the earth, they put everything, themselves, other people, animals, vehicles, buildings to use, and the cormorants were used for getting fish from the river. We had to avoid being run down by speeding tricycle rickshaws, some carrying as many as five Chinese trippers.

Before returning to Guilin we saw a university dating back to the Ming era, an art shop with many very attractive paintings, one depicting a fishing boat on the Li River with the peaks in the background, and I wish now that we had bought it, but at the time we felt that the equivalent of £100 was rather too much.

After a quick supper in Guilin we opted for the evening cormorant fishing trip. We sat in a boat looking through the window while a man standing on a flat fishing boat collected fish from his cormorants. They were not tethered to the boat and they dived into the water, disappeared, and then came up with a fish sticking out of their beaks. They had a ligature tied round their necks so that they were able to swallow only small fish, anything sizeable was taken by the fisherman who had between eight and ten cormorants in constant operation; his boat consisted of four bamboo poles lashed together, with a basket on one end into which he threw the fish.

On the way to the airport next morning to fly to Shanghai via Shanghai Airlines, we stopped at a Bonsai garden and learned that Bonsai trees originally came from China and not Japan, and there was a man here painting by putting drops of ink on paper and blowing them with his mouth into the shapes of trees. Last stop was the Reed Flute Cave, rediscovered in 1958, an enormous cave with stalactites and stalagmites everywhere and in the centre a huge space which could accommodate 5,000 people, all attractively lit with coloured lights. Outside there were people trying to sell things but they were much less persistent than in India and Egypt.

We were met at Shanghai Airport by Wang, who was our guide for Shanghai, and he took us to the Jade Buddha Temple which was unremarkable; the main Buddha was brought to China ten years previously. I was very much looking forward to Shanghai because I had read so much about it when I was younger, with its international settlements, and about what happened to it at the hands of the Japanese, and also at the hands of the British during the Opium Wars. We had recently read *Empire of the Sun* by JG Ballard and were both suitably armed with knowledge.

On tours throughout China you are in the hands of the China Travel Agency, who decide in each area where you will stay, and what you will see, and this is often not decided until you arrive. You are rarely allowed to eat in your hotel, and often after a long day of sightseeing there is barely time to freshen up before you are taken out to a local restaurant; for three weeks we had two Chinese meals every day in different Chinese restaurants. The reason for this is to save money, and if you opt to stay and eat a more leisurely meal in your hotel you are charged extra for it.

We had only one full day of sightseeing in Shanghai and needed rather more. Wang was excellent, he was an older man and talked much of the pre-war days in Shanghai, and he took us to the museum which had been recently refurbished. There we saw incredible bronze vessels, weapons and musical instruments, some of them dating back to 6,000 BC, we tried to place this with Egypt and realised that the Great Pyramid was 3,000 years younger. After the metal section we saw a wonderful collection of Ming porcelain dating from 1368 to 1684. As we crossed Shanghai in a bus Esmé was amazed by the washing hung out from every house, usually on a pole resting on the windowsill and on the electric cables across the pavement; some houses had a line right across tied to the house opposite, washing straggled the whole width of the road and they pushed it out and hauled it back with long poles; as we walked down the streets we were under a festoon of shirts, trousers and sheets. Shanghai was growing so fast and was already so big that the traffic problem was mounting, and they were frantically building underpasses and flyovers as fast as they could go. Wang told us that the Shanghai stock market was also growing at a rate which would soon make it the biggest and busiest in the world, and that Shanghai in ten years could make Hong Kong look like a small provincial city, and we believed him.

We passed a pleasant two hours in the Yu Gardens in the Old City, old fashioned Chinese wooden buildings in traditional style packed with Chinese tourists, just wandering around. Esmé had not expected that the majority of the tourists would be Chinese, she thought that we would be accompanied by Europeans, but in the event every place we visited was in the company of never less than a million Chinese. In the middle of the Old City was a small lake with fountains and wooden bridges leading to the central Teahouse, where we had jasmine tea with quails' eggs and other delicacies, all very much old Shanghai.

Travelling back across the city to the famous Bund we saw the old international settlements and very much liked the style of the colonial buildings, especially in the French settlement. The Bund is on the eastern side of the city; the bus set us down to have an hour or two on our own and we headed for the Peace Hotel, famous in the twenties and thirties, and here it was that Noël Coward wrote *Private Lives*. Walking into it took us back sixty years, marble walls and floors, heavy dark wooden furniture and a lot of brass everywhere. We went up to the rooftop ballroom which was featured in the film *The Last Emperor*, the young Emperor having a taste for Western living and dancing. We walked the length of the Bund which borders the Wangpu River, and you feel that you can reach out and touch huge cargo boats, tankers and even warships, as they come majestically round the long gentle bend as the river enters Shanghai. There were tugs pulling barge trains up to twelve at a time, as on the Chaio Phraya River in Bangkok. The Shanghai waterfront remains one of the sights of modern China; across the roadway from the river and lining it are the impressive buildings which were built by the British fifty and sixty years ago, and we imagined what sights they had seen along this wide road and river. We walked back to the corner of the Bund and Nanking Road, and waited outside the Peace Hotel for the bus. Esmé said that when she walked into the Peace Hotel it was exactly like walking into the Regent Palace in London before the war.

We were given a hasty supper opposite the Friendship Store in Nanking Road, and were whisked away to an Acrobatic Show where the acrobatics were very good, but we found the dog, elephant and chimpanzee performances rather degrading for the animals; we were amused by a man accompanying the elephant carrying a very large bucket on the end of a pole, the need for which was very soon apparent.

We had a 5 a.m. start to catch the train to Suzhou and were looking forward to our first train ride in China, having been told that Chinese trains were comfortable and pleasant, but the train that we caught was packed with people and dirty, although we had paid extra for "soft seats"; there were at least twenty coaches pulled by a single engine. Esmé was bearing up very well at this point in spite of periodic palpitations, and she was taking part in and enjoying everything. Suzhou is known as the Venice of China and we saw attractive Chinese Gardens, notably the Garden of the Fisherman's Nets and the Garden of the Humble Administrator. There are many smelly canals and apart from the gardens there did not seem much reason to include Suzhou in a tour. We saw a silk embroidery factory but were worried about the very young girls working so close to their eyes with very fine threads, they told us that they have to stop and rest for fifteen minutes every two hours and they work six hours a day. Esmé bought a length of silk, four metres for the equivalent of £28.

In retrospect we would have liked more time in the gardens which are beautiful, with many little pavilions with carvings and mahogany furniture and different shaped windows. There are many rocks of different shapes scattered about, all originally dredged up from the bottom of a big lake, ponds and streams and bridges and many trees, and scattered about in all these Gardens are little rest houses for sitting in contemplation. As you walk through the Gardens you become aware of the Chinese artistry in their combination of water, rock and trees; there is a theme about each Garden and they unroll before you like timeless parchments.

Later in the evening of that day we went to the City Wall, two thousand five hundred years old, which surrounds Suzhou, and we stood on an ancient bridge and watched the boats passing under. It was a peaceful evening and Esmé said that she felt so happy to be standing with me on that bridge. I thought that she looked tired and was constantly worrying about her, but I had to resist the temptation to keep taking her pulse; this tour would have been arduous for those who were fit, but for anyone with a cardiac irregularity and the symptom of frequent palpitations, it was exhausting at times. The unfailing lure of travel and discovery, and the knowledge that we were together and that if anything went seriously wrong we would cope,

fuelled Esmé with all the confidence and determination that she
needed, and only once during the whole three week tour did she opt
out of an opportunity to see something new.

After a breakfast of cold, solid scrambled egg, lukewarm coffee,
and some tired toast, we went to the Grand Canal and boarded the
boat for the journey to Wuxi. As we motored along the canal we
stood on an upper deck and watched the extraordinary activity of boats
and barges laden with everything imaginable: barges full of bricks,
straw; long trains of up to thirteen coal barges, pulled by tugs making
a terrible row, and added to this was the constant trumpeting of horns
and the wailing of sirens, and even the blowing of whistles. There
seemed to be no rule of the canal, you simply went straight ahead and
expected everyone else to get out of the way, it was quite
unbelievable, and not a little nerve-wracking; all the motorised barges
and tugs that we saw passing us in both directions on both sides,
hooting as they went, were family dwellings. Along either side of the
canal, which was dead straight, were the buildings of heavy industry,
interspersed with farms. The original Grand Canal was dug two
thousand four hundred years ago to facilitate troop movements in the
north. It runs from Beijing in the north to Hangzhou in the south, and
when it was completed it linked the Yangtse River in the south with
the Yellow River in the north, enabling junks in those early days to
sail down the Yangtse to the canal and then to ports up the Yellow
River, a journey that could take a whole year. The Grand Canal is
claimed to be the longest artificial waterway in the world and the
guidebooks will tell you that it was built by a million people with
teaspoons, we felt that many would have died in its construction.

Eventually we came to Wuxi, an enormous unattractive city, and
our railhead for Nanking; there was time in Wuxi for another silk
factory visit where we were shown the process of silk making from
silkworm pupae to bales of silk packed up for world-wide distribution.
The shop floor machinery looked primitive but the end result is the
silk trade for which China has been famous for so long. Esmé found
out that the women work in very dismal surroundings in these
factories for the equivalent of fifteen pounds a week, and she said that
whatever people may think and say about trade unions, as far as she
was concerned they would be a godsend to people who have to work
like this.

The train journey from Wuxi to Nanking was on a very comfortable double-decker train and we had seats on the top deck. At Nanking we were met and transported to the Jinling Hotel, big, modern and comparable with any five-stars hotel world-wide, but before we could settle in we were led as usual to a local restaurant, which meant a walk through the night streets of Nanking, and we mingled with the crowds of people who were cooking, eating and strolling about. Before bed we had a drink in the bar at the hotel and overheard two Englishmen trying to talk a Chinaman into doing some business with no success whatsoever, and as their frustration mounted the Chinaman smiled and smiled; here indeed was the urgency of the west so pleasantly rendered impotent by the timelessness of the east. Our suitcases caught up with us later that night; we found that throughout China we tended to precede all our baggage by about six hours, which made things difficult at times, but the inconvenience of tourists had near bottom priority as far as the China Travel Agency was concerned. Opening the curtains next morning we saw a vast building site below us, the workers looked like ants and the work went on day and night; in this part of China the towns and cities were one large building site and the countryside was one large allotment. On our one day of sightseeing in Nanking we began with the Sun Yat Sen Mausoleum, a large white building with a blue roof at the top of a steep hill. We walked up three hundred and ninety two steps to get to it, and I wondered about Esmé coping with this but she had no trouble; she said that she had never before marched fifty abreast with Chinese, and at the top we joined a long queue to get into the Mausoleum itself which lacked the atmosphere of mausoleums we had seen elsewhere, and this huge memorial lacked the simple dignity of the Rajghat in India.

We had two other sites to visit in Nanking and first was the Ming Tomb; little of the actual tomb existed but there was an interesting avenue of stone animals in bunches of six, standing up and sitting down, on either side of a long avenue leading to the tomb: elephants, camels, lions and unicorns. The final visit in Nanking was to the Yangtse Bridge, a huge structure with trains running below and road traffic along the top. We went in a lift to the top of a tower at one end of the bridge and had a marvellous view both of the bridge and of the Yangtse. The river was very wide and it was on the bend here that HMS Amethyst was bombarded by Chinese shore batteries, and the captain won a VC in 1949. In the building of the Yangtse Bridge the Chinese sought the inspiration and help for it from the Russians, but when it was half finished there was an international dispute, and the Russians dropped tools and left. To the great credit of the Chinese they managed to carry on and finish the bridge by themselves, and it now carries three hundred trains per day. In the hallway of the tower we ascended there is an enormous statue in stone of Mao, the only such statue left standing in the whole of China.

We flew to Beijing, collected our cases and were taken to the Holiday Inn Hotel where there were many Westerners, and I remember we had a drink on a balcony overlooking the main foyer and listened to music played on a grand piano and violin. Since I lost Esmé I have been unable to listen to music of any sort because of the pain that it causes me. Our feelings and emotions dance as puppet dolls on the chords of music; I do not need *Butterfly*'s 'Un Bel Di', nor *Tosca*'s 'Vissi d'Arte', nor Gladys Knight's 'The Way We Were' to make me weep, though most assuredly they would, any snatch of any shared song, any tinkle of any remembered tune can make my eyes brim and overflow with tears that I simply cannot control.

Tomorrow was the day for the Great Wall. Before we set out one of the group, who was a dental hygienist, put a dressing on Esmé's tooth which she had broken a day or two previously and was now becoming painful, and she had developed an ulcer under her tongue as a result; we were very grateful for this help and decided that in future we would add the wherewithal for dental emergencies to our medical equipment. On the way to the Wall we drove out of Beijing through endless suburbs of modern concrete blocks along a wide many-laned road lined by rows and rows of poplar trees. We stopped at the Ming Tombs and walked along an avenue lined by stone men and animals, twelve sets of them until we came to the Red Gate, with a giant stone tortoise inside with an obelisk on its back. These tombs were at a place called Dingling and were the only tombs which have been excavated, the rest of the Ming Tombs remain buried; further on there was another tomb at Changling where there were several halls; we walked through the Hall of Sacrifice and Ancestral Favour built in 1427, a museum containing articles removed from the tomb at Dingling.

We lunched at Badaling at the foot of the Great Wall and then walked along it; the incline was steep but Esmé and I felt that we could not leave China without walking along the Wall. The roadway on the top is wide enough for five horsemen riding abreast, and the north or Mongolian side is higher and with battlements; this part had been looked after but the greater part of the Great Wall of China lies in ruin. Originally built between five and three hundred BC, it was an extraordinary project then, but most of what you see now is of the Ming period. Like everybody else we had accepted that this was the only man-made structure visible from outer space, but we were told firmly that this was not so. I felt Esmé's pulse after climbing up the Wall; it was markedly irregular and she was in what is known as atrial fibrillation, but by the time we got down to the Verandah Bar in Badaling she had reverted to regular rhythm. She said that she felt fine and there was no question of aborting the tour; like her mother before her she was always unwilling to miss anything worth seeing, was never a quitter and what we saw that day was most certainly unmissable.

The next day we toured Beijing beginning with the Summer Palace, entering the main building, the Hall of Benevolence and Longevity, still containing the original furniture, including an ornate throne. Through this there was a huge lake which occupies most of the grounds of the Palace; it was misty but we could see halfway across the lake where there was an island with a long bridge connecting it to the mainland. One of the features of the Summer Palace is the Long Corridor and we walked the whole length of this and were amazed at the painting on the underside of the roof, very bright colours of blue, yellow and red, showing mythical scenes which extended also down the wooden columns which supported the roof at each side. At the end of the Long Corridor we came to the famous Stone Boat, a large stone paddleboat which we walked on.

The Forbidden City, which is familiar to everybody since *The Last Emperor*, is the main complex of buildings in Beijing; you enter it by walking between high red walls, through a gate known as the Meridian Gate and there are then three large buildings ahead of you, one behind the other. The Hall of Supreme Harmony, the Hall of Middle Harmony and the Hall of Preserving Harmony, built between the fifteenth and seventeenth centuries. Behind these great buildings are smaller ones, the Palace of Heavenly Purity which was a residence of the Ming and Qing Emperors, behind this the Hall of Unison which has a fascinating water clock built in seventeen forty-five, and at the extreme northern end of the Forbidden City is the Imperial Garden; each of these Halls has a large courtyard in front with white marble steps and balustrades. Along one side there were the living quarters for the Empress and the concubines, containing furniture with bedcovers and other fittings and charcoal burners; Esmé was glad to see these, she said that had she been a concubine she would not have wanted to be taken into the Emperor for his pleasure if she was cold; she liked the Hall of Mental Cultivation, she loved all these names and the serenity they suggested, and kept repeating them. It took a considerable time to walk through the Forbidden City and it was five o'clock in the afternoon before we got to Tiananmen Square. This is an enormous area, seven times larger than Red Square in Moscow, we were told with great pride by the young girl Sophie, who was our guide in Beijing.

Sophie was very pert and bossy, attractive in her tight jeans and knew it, and she marshalled us, ordered us about and heckled us all day. As we stood on one corner of this vast square I asked her if where we were standing was where the tanks came in on the orders of Deng Xiao-ping to crush the students in 1989. I hoped this would stop her in her tracks and indeed it did. She looked severely at me and said that there were tanks, but no people in the square. I then asked her why, if there were no people, was it necessary to send the tanks in and I thought she would kill me; she simply repeated that there were tanks but no people, and gave me a look which told me that there would be very serious trouble if I did not shut up. Esmé murmured that the Chinese were doing their best to rewrite their modern history and were making a pretty good job of it. As you stand at one end of Tiananmen Square with Mao's mausoleum at your back, straight in front of you at the far end of the square is the Gate of Heavenly Peace, with the large picture of Mao above the centre arch and Chinese writing, white characters on a red background on a large board proclaiming that the Republic will last for ten thousand years. On your left there is the Great Hall of the People and opposite on the other side is the History Museum and the Museum of the Revolution, two very large buildings. In the middle of the Square is the Monument to the People's Heroes, a tall white obelisk-like structure which we had seen on television as a centrepiece, when the massacre of the students took place; Mao's mausoleum was closed and so we were spared the queue for that.

Before we left the Square we walked along the length of it to the far end and we stood with the Gate of Heavenly Peace just behind us. We tried to picture the dreadful happenings of 1989 when the students revolt was crushed so brutally and we could almost hear the cries and screams as the tanks drove over the people, but as we stood there all was so peaceful. The evening sun cast its glow over this enormous space, the colour changing almost imperceptibly from topazine to saffron, the huge buildings lining it seeming small as cottage houses in the distance, so wide was this place. There were many people stroaming happily, flying kites and feeding the birds and it was difficult to believe that such mayhem and massacre could ever have happened here. Tiananmen Square is a much venerated place, sacred to all Chinese throughout the dynasties, and believed by them to be epicentral for all earthly human life.

By now we were tired and all we wanted to do, especially Esmé, was to go back to the hotel and have a leisurely meal, but we were given a short time to wash and brush up and were whisked out to an indifferent Peking Duck dinner and subjected to a terrible stage show. Esmé refused to accept that it was a Chinese Opera, she said that it was so unlike the dancing and singing we had seen elsewhere in the world and she had in mind the masked Batak dancing in Sumatra, the funeral Toraja dancing in Sulawesi and the trance dancing in both Java and on Bali. All of these were typical of ancient and mystical eastern dancing, with ritual body movement and the purpose behind much of it was to try to contact the powers of magic. The Chinese Opera was most missable and we ducked out at half time, hoping Sophie would not see us, and took a taxi back to the hotel. This was much too long a day for everybody, but curiously Esmé seemed to get second wind in the evening; the excitement and the interest in all that she saw seemed to fuel her, but I was worried to death about her.

There was another 5 a.m. start the next day and we caught the train to Chengde. This was an optional side trip but we wanted to do it because it would take us up into Northern China, which is the mountainous part of this huge country, and we wanted to see the Summer Palace of the Empress Dowager. The experience of Beijing Central Station was quite shattering. There were thousands of people milling about, quite a lot of them lying on the floor and sleeping. We had to get on to an escalator to take us up a floor to the platforms; the only problem about this was that thousands of Chinese were aiming to do the same thing and not only did they just have bags and suitcases but all sorts of produce, sacks of this and that, pieces of furniture, crates of ducks and chickens, and many of them had bicycles. Eventually somehow we got a foot on the escalator and made the upper level. Esmé said that she had never travelled up an escalator before with a crate of ducks up her backside and she hoped that she would never have to again. My problem was avoiding castration by the handlebars of a bicycle. The train journey was interesting and we were able to relax for four hours and take in the topography of this strange land of the East. We spent that night in a three-star Chinese hotel, the sheets were stained with we knew not what and there was dust everywhere. We needed a mixer for Esmé's duty-free rum but were unable to obtain any fruit juice, so we tried almond juice which she said was indescribable; the lifts did not work, everybody had to use the staff lift and we got stuck in it just below the fifth floor for ten minutes. The next day we went to three of the eight outer temples, the first was Puning Temple, the Temple of Universal Tranquillity. It was modelled on a Tibetan temple, and housed a huge wooden Buddha with twenty-eight pairs of arms, and was twenty-two metres high; at the exit there were three tall stone tablets inscribed in Tibetan, Mongol, Chinese and Manchu Writing; the Qing Emperors who were dominant in Chengde were anxious to promote unity of the peoples. The second temple was Putuozongsheng Temple, a mini replica of the Potala Temple in Lhasa; it looked a little like a prison, with very high walls and many small windows along the top, the whole thing four square. We climbed one hundred and four steps to the terrace at the lower part of it, and Esmé did not feel like going any farther, I felt her pulse and her heart rate was two hundred per minute, so she rested and we went straight down again. The last temple was Xumifushou Temple built for the Panchen Lama, with a pagoda on a hill at the back; we did not attempt to climb this one and took in what we could from the road. On the train on the way back to Beijing Esmé noted that the lavatories seemed to empty straight out onto the track; she said it reminded her of the Swansea valley in her youth.

Back in Beijing we were delivered again into the hands of authoritative Sophie who arranged the next day to take us to the Temple of Heaven. The strap of my camera bag had torn off when entering a coach in Chengde and when I opened the bag I realised that the camera had been forced open, and I feared that the whole roll of film had been ruined, which included not only Tiananmen Square but the Great Wall and the Forbidden City and the Summer Palace as well. Fortunately, when we got home this was not so, and I had lost only some of Tiananmen Square on the end of the roll. The Temple of Heaven is very impressive, there is a large circular tower with three main buildings around it, all in good repair and recently repainted and we viewed the scene standing on a round raised area surrounded by ornate stonework, which was a sacrificial altar.

We flew from Beijing to Xian for the Terracotta Warriors. Esmé had gone at some length into the currency situation; in China they issue you with special tourist money and all the locals want to get their hands on this if possible. Sophie was busy trying to pay for everything with her own people's money and she tried to get us to pay her back with our coveted tourists' notes, which were not subject to the same inflation, and could be used to buy otherwise unavailable goods. Esmé wrote in the journal that Sophie with her sweet little face and tight jeans was not only bossy, but also an accomplished liar, and should go far in modern China. At this point, before we saw the Terracotta Warriors, we had reached the two-thirds stage of the whole tour, and felt that this tour of China made our earlier trip to South America seem like a gentle stroll.

The next day was a public holiday and Esmé observed that the million Chinese who had accompanied us all through the tour had now grown to two million. They took us to the Bampo Neolithic Village dated four thousand five hundred BC, of which only the foundations remained, discovered in 1953. We went on to Huaquing Pool where the emperor relaxed in water from hot springs; there were some rather attractive pavilions here but the crush of Chinese sightseers was a nuisance. The more modern history of this place was that Chiang Kai Shek was kidnapped here by two of his generals and forced to stop fighting the Communists in 1937, and instead made to fight the invading Japanese, who had already overrun three provinces in the north-east. The Japanese had by then perpetrated the Rape of Nanking during which three hundred thousand civilians were butchered in two weeks, mostly by bayonet. We bought a model Terracotta Warrior at a pottery works where they make these replicas at the rate of five thousand per month. The warriors are of three types, generals, officers and soldiers, and we bought a general one foot high. The Terracotta Army itself is in three large pits, the first is a huge hall like

Paddington Station and you enter and look down from a high balcony on a large area of parallel trenches, in which stand hundreds of warriors facing you, all restored from fragments. The warriors were destroyed when an enemy of the emperor set fire to the wooden roof which covered the army and which then fell in upon them. Excavation continues, but when I asked the guide he said that experimental diggings have been carried out over a wide circumference around the main site, and it is believed that there is no more to be uncovered. Number two pit was closed to us and number three was small. In China they refer to this whole site as the Eighth Wonder of the World, and it is incredible to behold these soldiers each with a different face; we were looking at unique art two thousand years old. In a small museum there was a case showing two chariots, each drawn by four horses, almost intact, that had lasted so well because they were made of an alloy of brass, tin and copper; the chariots being pure brass had to be reconstructed from thousands of small pieces.

The next day we were off at 4.30 a.m. which was the earliest start of the whole trip. The flight to Chongquing was uneventful, but we had to hang around until midday because the hotel could not receive us and it was pouring with rain. The real purpose of coming to Chongquing was to pick up the boat for the down river Yangtse cruise. I was interested in Chongquing because it had been Chiang Kai Shek's headquarters during the Second World War and was one city the Japanese Imperial Army did not reach, though they bombed it almost to destruction. It is a remarkable city, built on three cliffs where the Jialing River joins the Yangtse, and they showed us hundreds and hundreds of bomb shelters, tunnels dug far into the cliffs.

We boarded the Yangtse cruiser, the White Emperor, and found that it had been grossly overbooked with a large bunch of Taiwanese tourists. There was a great deal of shouting, and Debbie, our stalwart courier, stood her ground against many gesticulating Chinamen and we eventually got our cabin with a big window which gave us a good view of the banks of the river. The corruption and lying of the Chinese officials was breathtaking, nobody admitted the overbooking, and they left the tourists to sort it out for themselves; some Taiwanese ended up three or four to a cabin and somebody was obviously getting a rake-off.

The first part of the cruise was down a wide river half a mile or more across; there were many barges and tugs and fishing boats, the banks were all cultivated and looked like a million allotments coming down to the water's edge. On the second night we were invited to the Captain's Party, the food and drink, which was free, was limited, and most of it was seized by a stampede of Taiwanese before we could get any at all.

We came to the first of the Yangtse gorges, and it was explained to us that when the proposed Great Dam much lower down the river was completed, these magnificent gorges would disappear, and the river would simply become a series of interconnected lakes. In the first gorge which was the Qutang, the river was only some two hundred yards wide and the mountains towered up on either side to thousands of feet. We moored at the mouth of a tributary, the Daning, and boarded sampans which had been converted into twenty-eight seaters for this diversion. We passed through the Three Lesser Gorges on this interesting cruise; we had some semi-rapids to negotiate as the river churned round beaches of pebbles and the boat had to be helped over by two men with long bamboo punt poles. There was much cultivation of crops and there were many sampans belonging to farmers, these boats were typical of China, long and narrow with a rounded covered central section and a square roof area at the stern over the engine and the driver. After three hours we came to Double Dragon Pier where all the boats tied up and we fought for our lunch. The journey back downstream to the Yangtse was much quicker, and at one point there was a bridge across the gorge which seemed to be suspended in the sky above us.

On the Yangtse the next gorge was the Wu Gorge, forty-four kilometres long, very dank and misty as is often the case. Esmé was really very tired now and rather than go up on deck she sat by the window of the cabin watching the banks of this magnificent river slip by. The mountains on each side were three thousand feet high and only a few hundred yards apart; when the Yichang Dam is built they will be reduced to one thousand five hundred feet, and two million people living along the river will have to be rehoused. There is much barge traffic on the Yangtse and the main method seems to be to have one large tug pushing and pulling up to five barges, which are lashed all around and to each other. On the last night on the river, we were entertained to a Captain's Banquet which was fun, and we made a presentation to Debbie who had tried so hard to make this difficult tour worthwhile for us, especially as she had done another trip immediately before ours, and was very tired and keen to get to America to see her boyfriend. We thought she was very like our daughters Cathy and Emma in appearance and had many long talks with her. Esmé could not really understand the fact that neither Debbie nor her boyfriend seemed to mind being apart for long periods. She was never one who believed in loving at a distance, for her it had to be close always, she craved being touched, held and caressed, and during the interminable weeks of her grievous distress before her awareness was finally plucked from her, this was one small way in which I could try to mitigate her suffering.

Esmé repeatedly wrote in the journal how much she enjoyed everything and especially the Yangtse cruise. Looking back now I know she must have felt unwell much of the time, but never once did she complain or grumble, and when I remember her sitting by the window of the cabin and appreciating everything on the Yangtse, and when I think that within two months of that she was to suffer her first two strokes, I feel sad beyond words.

We eventually got off the boat at Yichang and had a beer in a hotel bar, preferring to give the sturgeon farm a miss. We flew from Yichang from an airfield thirty kilometres out of the town where there were old single storey buildings dotted around built by the Japanese when it was used to bomb Chongqing during the war. We flew to Wuhan, an enormous industrial city, where we had an overnight stop, and then next day caught a plane to Guangzhou where we would have liked more time, but we had to catch the train to Hong Kong in the early afternoon. Esmé and I did make time to go the White Swan Hotel on the Pearl River, where we sat and watched the busy shipping passing by. The hotel had some gorgeous shops; Esmé bought a quilted hand-painted silk jacket for forty-five pounds and we found two Chairman Mao caps with red stars on them for our grandsons.

The train left at 4 p.m., we arrived back in The Lee Gardens Hotel four hours later and for the first time in three weeks Esmé dressed for dinner; I must have watched her make herself up for the evening in a hundred hotel rooms and more, and this night I stood behind her and watched her face in the mirror. She said that her long and sensitive Welsh nose could have been a total disaster, but she was saved by her high cheekbones and her enormous wide-set brown eyes. For so long those lovely eyes had beamed to me her humour and happiness, and had shone like the rising sun with the light of love. I could never have known that evening in Hong Kong that my pitiless punishment, my life sentence without the option of death, would be to stand powerless as those limpid pools of laughing brown beauty became eyes of night, as first they clouded and darkened with doubt and worry, then gyrated in the hideous spasms of her foul distemper. Finally they were lidded for ever in the too tardy mercy of her terminal coma, and my eight week vigil began when all I wanted to do was lie in the bed with her, hold her very close with no space between us, and share her dying as I had shared her living.

She had always hoped she would die in her own bed and I was thankful she never knew that she would not.

We spent our final morning before boarding the plane for London shopping with Debbie. Esmé announced that she would like to go to a jeweller's to give me the opportunity to buy her some pearls, which rather surprised me because she had never been really interested in jewellery. We bought a lovely three-rope pearl necklace with earrings to match, and she loved it.

On the plane home she said that we must relish our travel together and savour every morsel, because one day very soon, and she used those words, it would all come to a sudden end; within two months the first two clots hit her brain, missiles of destruction and death, brutal wounding bullets so undeserved by my darling, who had never willingly harmed a living soul. She never wore the silk jacket, and the rope of pearls never graced her lovely neck.

Postlude

Beauty transmits a mystical tranquillity, whether created by man, such as the changing light of a Turner skyscape, a Beethoven symphony or a shrine like the Taj Mahal, or part of nature, such as the first shy glimmer of a sundawn emerging round the corner of the night while all the world still sleeps, or that sudden hush of reverential wonder which heralds a tropical sunset, or the silver lane of the light of a moon on a distant solitary sea. The world showed us so much beauty that almost passed our understanding and it showed us the beauty of its peoples, so many unconscious of their grace. I have tried to convey the effect upon us of the sensations and happenings which were our so privileged experience while we travelled. I have tried to do justice to the richness and abundance of all that impinged upon our minds, year upon year and now locked in memory. The first sunset on Tobago, the first dawn on Bali, the singing and dancing on Tahiti, the coral reefs of the Seychelles, the moai on Easter Island, the temples of the Nile and the pyramids, the Andes and Macchu Picchu, these were the wonders of our world and we saw them all together and in love.

Esmé was my rhapsody; with her I could string together all my poems, with her I could set free larks to soar and soar and sing and sing in the high blue heaven, our songs of love and passion. She was the leitmotiv on the whole wide stage of my world, always so full of light and colour, music and pageantry, but empty now and silent for ever. She who showed me the sun and all the rainbows, and convinced me that the good things and the power and the glory were possible, she who took me to the moon and whose effect upon my mind and body was simply electric, that lovely warm feminal woman with whom I shared such loving and living was torn from me in sunderance so cruel. She wrote the music that made my heart a dancer, now the ice that holds it fast never will melt and set it free.

Those quiet still dews of peace and contentment that so sweetly refreshed my soul when we were together now are washed away by such mountainous waves of black depression that I cannot help but drown. Kind and feeling friends, try as they may and do and will, cannot enter the cell of my solitude, nor can they cross the desert of my desolation.

Please take me back to that lakeside in Udaipur, let it be evening and let it be quiet, and leave me a while to think of her there. Take me back to Bora Bora, let me hear the song of the islands wafting across that lagoon, leave me to try to remember her there. Take me back to the Andes, let me hear the mountain music, let me hear those pipes again, let them play my threnody of sadness, my sorrowful lament. Then take me home to the cliffs of Gower where first we ever made love; let it be mellow autumn, let leaves of russet litter the fresh green grass, let me smell the gorse and the bracken, the sage and the wild thyme, let me look at the sea and cry for her there with the gulls and the gannets, the puffins and terns, the wild seabirds she loved so much.

Then take me away and play songs of love, let Mahler's love-letter to his beloved, the adagietto from his fifth symphony, and the heart-rending beauty of Isolde's 'Liebestod' fill my mind with such a swell of sound and feeling as beseems the last music I ever shall hear.

Please hold my hand, I need you to hold my hand to give me courage, and we will walk together a little of the way toward the ultimate sunset of my life, and then I will walk alone and with confidence into that blessed oblivion waiting to embrace me.

Please understand that I cannot live without my love, not one more lonely night nor one more endless day. I love her so very much, her hurting broke my heart, and no longer can I bear this pain.